# COME OUT
## OF HER
### MY PEOPLE

PAUL SHIRK

Paul Shirk
5817 N Salem Rd
Dover, PA 17535

ISBN 1-890050-61-X

2.5M - 2002

Carlisle Printing
WALNUT CREEK

2673 TR 421
Sugarcreek, OH 44681

# Dedication

This work we dedicate to the universal church of Jesus Christ that has been faithful to Him down through the ages from Apostolic times, and has not wavered in her doctrines, though beset by many foes from without and from within; remaining true during both peace and tribulation, being ever the sufferer and never the persecutor, keeping her wedding garments white as a chaste bride, in anticipation of the blessed appearing of her Bridegroom.

# Contents

# Preface

What is being accomplished here? Why this book? The relationship between the church and state tends to be discussed from the viewpoint of the state. What happens to the state when the church is a major political force? It is commonly believed that this always results in a loss of freedom. The fact that other moral value systems may restrict freedom even more is ignored. Getting the church out of the state is the current thinking.

There is another side to this. What happens to the church when it is a major political force? What kinds of theological and doctrinal changes occur? How do the members of the church practice their beliefs when the church and state walk together?

The Bible has a good bit to say on the topic. When approaching the Bible, one must keep in mind that all of it is important. There is no good in ignoring any part of it. The Bible fits together, with a common theme and focus. Every doctrine and every practice must be in agreement with every other and with that theme and focus.

History has a good bit to say, too. The working out of moral codes, the desire for justice and mercy, the need for order of some kind, the powerful urge for freedom, all have been dealt with across the span of human existence, over and over. The church has been involved in these problems, from persecuted to persecutor, from politically powerless to powerful. The results of the church's actions on the church itself are a matter of history which can teach much to those sensitive to the Bible's standards.

Paul Shirk, the author, brings both the Bible and history to bear on this topic. He goes through moral law, Old Testament Law, New Testament grace, prophecy, and God's sovereignty. He points out that this is not just a matter of opinion or preference, but has been dealt with and demonstrated over and over again. Is he right? Has he handled Scriptural and historical evidence correctly? Turn the page and see, and learn the basis of what you believe.

# Acknowledgments

A special appreciation is expressed to those that have aided in the development of this work.

The doctrinal evaluation from Charles Lehigh and Harold Martin has both been very helpful in refining the expression of some of the tenets of our faith.

The art on the front cover is the result of the labors of my natural sister, Anna Ruth Mills. The ability to take a concept and give it credible artistic form is beyond the abilities of this author and it seemed as though no picture could be found suitable to express the thesis of this book; so it is with much gratitude her services were accepted.

Without the aid of David Esh the publication of this book would need to have been postponed due to mitigating circumstances in the Author's life. Through his benevolent assistance the fruit of many hours of labor will be available to those who have expressed an interest in a work of this type.

The printing of this book was done by a firm that has shown tremendous flexibility in working with the Author under somewhat rigid time constraints. The ways in which they have been accommodating has been quite rare in these times and has been a great blessing.

The interest and support that has been expressed by many people in the publication of a work on such a topic has been a great encouragement and impetus to the Author during the many late nights laboring over the manuscript of this book.

May God's richest blessing be to all that have shown such kindness and generosity.

come out of her my people

# To the Reader

The intent of this work is comprehended in a few premises that have impressed themselves upon me.

It is my desire to illustrate that history has a way of repeating itself so that we may learn from it in the same manner that Paul speaks to the Corinthians (1 Cor. 10:1-11) to learn from the history of Israel. As Jesus says, a tree is known by its fruit, so that if a fig tree is planted in the twenty-first century, it will bear figs the same as the tree planted in the first century. The fruit may vary in some respects due to the differences in seed, but a fig tree will always be a fig tree, if that is what is planted. In the like manner the same doctrine will always generate the same fruit if given the proper conditions for expression. Beliefs are not held in a vacuum, nor are they innocuous, but are the catalysts of action. Jesus told the Pharisees that they were guilty of the same sins as their fathers who murdered the prophets; this being not because they committed the exact offenses in every case, but because the same doctrine moved both they and their fathers to reject the truth and exterminate the messenger (Mat. 23:28–36). If a doctrine has historically borne fruit in a particular manner, we can rest assured that it will again in the future if given the right opportunity, or Jesus' own words on fruit bearing are untrue.

From early in the history of the church on down to the present times, there has been a conflict between the pilgrim (independent and persecuted) church that is founded upon the primitive doctrines and practices of the Christian faith, and Christendom at large with its doctrines and practices, that has often obtained the privilege of being a nationally established religion; which though appearing in a variety of forms, yet all bore similar fruit.

History has always been a very controversial subject when men seek to draw conclusions from it, so it has been my intent to let the quotations of certain men speak for themselves. Yet even here we can have different understandings of meanings of quotations at times: but yet if the same message is repeated regularly in a similar manner the unprejudiced reader can usually ascertain the intent of the quotation. Whatever your views as the reader may be on certain historical data within this book, be informed that the thesis of this work is not contingent upon history but upon the truths of God's infallible Word. History is merely the means of illustrating the truths that the scriptures declare.

It is my desire that the faith of the Christians who adhere to the views set forth in this work be strengthened and equipped for better articulation and that those Christians who have a different understanding would consider the material set forth here before rejecting it. Though this work may at times appear to be polemical, it is not my intent for this to be a polemic against any particular sect, though it could be said to be one against certain theology. When propounding a certain view it is necessary to critique the opposing view/views and examine the fruits of both doctrines in order to make a better decision for holding a particular belief system.

It is not my intent to pass judgment on any individual's character but rather to evaluate certain theology and illustrate the fruit of it in the lives of those that hold it. God will be the judge of each man's destiny and there is not any intent on my part to imprecate any person quoted in this book. Further, it is recognized that there are children of God in the churches whose theology we reject in certain areas. It is my hope that these believers would consider some of the tenets taught in the following pages. I am sure that this material may disturb some people and others even incense, but this is not to be expected whenever a position is refuted that some hold dear. I make no apology in this regard as I do not create truth, but only attempt to expound it.

If I have made any historical errors it was not by design, nor do I wish to falsely characterize any individual. If I made any exegetical errors, may God bring it to nothing so that it may deceive no man, and send me brethren who will lead me into a better understanding of His truth.

# chapter one

# The Relationship of the Moral Law to the Gospel of Christ

As we look at the unfolding drama of history, whether Biblical or secular, we see that its focal point was approximately 2,000 years ago.

Before that time, the earnest expectation of prophecy was the coming of a Redeemer that would crush the head of the Serpent. Men of faith saw these promises of a coming Christ and embraced them and lived their lives in view of the reality of their fulfillment (Heb. 11:13).

Regenerate men of today look back and embrace these events with the same faith as those that anticipated them.

Paul speaks of the first Advent of Christ as taking place in the "fullness of time" (Gal. 4:4).

It is one of the purposes of this book to demonstrate that God's redemptive plan from its very beginning was to point man to Christ. The giving of the law was an ordered design by God to bring man to a Savior. To look at the old and new covenants as merely plan A and then plan B is to ignore a large body of evidence in the Scripture that shows a well ordered, calculated plan of God's providential dealings with man.

It is very significant to note that Moses, who was revered by the Jews as the lawgiver, (in conjunction with God, John 1:17, 7:19) should speak of One who was to follow him, whom all were to obey (Deut. 18:15-19). God promised that there would come a time when He would speak no more from Horeb (Sinai) but directly through His Son.

Mount Sinai shook with the awful and very visible sight of the glory of God being manifested to man, when giving us His law, and yet this whole event spoke of another, when God would speak His Words to us through His Son; "This is my beloved Son, in whom I am well pleased, HEAR YE HIM." This event was upon a mountain also, and the voice that endorsed Christ was God Himself. The former experience anticipated the latter.

We want to examine the importance and necessity of what happened on Sinai with the giving of the law, and then relate it to the Gospel of Christ.

## The Necessity of a Moral Law

In order to fully appreciate the significance of Sinai it is important to understand: "The Reality of Natural Law".

One of the principles of creation, portrayed in the Scripture, is that man is created in God's image. By this it should be understood that in bearing God's image we have an inherent knowledge of a Divine Being, a need to worship and communicate with Him, and a sense of morality that has been conveyed from His character to our conscience.

God's creation is a great evidence of His existence. In Psalm 19:1-4 this concept is outlined to illustrate how the united voices of the heavens, the firmament, the day, and the night all speak to the reality of God. This is a facet of His natural law by which He speaks to man throughout all the earth; their words going even to the end of the world.

This passage is quoted in Romans 10:18 in the context of faith coming by hearing and hearing by the Word of God. Paul then says that the people in all the earth have heard the Word that goes to the end of the world. The Word is what is spoken by God to man, through nature, which also affirms the truth of the Gospel, by way of His natural laws.

In Romans 1:18-27 Paul claims that the wrath of God is revealed against man because they have not acknowledged what is clearly seen by Creation, specifically the Creator, but rather substituted this truth with idol worship. Paul states emphatically that creation leaves them without excuse for belief in God. What then shall be the judgment of those who seek to use creation to disprove the existence of God?

The passage further states that those who do not acknowledge nature's God will also transgress the natural law of God by performing UNNATURAL ACTS (homosexuality vs. 26, 27), which are the ultimate expression of their depravity. The need for man to worship deity is also outlined in this passage in Romans. The refusal of men to worship God did not alleviate their natural desire for worship, but rather it found expression in false (idol) worship. They changed the truth of God into a lie and worshiped and served creation rather than the Creator.

The image of God produces a natural affinity toward worship and communication with the Divine. Natural laws are given by God as an intuitive sense of ethics and morals that are rooted in the conscience. Romans 2:14, 15 speaks of Gentiles who do not have God's (written) law, yet by NATURE are able to do things contained in the law, because of the guide of their conscience. So the conscience is a God-given guide to moral behavior. It is the faculty in every man, a result of being created in God's image, that gives him a sense of right and wrong.

Another passage that speaks of nature guiding men to truth is I Corinthians 11:14, 15. The text argues for long hair for women and shorter hair for men, as a precept that is evident even from NATURE'S teaching.

When Paul gave his address on Mars Hill to the Stoics and Epicureans, he began his arguments from the basis of natural law. Now the Stoics especially believed in natural law. They became well known for their teachings of One Supreme Being who was Creator, (in spite of their idolatry), and the use of reason or intelligence to determine equity and morality. They were strict moralists, at least in belief, if not always in life. They developed concepts of natural law as the basis for judicial law. Their thoughts affected even our American founding fathers.

In his address to the Athenians Paul quotes the Greek poet Aratus, a native of Cilicia, from his book, Phenomena, "For we also are His (singular) offspring." From this common ground between them, he showed how foolish it is to worship what you create, when you yourself are the offspring of God. It is impossible to assign form to what we have not seen. Or how can you create an object for worship when you yourself have been created by a greater power? Our worship is always reserved for that which is greater than ourselves, never a lesser being. So if in Him we live, move, and have our being, let us live for Him, move towards Him, and be like Him, for we bear His image.

A study of Greek and Roman stoicism will verify that they had a firm belief in natural law. This is an outside confirmation of the truth of Romans 2:14, 15. Those outside the written law still could be spoken to by God's natural law.

The following are some quotations from them:

*"Tis the Divinity that warms our hearts"* - Ovid, Fast. VI

*"No lash is heard, and yet the guilty heart is tortured with a self-inflicted smart"* - Juv. Sat. 13

*"A sacred spirit dwells within us, the observer and guardian of all our evil and our good"* - Seneca

*"There is no good man without God"* - Seneca[1]

*"Think of God more often than you breathe. Let discourse of God be renewed daily, more surely than your food"* - Epictetus

*"If a brother wrongs me, that is his fault; my business is to conduct myself rightly towards him."* - Epictetus[2]

*"Do not act as if thou wert going to live 10,000 years. Death hangs over thee. While thou livest, while it is in thy power, be good"* - Marcus Aurelius

*"Oh Nature: from thee are all things, in thee all things, to thee all things return."* - Marcus Aurelius[3]

These were all Greek and Roman philosophers, with no profession of Christian faith, yet with a profound understanding of a Creator and natural law.

The following are some words from a Jewish teacher, Hillel III, who also was not a Christian.

*"Men are led to God by their understanding and by their moral nature. On the first dawn of his faculties man experiences within him certain moral perceptions. ...*

*This moral nature he finds exists not only in himself but in others. It is a universal attribute of man. ... It is given to man by his Creator as the law of his action. ... Such are the convictions of the heathen world. The great men of the old world, poets and philosophers, have entertained such opinions in all time. They all take for granted one superior Being and all other inferior beings that are responsible to Him. This is not only the last and highest conclusion of human intellect, but likewise the consenting voice of the most ancient tradition."*[4]

So if natural law led man to God and provided a sense of morality, is it not adequate for the development of morality? The testimony of Scripture and the history of human experience both confirm that while nature may instruct, it is an incomplete catechism of truth.

Man may feel the need to believe in God and worship Him, but he does not know who God is, or how He desires to be worshiped. This was the reason that many stoics allowed for idolatry, as it became a tangible expression of worship for something that was relatively unknown. They also acknowledged the presence of good and evil but could not authoritatively define the difference between the two.

The Greek philosophers were often at odds with each other, and then to confuse matters even more, they could not make their lives completely adhere to their own teachings.

The result was, though God was believed in, He was UNKNOWN to them.

Though they sought morality, they could not define to what they aspired.

They taught the necessity for virtue but could not agree on what it was.

Here again Hillel's observations are most appropriate.

*"But even in the best minds the subject was surrounded with great doubt and difficulties. God, Himself, is an object of none of the senses. It is in vain, therefore, for the human mind to form an idea of the mode of His existence. Not being then, a matter of sense or of demonstration, the wisest of men, though he might arrive at truth, could not feel sure that it was truth. Wanting certainty for himself, he could not impart certainty to others. He could not propagate his doctrine with confidence. ... While religion, therefore, was in the hands of the philosophers (that is, the thinkers), it affected next to nothing in guiding and restraining mankind, it being merely a matter of opinion - that is, of dim probability. One man felt that he had just as good a right to his opinion as another. One philosopher differed from another, and thus weakened the authority of the opinions of both. A religion, therefore, in the true sense of the word - that is, one that shall take hold of faith and control the conduct of mankind - must have certainty and authority. Neither of these can be obtained without revelation, inspiration, and miracles."*[5]

Paul brings this issue to the forefront while speaking from the Areopagus (Acts 17:16-34). The God you claim to believe in and have built an altar to, is to you unknown (vs. 23). You may recognize His existence (vs. 28) but you can only feel (seek after or grope for) for Him somewhat blindly even though He is not far away. Why? Because you dwell in ignorance concerning who He really is (vs. 27, 30). Paul says, the One who is to you unknown, now I declare in truth to you, (vs. 23) that He may be rightly worshiped (vs. 24,25). Paul first acknowledged the truth of natural law in bringing man to a knowledge of God by quoting one of their poets, then he exposes their ignorance of God by showing how their idolatry is inconsistent with their professed beliefs. What is demonstrated here is first the reality of natural law, then the necessity for an absolute knowledge of truth in order to worship and obey God.

# The Insufficiency of Natural Law

Natural law may give evidence for the existence of God, but cannot define the difference between truth and error like a moral law can.

The primary need for a moral law is because in the fall of man the image of God became distorted by sin. Conversion is a renewing of the image of God in man (Col. 3:10). Man did not totally lose God's image in the fall, for even after it had taken place God said murder was forbidden because man still bore the image of God (Gen. 9:6). Sin brought a perversion to man's faculties, specifically the conscience, by deadening it to guilt for sinful acts (Eph. 4:17-19; Titus 1:15).

With man being separated from God, he lost a distinct knowledge of the good, hence the need for a moral law. A moral law shows man his sin, a righteous standard, and his need of a Savior.

Man's heart became the seat of a sinful nature that produced only evil continually (Gen. 6:5; Rom. 3:9-20). The great wickedness of man in the earth was moving him farther away from his Maker, as he removed God from his knowledge (Rom. 1:28). There needed to be a moral law, an unchanging standard of God against sin, whereby man could rightly discern truth and know God's moral will for himself.

The law of God was given because of the sin of man.

"Wherefore then serveth the law? It was added because of transgressions, ..." (Gal. 3:19)

"What shall we say then? Is the law sin? God forbid. Nay I had not known sin, but by the law: for I had not known lust, except the law had said, Thou shalt not covet. ..." (Rom. 7:7)

"But sin that it might appear sin, working death in me by that which is good; that sin by the commandment might become exceeding sinful." (Rom. 7:13)

The consensus of these Scriptures is that the law identifies sin. Without the law we could not accurately define sin nor would we have an unchanging standard of righteousness. Man, without the law, would be left to human reasoning, opinions, and emotions to determine right from wrong. The obvious dilemma would be that no one could absolutely determine the difference between virtue and vice.

Conscience can convince a man of the reality of God, lead him to worship God, and create a prompting to obey God, but without a moral law, he cannot understand the character of the God he believes in, know how He is to be worshiped, or understand what the obligations are to obey Him.

The reason for man's blindness is his sin. It has alienated him from a true knowledge of God and His requirements.

"Having the understanding darkened, being alienated from the life of God through the ignorance that is in them, because of the blindness of their heart." (Eph. 4:18)

As it has been proven that a moral law is necessary in addition to natural law, to give man a knowledge of sin; it is then an obvious determination that sin is a transgression of God's moral law. Sin is not defined by guilt of conscience or emotional distress but by the clear standard of God's holy law. The law is the necessary medium whereby the conscience can be pricked, the emotions stirred, and the understanding enlightened, to motivate man to a proper and specific course of action, because of an absolute knowledge of truth.

"Whosoever committeth sin transgresseth also the law, for sin is the transgression of the law." (I John 3:4)

This leads to another conclusion; a law of God is necessary if man is to be judged a sinner before Him. God does not hold a man accountable for that which he cannot know (James 4:17). God's law then, is crucial in bringing man into judgment for his sin. Paul acknowledges this principle in the following statements:

"For where no law is, there is no transgression." (Rom. 4:15)

"For until the law sin was in the world; but sin is not imputed when there is no law." (Rom. 5:13)

For a man to be saved there must be a knowledge of his transgression of God's law and the fact that these violations place him at enmity against the character and moral will of God, thus incurring His wrath upon them.

"Because the law worketh *wrath*." (Rom. 4:15)

"Moreover the law entered that *offense* might abound." (Rom. 5:20)

"We shall be saved from *wrath* through Him. For if when we were *enemies* we were reconciled to God by the death of His Son; ..." (Rom. 5:9, 10)

"Because the carnal mind is *enmity* against God: for it is not subject to the *law* of God, neither indeed can be." (Rom. 8:7)

It is imperative that the sinner be showed that his sin is a transgression of God's law, and has made him an enemy of God, and placed him under His wrath, and were it not for Christ's death no reconciliation would be possible.

"He that believeth on the Son hath everlasting life: and he that believeth not the Son shall not see life; but the *wrath* of God abideth on him." (John 3:36)

The law of God was specifically ordained to expose sin.

God also uses His law to restrain sin. The threat of its penalty for disobedience serves to keep even unregenerate man from an unbridled indulgence in it.

"For I the Lord thy God am a jealous God, visiting the iniquity of the fathers upon the children unto the third and fourth generations of them that hate me;" (Ex. 20:5)

"If ye will not for all this hearken unto me, but walk contrary unto me; then I will walk contrary unto you also in fury; and I, even I, will chastise you seven times for your sins." (Lev. 26:27, 28)

"Knowing this, that the law is not made for a righteous man, but for the lawless and disobedient, for ungodly and for sinners ..." (I Tim. 1:9)

It is the wrath of God, which is promised against all individuals and nations who do not walk in His ways, that serves as a deterrent against unrestrained passions.

God's natural laws that were implanted in man have been distorted by man's sin, but His moral law, written in stone, by the finger of God, represents a clarion call to repentance for men of all ages. The need for such a moral law is evident, or sin is reduced to ethereal emotions of guilt and remorse. As man becomes more wicked it becomes increasingly easier for him to ignore his conscience and to eventually silence it.

God's moral law can awaken man to see his sin. It is an absolute standard from God to expose man's sins and is a revelation of God's will for him. Most people would agree that not all men will be saved from a life of sin, and so even for those unrepentant people there must be a moral code of ethics for society to govern itself by. If governments are to uphold good and punish evil, they then must have a standard to establish their civil laws on. God's moral law is such a standard.

The most critical determination then is; what represents God's moral law?

All the arguments for its necessity mean nothing unless we can succinctly demonstrate what God's moral law is. We may argue for God's law over man's law but unless we can define God's law, specifically His moral law, we have created a need with no remedy, and will eventually cause men to doubt whether such a need really exists at all.

It is natural for a man to strengthen his arguments against a societal evil by calling it immoral; but by doing so he acknowledges the presence of a moral law, which presupposes a Moral Lawgiver, which also means that his own arguments are now subject to review for coherence with God's moral law. By introducing morality to buttress an argument, he may, in effect, destroy that which he has set out to accomplish, for the moral law may condemn what he advocates (Rom. 2:1,2, 21-23).

It is very important to understand that while God's moral law does restrict sin in a society (otherwise what good is it?), it does not negate the principle of freedom of worship, especially for the Christian faith.

All civil law is undergirded by a moral foundation. When therefore morality becomes obsolete it will only be a short period of time until lawlessness will manifest itself. Once the moral foundation has been discarded by society, it will be only a short period of time until the validity of civil laws will be questioned, because they now are based upon precepts that have lost all value. Society will then view all attempts to reestablish a moral foundation as an infringement upon their rights. But if morality becomes void then we have created a scenario whereby all laws and ethics are merely the product of human philosophy, or at best natural law. We are then relegated to an imperfect knowledge of truth at best, and a gross distortion of truth as the inevitable end of a society's decline. The Scripture says, "If the foundations be destroyed, what can the righteous do" (Ps. 11:3)?

If man is not a moral creature, what right does anyone have to place him under any ethical guidelines? May I not then steal from another if he has what I want and I have the ability to take it? Shall my actions be judged by a moral code that does not exist? If there is no such moral code then there can be no compunction to obey it. And what right does even the government have to make a civil law on an ethereal premise of what constitutes right and wrong? Is government to be arbitrary in its enactment of ethical statutes? Does government become the Supreme Authority in moral matters? Does government have the right to impose its morals upon me without my consent? Are morals merely the product of group consensus? Does the majority have the right to impose its will upon the minority? What is morality anyway, and how did it attach itself to the human race in the form of a "value system"? If we are the product of a mutating and evolving species, without any moral makeup, shall we not take from the weaker to strengthen the strong in order to produce a superior race (survival of the fittest) and thus advance mankind's evolution? The Nazi rationale was clearly such, and revealed to the whole world the horror of such a philosophy.

Man is a moral creature that is under moral obligation. Once more, it is imperative to know God's moral law if we are to establish morality, and without morality we will have either tyranny or anarchy. We cannot create a moral foundation unless we can delineate the moral law. We must understand the definition of God's moral law.

## THE MORAL LAW

In an effort to determine the moral law of God some practical guidelines need to first be established.

*Firstly*, a moral law represents a foundation upon which all other laws are established. It must precede the giving of other laws. The edifice always follows the foundation, it never precedes it. So to find God's moral law we would look at the first laws He gave. The first step in the formation of a country is to write a Constitution, from which all law may be legislated. If the moral law is foundational, which it is, it needs to be given first.

*Secondly*, a moral law must be an unchanging standard. If it is to be the basis upon which other laws are enacted it must remain firm, or the legislated laws will lose their authority.

*Thirdly*, a moral law must be beyond debate or skepticism, for if the truth of it be questioned, then all its subsidiary and derivative laws become suspect. The framers of the American Constitution realized this, and began by observing that some truths are "self-evident" and as such are beyond debate. The stoics appealed to natural law as an absolute foundation for their statutory laws.

*Fourthly*, it must be recognized that all laws deriving from a moral law may change without in any way altering the immutability of the moral law itself. The changing of times can bring changes to a society's needs and thus call for new legislation, but new legislation still needs to be consistent with its moral foundation. The moral law must stand as a bulwark against the deception of changing times, and yet be flexible enough to accommodate relevant legislation.

*Fifthly*, moral law must be transcendent above the human experience and represent Divinity itself, and not the mere opinion of man. This enables man to legislate from it more authoritatively because the basis of the law can never be questioned.  Were moral law the product of man, its authority could be weakened by an opposing view that sounded logical to the human ear but in the final analysis could produce disaster. There must be a connection between the moral law and the divine character of the moral lawgiver so that it may be unquestionably true, even if it proves all men to be liars (Rom. 3:4).

It is important to understand that these five premises are foundational criteria of a moral law. A person may add other principles to these five, although this writer feels these five are comprehensive enough. It must also be understood that although the premises are listed before the scriptural support is produced, these premises were deduced from Scripture and not any work of philosophy or jurisprudence. The reasoning is the product of scriptural evidences that were given by God Himself to elevate the moral law to a superior position over the many other Hebraic laws and ordinances. The Scriptures provide their own criteria for these premises and are not answerable to any other moral or legal code of ethics or interpretations.

The truth of these premises should be immediately clear to any reasonable, thinking individual with a rudimentary knowledge of the relationship between law and ethics. There is only one body of law that fits this criteria; it is the Ten Commandments. It was the first law given to man (Ex. 19:20).

There were oral traditions among the ancient world that preceded the Ten Commandments but they were not given as a written law. The patriarchal book of Job represents a knowledge of God's will but there is no evidence of His law. Man is primarily instructed by the tradition of elders and inspiration from the Almighty (Job 5:1, 8:8-10, 15:17,18, 21:14,15,29,30 32:6-9).

All the Scripture references referring to the law place it in the time of Moses. Yet in that time frame it is seen that the Ten Commandments preceded the giving of the rest of the law. So the Ten Commandments meet the first qualification of a moral law. They represent the first body of commandments given by God.

Secondly, are the Ten Commandments an unchanging standard of God against sin? In order to answer that question we need to examine the significance of some Scriptures. In doing so we will really answer the third and fifth requirements also for a moral law. The second, third, and fifth principles are so closely related that some may think it unnecessary to differentiate between them. Although there is a distinction in these principles, they are so closely related that they will stand or fall together and so they will be treated together in the Scriptures that we examine.

One of the most significant facts about the moral law is that it was etched by the finger of God Himself on tables of stone.

"And the Lord said unto Moses, Come up to me into the mount, and be there; and I will give thee tables of stone, and A LAW, and commandments which I have written; that thou mayest teach them" (Ex. 24:12). Now the law had already been spoken by God in Exodus chapter 20, but it had not yet been given in written form. The first writing of this law was with the finger of God. The only law written on the tables of stone by God was the Ten Commandments.

The giving of this law was accompanied by an awesome demonstration of the majesty and holiness of God. This manifestation of Divine glory removed all doubt to those present that God was giving man His law.

*"And Moses brought forth the people out of the camp to meet with God; and they stood at the nether part of the mount. And mount Sinai was altogether on a smoke, because the Lord descended upon it in fire: and the smoke thereof ascended as the smoke of a furnace, and the whole mount quaked greatly" (Ex. 19:17, 18).*

*"For ask now of the days that are past, which were before thee, since the day that God created man upon the earth, and ask from one side of heaven unto the other, whether there be any such thing as this great thing is, or hath heard like it?*

*Did ever people hear the voice of God speaking out of the midst of the fire, as thou hast heard, and live?*

*Out of heaven he made thee to hear his voice, that he might instruct thee: and upon earth he showed thee his great fire; and thou heardest his words out of the midst of the fire." (Deut. 4:32, 33, 36)*

Now these words were spoken by Moses to Israel and prove that God spoke His Words of the Ten Commandments audibly in the ears of all Israel. God had to make the giving of His law incontrovertible, beyond all dispute, making it an immutable standard of holiness against sin. By all Israel gathering together and hearing God's voice speaking the commandments, it could never be construed as the philosophy of Moses.

"And the Lord said unto Moses, Lo, I come unto thee in a thick cloud, that the people may hear when I speak with thee, and believe thee FOREVER" (Ex. 19:9).

Moses said that this was the most momentous event of all times from the creation of the world until now. Because of the importance of it God wanted Israel to personally hear His Words, so that God's law would be believed FOREVER.

This audible speaking of the Ten Commandments before their writing of them upon stone is also testified of by Josephus, the Jewish historian.

*"When he (Moses) had said this, he brought the people, with their wives and children, so near the mountain, that they might hear* God Himself *(author's emphasis) speaking to them about the precepts which they were to practice; that the energy of what should be spoken might not be hurt by its utterance by that tongue of a man, which could not but imperfectly deliver it to the understanding. And they all heard a voice that came to all of them, which Moses wrote on two tables; which it is not lawful for us to set down directly, but their import we will declare."*[6]

After the giving of the Ten Commandments the people said to Moses, "Speak thou with us, and we will hear, but let not God speak with us, lest we die" (Ex. 20:19; Heb. 12:18-20).

The rest of the law was not given in such a manner (Deut. 5:28-31). So actually the law was first spoken by God to all Israel, then written by God on tables of stone, to be placed in the ark of the covenant, and then inscribed by Moses to be delivered to the people for regular referral (Ex. 32:15, 16).

"And the Lord delivered unto me two tables of stone written with the finger of God; and on them was written according to all the words which the Lord spake with you in the mount, out of the midst of the fire, in the day of the assembly." (Deut. 9:10)

"And thou shalt put into the ark the testimony that I shall give thee" (Ex. 25:16).

"And the Lord said unto Moses, write thou these words: for after the tenor of these words I have made a covenant with Israel. And He wrote upon the tables the words of the covenant, the ten commandments." (Ex. 34:27,28, see also Exodus 31:18  Deut. 5:1-5,22-26, 10:1-5.)

These passages make it clear that the Ten Commandments were the basis for Israel's covenant with Jehovah. They are the moral law of God. They are the standard of God that abides forever (Ex. 19:9). They were the only law that was placed in the ark of the covenant, and as such occupy a place of greater significance than the civil or ceremonial laws of Israel. The Decalogue (Ten Commandments) meet the requirements of a moral law on the following grounds:

1. It preceded all the other laws given to Moses.

2. It is unchanging, in that God told Moses He was to be believed "forever." There is no New Testament precept that nullifies the moral law, as we shall see later.

3. It was beyond dispute, for all the people personally heard the voice of God in these ten utterances.

4. The giving of it was accompanied by an awful display of God's majesty and holiness.

5. It was transcendent over human experience or opinion, for it was given by God Himself.

Because God is absolute in His character and attributes, and His moral law is a reflection of such, it becomes a standard that has not been perverted by human influence, and stands as a pristine insight into the will of God for man.

The fourth requirement states that laws that are based on a moral law may change without in any way calling the moral law, itself, into question. As an example, our Constitution is the foundation of all our legislated laws. The legislation may change but it must always be consistent with the Constitution. In a much greater way does God's moral law provide an unchanging foundation for other Old Testament laws.

While it is clearly seen that the sacrificial system of laws were rendered obsolete at Calvary, yet God's moral will for man has not changed. In fact, Christ's sacrifice accomplished for man what animal sacrifice could not. And so the change in law for atonement does not represent a change in God's will for man, but rather God's will is revealed in bringing man to the place where he would have no other gods before Him, by no longer being a servant to sin. This principle may be also represented by a father's moral will for his child. As the child grows, the father changes his methods of nurture and correction and yet there is no change in the father's ultimate will for his child. And so upon these grounds the Ten Commandments also meet the fourth criteria of a moral law; they represent a standard from God that is not made obsolete by the gospel, as many of the Old Testament laws are.

## THE MORAL LAW IS AN EXPRESSION OF GOD'S CHARACTER

It is this fact above all others that transcends the moral law above the other laws of the Old Testament. Because of the relationship between God's character and the Ten Commandments, along with the significance that God gave it Himself, we ascribe to it the term "moral law." The Ten Commandments are divided between our relationship to God, firstly, and then to our fellow man. The order in which they are given expresses the proper sequence, with our relationship to God being foundational to our relationship to others.

These standards as we have seen and shall see more fully have never been revoked by the gospel of Christ but instead have been strengthened.

"Do we then make void the law through faith? God forbid: yea, we establish the law." (Rom. 3:31)

When Paul speaks of the law showing him to be a sinner, it is the Ten Commandments, or moral law, that has the continuing relationship to faith, not in justifying the sinner, but in showing him wherein he has sinned (Rom. 2:21-24, 7:7-14). The moral law is comprehended in two basic concepts, of love for God and love to our fellow man. Jesus affirmed these two concepts in Matthew 22:34-40 and Mark 12:28-34. "On these two commandments hang all the law and the prophets" (Matt. 22:40). Note also the wording used in Romans 13:8-10.

"... he that loveth another hath fulfilled the law. For this, Thou shalt not commit adultery, Thou shalt not kill, Thou shalt not steal, Thou shalt not bear false witness, Thou shalt not covet, and if there be any other commandment, it is briefly comprehended in this saying, namely, Thou shalt love thy neighbor as thyself. ... therefore love is the fulfilling of the law." There is a direct connection between God's intention that we love our neighbor and the giving of the Ten Commandments. There was a moral intention to these physical acts.

Now if the Ten Commandments are the basis of God's covenant with man (Ex. 34:27, 28), and they are comprehended in love, then there is a direct connection between them and the fact that God Himself is love. There is no love outside of God, and if these precepts result from love then they are inextricably linked to the character of God (I John 4:7-21). If they proceed from the character of God then they cannot change unless God Himself would change, in which case He would no longer be God.

"... God is love; and he that dwelleth in love, dwelleth in God, and God in him (I John 4:16).

If God is love and His commandments are based on love, then they represent to man His unchanging moral will that is the expression of His character. This relationship between the character of God and His will for man is expressed in the following verses also:

"Ye shall be holy: for I the Lord your God am holy" (Lev. 19:2).

"Be ye holy; for I am holy" (I Pet. 1:16).

"Be ye therefore perfect, even as your Father which is in heaven is perfect" (Matt. 5:48).

If God's moral will for man flows from His character, then His moral will can never change without there being a change in God Himself. Can God change?

"Every good gift and every perfect gift is from above and cometh down from the Father of lights, with whom is no *variableness*, neither *shadow of turning*" (James 1:17).

"For I am the Lord, I change not..." (Mal. 3:6).

"The counsel of the Lord standeth forever, the thoughts of his heart to all generations" (Ps. 33:11).

The fact that the moral law springs from God's attributes is the reason that the moral law has preeminence over all the other Jewish laws. This is why the gospel of Christ may abrogate the other laws but serves to strengthen the moral law.

Concerning the ark of the covenant and the tables it contained, the Jew, Hillel, writes:

*"It is the written testimony of God against idolatry. It contains the fundamental articles of our nation's constitution."[7]*

He gives it the same distinction that the scriptures ascribe to it. There is a direct relationship between "I Am" and "Thou shalt" and "Thou shalt not."


## THE GOSPEL OF CHRIST IS THE FULL REVELATION OF THE ORIGINAL INTENT OF GOD'S MORAL LAW

We have established the necessity and importance of a moral law and now maintain that it is a catechizer to the gospel of Christ, which now raises another very important question (Gal. 3:24). Why did God wait so long to introduce a moral law and then wait again so long to reveal the gospel through His Son?

The full answer to this question exists in the inscrutable counsel of

God. But the providence of God has also made some things evident in the affairs of history. The giving of the moral law is largely relevant to the development of alphabetic writing. The Sumerians had a cuneiform style of writing as early as 3200B.C. The Egyptians used a hieroglyphic style that dates to 2800B.C.

Now we know that Moses was trained (Acts 7:22) *in all the wisdom of the Egyptians.* It mentions specifically that he was mighty in WORDS. His training obviously familiarized him with both cuneiform and hieroglyphic writing. He was responsible for developing the Semitic alphabet from these two forms of writing, although he possibly got some ideas from the Phoenicians. At any rate, all current alphabetic writing has its origin in the Semitic alphabet. (Reference an encyclopedia.) His training in language allowed him to develop writing to a new level, which moved from expressing mere concepts to precise wording. This development led to the giving of the moral law in a very exact form. Moses became then, also, the first author of Scripture. God brought Israel to Egypt, it would seem, to train Moses in language so that God could give and preserve His Word in a very accurate manner.

Many scholars feel that the early Semitic writing was a composition of the best of Sumerian, Egyptian, and Phoenician developments. Moses, being a privileged son of Pharaoh, would have had access to the best education available at that time. It would seem then that from this educational background Moses was able to develop an alphabetic style of writing. This assumption has its validity in the fact that there is presently no record of Semitic alphabetical writing before the authorship of Scripture. Even the learned Greeks, who came on the scene of history somewhat later, adopted the Semitic alphabet and modified it slightly by adding two letters and introducing vowel sounds to some consonantal symbols.

But the fact remains that history correlates Moses, alphabetic writing, and Scripture to the same relative time frame.

Here again, we quote Hillel, the Jew:

*"The world was overrun by wandering tribes, scarcely having bound-*

*aries or fixed habitations. Chaldea, the cradle of the human race, and Egypt, the birthplace of human learning and the arts, were the only nations of consequence at that time. It is not probable that any such thing as* alphabetic writing *existed; for we read that Abraham took no other evidence of the purchase which he made of a burying place for his family then living witnesses of the bargain. At that period, therefore, divine communication must have been confined to individuals. The* Fullness of Time *had not yet come even for that partial revelation which was made by Moses. There was no mode by which it could be recorded and preserved. The invention of writing was necessary to prepare the world for it. That invention took place some time within the five hundred years which elapsed between Abraham and Moses.*

*....Moses, the child of a slave, his life exposed in infancy in a frail cradle of rushes upon the waters, yet destined to be the mightiest agent in the affairs of men that the Almighty had ever employed on earth. Who can but admire the wisdom of Divine Providence in the education of this great founder of nations, this prophet of divine truth, this enlightener of the world?*

*Who can apprehend the glorious position which he holds in the world's history? What a distinction to have framed the constitution of a nation which lasted fifteen hundred years* (Hillel lived during Apostolic times), *and stamped a people with the marks of nationality which time itself has not obliterated!*

*...What a noble use did the Almighty make of the recent invention of man's ingenuity, the invention of letters, to engrave upon stone His awful testimony against the great, fundamental, and all-polluting sin of the world, the worship of idols: 'Thou shalt have no other Gods before me; thou shalt not make unto thee any graven image, or the likeness of anything that is in the heaven above or in the earth beneath; thou shalt not bow down thyself to them nor serve them.'"*[8] (emphasis mine) Hillel's observations correlate with modern research on the subject. He rightly links the giving of the moral law to Moses' education, alphabetic writing, the Providence of God, and the *Fullness of Time.*

The time frame and factors that contributed to the giving of the moral law are well established. Now the critical time line moves from the introduction of God's moral law to the birth of Christ and the giving of the gospel. In Galatians 4:4, 5 Paul lays down some very important points concerning the incarnation of Christ into this world.

"But when the *fullness of the time* was come, God sent forth His Son, made of a woman, made under the law, *to redeem them that were under the law,* that we might receive the adoption of sons.

There are two important principles here:

a. God had a specific time frame for the sending of His Son.

b. The purpose of Christ's coming was to bring redemption to those under God's law, implying that the law, while an unchanging standard against sin, could not in any way save man from sin, specifically from his own sinful nature.

The first principle is critical to the present subject, while the second will be illustrated throughout this work. So if Christ's coming had specific reasons for its time frame, then the providence of God should be evident throughout history relative to this event. With the giving of the moral law and then the other laws by Moses, the Jewish identity became established in this world.

From the infancy of the Jewish nations to the rise of the Grecian Empire, the various world empires all came into contact with the Jewish faith by their conquests. This was for several reasons the providence of God; it was remedial judgment for Israel, and it brought heathen nations into contact with truth and a knowledge of one true God.

After the final captivity of the Jews in Babylon and their return to Israel under Cyrus, the Persian, they were completely cured of their idolatrous tendencies. During these two empires, the Babylonian and Persian, the Jewish faith confronted the best heathen philosophers of the time. During Daniel's life, which spanned both the Babylonian and the Persian powers, he was in prominent positions of leadership. His influence and life demonstrated the superiority of his faith, provoking both Babylonian and Persian kings to acknowledge the pre-eminence of Jehovah (Dan. 2:47, 4:34-37, 6:25-28). The Jews demonstrated their superior knowledge of truth to both these empires (Dan. 1:17, 5:11-12, 6:3-5).

The interaction between these Jews and the heathen philosophers (Magi) acquainted the pagan world with the principles of one true God and other elements of the Jewish faith. It was under Darius I that the teachings of monotheism gained widespread acceptance among the Persians, as taught by their philosopher Zoroaster. Hillel records that due to Jewish influence of monotheism, the teachings of Zoroaster were introduced as an alternate to both pagan polytheism and Judasim and became the prominent philosophy of their Magi.[9]

Although the Persians did not convert to Judaism, they modified their own beliefs because of it, and were very friendly to the Jewish faith, aiding in the return of the Jews to their land to rebuild their temple. God was using the captivity of His people in world empires to begin the infusion of truth to all peoples of the world.

The next significant event was the establishment of the Greek empire, which united the world by one language and culture. During the Hellenistic (Greek) age, the Jews translated their Scriptures into the Greek language (Septuagint) and established synagogues and schools of learning throughout the whole Greek world, bringing more pagans to a knowledge of truth. With the world adopting one language, truth could spread much more rapidly. The Greek philosophers came into contact with Judaism and again there was a profound influence upon Greek thought. Josephus relates the following account that was a conversation between Aristotle and Hyperochides as recorded by Clearchus:

*"This man, then, was by birth a Jew, and came from Celesyria; these Jews are derived from the Indian philosophers; they are named by the Indians Calami, and by the Syrians Judaei, and took their name from the country they inhabit, which is called Judea; but for the name of their city it is a very awkward one, for they call it Jerusalem. Now this man, when he was hospitably treated by a great many, came down from the upper country to the places near the sea, and became a Grecian, not only in his language, but in his soul also;* (probably referring to culture, for his beliefs

remained distinct*) insomuch that when we ourselves happened to be in Asia about the same places whither he came, he conversed with us and with other philosophical persons; and made trial of our skill in philosophy; as he had lived with many learned men, he communicated to us more information than he received from us.*[10] (emphasis and clarifications mine) Josephus catalogues other instances of Jewish interaction with Greek philosophers, and the influence it had upon Greek thought and law.

Now it might be argued that if the Greeks were influenced by the Jews, then the Greeks did not believe in natural law but rather in Jewish morality. On the surface this argument may seem plausible, but if Greek thought is studied what one finds is that they only accepted from the Jews what could be supported by human reasoning. They did not accept the Jewish ideas of inspiration or revelation, to any large degree. They believed the ideas of one Supreme Being, a moral code of ethics, and life after death were three elements that could be supported with good rationale and were profitable to establishing a just society.

Their arguments were always based on reasoning and what was defined as natural law rather than from special, divine revelation. But even these developments were a move away from pagan myth and legend, toward logic and truth, a move for which the Jewish faith provided a lasting contribution. The element most significant here is that with a universal language in place, the spread of truth and specifically the gospel would occur far more rapidly.

The next empire was the Roman. What they brought to the world was a continuation of the Greek language and culture, which they combined with relative world peace over a long period of time and an extensive system of roads. As someone has observed, "They literally paved the way for the gospel." Not only were world conditions physically ripe for the gospel, but the Jews had spread their anticipation of a Messiah throughout the world. The prophecies of Daniel's sixty-nine weeks, from the building of Jerusalem until the time of the Messiah (Dan. 9:25), had given the world a specific time to expect the appearance of Christ. Both of the Roman historians, Tacitus and

Suetonius, record that there were many with an air of expectancy for the appearance of a Jewish ruler coming to the world scene.[11]

So what Paul referred to as the "fullness of time" was a specific reference to the providence of God in history leading up to the birth of Christ. The world was given one language and one government, and many roads to facilitate the spread of the gospel of Christ. God's hand is seen guiding history in all these events, from the giving of His moral law to the full revelation of His gospel.

We have seen how the Jews influenced the world with God's law, yet we realize that all this was only preparatory for Christ. The law was never intended as an end in itself, it was a schoolmaster to bring us to Christ (Gal. 3:21-25). The reasons for the giving of the law are the same reasons for which it is still retained today; the same reasons why faith in Christ does not make it void. The world still needs an unchanging standard of morality. Sinners still need precise precepts to show them wherein they have sinned, so that their mouths may be stopped and they may become guilty before God. Sin is not ethereal, guilt is not merely emotional distress, and morality is not relative.

Christ's pardon is only effectual to the man who sees himself as an enemy to God, under His wrath, with no hope of saving himself outside of Christ. This is the work of the moral law, to bring a man to Christ, by showing him his sin.

The other Jewish laws have relevance to their culture and nation in pointing the Jew to Christ, but the primary catechizer is the moral law, especially for Gentile unbelievers, in showing man his sin and need for a Savior. It is the moral law that is continually used in reference to sin and a need for salvation.

"I had not known sin except the law had said, Thou shalt not covet." (Rom. 7:7)

James 2:8-11 shows that offending God in any part of His moral law will make us transgressors. Why? Because the second table of the law is comprehended in love to our neighbor, and to violate any of those six precepts will condemn us in a lack of love.

In Jesus' dialogue with a rich young ruler he used the moral law to answer the man's question, "What good thing shall I do, that I may have eternal life?" Jesus' answer was, "Keep the commandments," and He quotes from the moral law.

This young man still did not see his sin, "All these have I kept from my youth up," he replied, but yet he knew there was a lack. "What lack I yet?" he asked.

Jesus pointed to his possessions as the great hindrance, which in effect showed the young man's disobedience was in the first command, "Thou shalt have no other gods before me." Jesus was not establishing salvation either by the law or by poverty. Christ introduced the law to the dialogue as a code that He knew the young man would profess to believe in. He did it to show the man his sin. The man felt that the law would vindicate his righteousness. Christ showed the man his sin by pointing to a specific area of idolatry. As Christ's methods often were, He let the individual think through the final point.

Thought process: *"If I cannot give up my possessions to follow the One whom I called "Good Master" (and "Good" implying His Deity), then I cannot say that I obey the first commandment, which shows that I do not love God with all my heart, soul, mind, and strength. If I cannot give up my many possessions to those who have need (the poor) then I do not love my neighbor as myself. So I am a sinner before God, for I love my possessions more than Him. I will not follow Christ whom I acknowledged as God and I will not help my neighbor in need; the law has shown me a sinner."*

Did the young man have all these thoughts? We do not know. But what is clearly evident is that a self-righteous man sought salvation. Christ introduced Himself as God, and then the law to show his sin. The man wanted salvation without necessary repentance. Christ showed him that materialism was an idol held above obeying God and loving his neighbor. The law that he professed righteousness in showed him to be a sinner.

There is a very close relationship between the moral law of God and the gospel of His Son. This is manifest again in the defense

Stephen gave against the indictments brought forth by the Hellenistic Jews. (Acts 6:11,13,14) The charges were (as they relate to this subject):

He spoke against Moses and against God (vs. 11)

He spoke blasphemous words against the law (vs. 13)

The evidence was:

He said that Jesus of Nazareth would change Moses' customs.

The Jews equated changing Moses' customs (ceremonial law) with speaking against God, Moses, and the law; and obviously if the temple were destroyed, as Jesus said, their customs would change. What they were forgetting was that the foundation or constitution of the law would never change, only the interim laws given by Moses.

Stephen in his defense answered their charges so powerfully that the Jews stopped their ears. Notice now how Stephen argues for first the Deity of Christ and then for the gospel of Christ (Acts 7:30-38; Ex. 3:1-6). Stephen tells how Moses was spoken to by the angel of the Lord from the bush. Now Moses clearly saw the Angel (no man hath seen God at any time, John 1:18) in form, but yet when the angel spoke, He said, "I am the God of thy fathers." There was a visible form that said, "I am God." Then Stephen quotes Moses as saying that a greater one than him will come who is to be obeyed (vs. 37). Stephen shows that this same Angel who called Moses was also with the assembly (church) at Sinai when Moses received the Law, specifically saying that this Angel spoke the law to Moses and to their fathers (vs. 38).

Now if this Angel was God, but not Jehovah, then it had to be His Son, which was who Jesus claimed to be, and He who gave the law to Moses surely had the authority to change their customs. This Angel is also spoken of in the Old Testament and by its description must be Christ, as Stephen argues. In Exodus 23:20-23 God says that He has put His name in this Angel and He demands obedience to Him. The Angel is also the one who drives out the heathen before them (Ex. 33:2). Moses himself describes Israel's deliverance as being by the Angel (Num. 20:16). If Christ was the Angel who spoke at Sinai, then there was only one lawgiver and it was Christ (James 4:12). Christ spoke the moral law and also came in person to bring His gospel.

All the religious ceremonies of the Jews were types and shadows of one man, Christ. They would all pass when the fullness of time brought Christ. But the moral law was the heart of God's covenant with His people, rooted in the very character of God, given by Christ, and as such has a continuing relationship to the gospel of Christ, by bringing them to his Redeemer.

One of the chief distinctions between the moral law as it was originally understood and the gospel of Christ is that the law under the old covenant could only identify physical and external transgressions, while the gospel spoke to the heart and identified motives and affections.

The first required a commitment of the will, while the second required, along with a choice of the will, a quickening of the spirit.

Under the covenant of law, those who could physically conform to the external act were deemed righteous or moral, with the perfect heart being one that was fully committed to God and His law.

Under the covenant of grace, a man sees his sin because of Christ's spiritual interpretation of the law by His gospel, realizes his will as insufficient to reform himself, and casts himself upon Christ for pardon and a new heart that will walk in obedience, not for salvation, but out of a heart of gratitude for what Christ has done for him (Rom. 7:7-25, 8:4).

This is why Paul could say that he was blameless in the law (Phil. 3:6) as an unconverted man, and then say that the law was spiritual and he was carnal, sold under sin (Rom. 7:14), and found a sinner by the law. He was externally blameless but internally sinful. This illustrates the difference between the law and the gospel. (See also Matt. 5:21, 22, 27, 28). Yet the law retains its value by helping a man see his sin and by bringing him to Christ.

It has also a use as a moral standard for the establishment of a just society, which shall be shown in another chapter.

The primary purpose of the law, though, is to stress the importance of love for God and our fellow man (Mark 12:28-34, Matt. 22:40).

Love is primarily a condition of the heart and the will, and manifests itself in actions. No man, in an unregenerate state, can love God as he ought, because his heart is deceitful and desperately wicked, and yet this is what God requires by His law. Christ's love for us, when appropriated to our hearts provides for us then the ability to love. In our sins we were God's enemies, unable to love Him, but through Christ's death we are able to be reconciled to God and love Him (Rom. 5:8-10). Our ability to love God lies in the fact that He has chosen to first love us (I John 4:10, 19).

Our ability to love God enables us to love our neighbor, which fulfills the original intent of God's moral law (Rom. 13:8-10, Gal. 5:14). Our love to our fellow man is to be exemplified in the same manner as Christ showed His, unconditionally and unlimited (John 13:34). Christ called this a new commandment because it was to be instituted by His example.

Therefore, love, while being an old concept, is a new commandment when it is instituted after the pattern of Christ's life. The world had never before seen the love of God manifest in flesh and blood. The Old Testament saint was to love God and his neighbor but was allowed to hate his enemy (Matt. 5:43, II Sam. 22:41, Ps. 139:21, 22, Eccl. 3:8).

Christ exemplified for us how to love our enemies, pray for our persecutors, and bless those who curse us. Only a regenerated heart can love in this manner; only one born of God's love (I John 4:7, 8). Thus the weakness of the law to institute love was overcome by the gospel and grace of Christ and is now the preeminent attribute of the Christian (John 13:35, I Cor. 13). The righteous intent of God's moral law is realized by those who walk in the Spirit of Christ (Rom. 8:3, 4).

The gospel of Christ strengthens the moral precepts of each one of the Ten Commandments. The following numbers indicate the particular commandment, while the New Testament references affirm the precept.

1. Romans 1:25; I Corinthians 10:14, 20; Acts 14:15; I Corinthians 8:4-6

2. Acts 17:24-26; I John 5:21; Romans 1:22, 23; Revelation 9:20

3. Matthew 5:33-37; James 5:12; Ephesians 4:29; James 3:6-12

4. Hebrews 4:4-11; Acts 20:7; I Corinthians 16:2; Revelation 1:10; Mark 2:27

5. Matthew 15:3-6; Ephesians 6:2, 3

6. Matthew 5:21, 22; I John 3:11-15; Matthew 10:16, 26:52

7. Matthew 5:27-32, 19:1-9; I Corinthians 6:9

8. Ephesians 4:28; Mark 11:17, 7:21, 22; I Corinthians 6:8-10; I Peter 4:15

9. Luke 19:8; John 16:13; I Corinthians 13:6; Ephesians 4:15; II John 4

10. I Corinthians 6:10; Ephesians 5:5; II Timothy 3:2; II Peter 2:14; Luke 12:15; Hebrews 13:5

Perhaps someone might object that the fourth commandment does not apply to the gospel age. Without digressing from the main emphasis of this chapter it may still be profitable to point out a few principles concerning the Sabbath observance.

First of all the word "Sabbath" means rest, repose, or cessation (from labor). Even with the Apostolic practice of moving its observance to the first day of the week, the basic principle of rest every seven days remains in effect. While Jesus and the Apostles both modified its practice and the rigid guidelines for its observance under the Mosaic code, the foundational principle of a day of rest and keeping it holy remain in effect by their observance of what the Apostle called "The Lord's Day" (Rev. 1:10).

Jesus also in His statement that the Sabbath was made for man, was speaking clearly of man's need for physical rest and a spiritual focus. Although He violated the Mosaic observance of it repeatedly, here He affirms the validity of the principles for it. Did man's physiological composition change with the Advent of Christ? Surely it did not, so the need for it remains. Did man's need for focus on God change with the Advent of Christ? Surely it did not, so the need for a Sabbath remains; for the Sabbath was made for man.

In the Hebrews 4:4-11 passage the writer establishes the "rest" of the believer upon the principle of a Sabbath "rest." Now if the principle of rest has become obsolete, then the writer was seeking to rest a future promise upon a destroyed foundation, which if true, would also leave us with no guarantee for an eternal rest.

While the New Testament in many places nullifies the ceremonial ordinances, it nowhere nullifies the moral precepts of the Decalogue (Ten Commandments). In fact, the opposite is true, it strengthens them and gives them spiritual meaning. The whole law and the prophets hinged on the concepts of love to God and love to our fellow man. These concepts are clearly expressed in the moral law. It is an external test of love. There is always a relationship between love and obedience.

This same principle Jesus upholds by saying, "If ye keep my commandments, ye shall abide in my love" and "Ye are my friends, if ye do whatsoever I command you." (John 15:10,14) The first four commandments teach us to love God with all our heart, soul, mind, and strength. But this is impossible with an unregenerate heart that by nature is a child of wrath and is at enmity with both the person and law of God (Eph. 2:3 Rom. 8:7,8).

The unconverted heart always lives for self and cannot give God all his love. Yet the heart is so deceitful and self-righteous that it imagines itself to be quite good. It finds assurance in all its benevolent deeds and outward acts of piety. So God has chosen ten key areas where He can show man where his sin is quite evident. Christ showed how hatred in the heart is fertile soil for murder and is a violation of love towards one's neighbor.

God has provided His preachers with a law that they can use to make sin appear exceeding sinful; for he who violates God's law in one point only is convinced of the law as a transgressor and is in open rebellion against God. To continue in such a state is to declare oneself as an enemy of God and His law and to incur God's wrath and judgment upon his life. The love of God has provided for only one escape from the death penalty and it is through His Son. He that believeth on the Son hath life and he that believeth not has the wrath of God upon him (John 3:36). Through the gift of God's Son He has expressed to us His great love. This is the means by which we may flee from the wrath to come. It is the purpose of the law to work wrath, that is, to show that our every affection is against God, and His law is against us for our sin (Rom. 4:15). When we see our desperate wickedness, and how sin has polluted our very nature, and acknowledge our inability to reform ourselves, then we are led by the law to the only pardon it will accept, the Lamb of God. Christ has taken the full punishment for sin and bore it in His own body on the tree, with the reproaches of those that reproached God falling upon Him. His travail of soul has wrought our redemption. He cried, "My God, My God, why has thou forsaken Me" that He might say to us, "I will never leave thee nor forsake thee," and "Lo I am with you always." He was made the curse of the law for us that He might redeem us from its penalty (Gal. 3:13). This great redemption not only obtained our pardon but it united our old man to that cross and slew that rebellious nature, so that the body of sin might be destroyed and the new man might resurrect (Rom. 6:1-11). This new man has a "divine nature" (II Pet.1:4), one that is truly capable of loving God with all his heart, soul, mind, and strength.

Because of Christ's work alone this man now has the ability to both love God and keep His commandments. Our ability to love God is due solely to the fact that He chose to first love us (I John 4:19). The heart that now loves God because it has experienced God's love has the ability to keep His commandments. It is an impossibility to possess a heart of love and not have a burning desire to obey God, for this is the love of God, the obeying of His Word (I John 4:7-5:5). What the law failed to accomplish because of being limited by a corrupted human will, God by His Son is able to perform in our hearts by the work of His Spirit. So God's law brings man to faith, and the justified man is now able to walk in obedience to the commands of the gospel. Where before he could not truly love God or his neighbor, now he can love God, his neighbor, and his enemy.

The man that "labors" for his redemption is filled with frustration in his attempts to overcome sin; it is a war against his own nature which he cannot win, but he who "accepts" his salvation labors the more diligently, not for salvation, but rather from love and gratitude for what Christ has already done. And so it becomes evident that the original intent of God's moral law is revealed fully only in the gospel of His Son.

Mount Sinai was an awful demonstration of the holiness of God. The moral law was given to expose and restrain sin by producing the fear of God through a visible manifestation of holiness. The law, though, could not regenerate the sinful heart, and so was unable to cure the malady of sin.

Someone has said, "Truth without relationship breeds rebellion." Also, moral precept without love generates either animosity or hypocrisy, which is just disguised rebellion; which in either case places a man at odds with God and His law. But by exposing the problem, the law could anticipate the solution.

Christ Himself, the Word of God, gave the law, knowing full well that one day He would pay for the full sentence it had given to the transgressors.

Moses, who was the earthly mediator for Israel, who spoke with the Angel (Christ), confessed to all the people that one day they would hear a greater prophet, one who has been given the name, "The Word of God." God confirmed also the gospel and deity of His Son, audibly, on different occasions; "This is My beloved Son in whom I am well pleased, HEAR YE HIM."

In Hebrews 12:18-24 the Hebrew writer also shows how the gospel of Christ has superseded the moral law by establishing a new covenant relationship with the people of God. *"For ye are not come unto the mount that might be touched, and that burned with fire, nor unto blackness, and darkness, and tempest, and the sound of a trumpet, and the voice of words....But ye are come unto Mount Zion, and unto the city of the living God, the heavenly Jerusalem, and to an innumerable company of angels, to the general assembly and church of the firstborn, which are written in heaven, and to God the Judge of all, and to the spirits of JUST MEN MADE PERFECT, and to Jesus the mediator of the NEW COVENANT, and to the blood of sprinkling, that speaketh better things than that of Abel."*

The covenant of Sinai was one of works and bondage (Gal. 4:24) for it condemned man for his sin but could never perfect him. Even those like Paul who could walk blameless in all the external moral precepts could become "just" because of their obedience, but could never become "perfect" because of a heart that was ruled by a sinful nature that could not fully love God. These just men could never be made perfect until the new covenant made it possible for the law to be written in their hearts. They could obey it externally but could never obey it spiritually. He who has a perfected heart by the blood of Christ, in adhering to the gospel, will also automatically obey both the physical and spiritual precepts of the law without it ever really being his focus, for its spiritual precepts have largely been comprehended by the gospel commands that he obeys. He will not focus upon that which he has died to (Gal. 2:18, 19). His heart is intent on loving God through obedience to the Gospel of Christ. It is God working in him both to "will" and to "do" of his good pleasure (Phil. 2:13).

If the "life" of Christ be in him it is only natural for it to produce the "actions" of Christ. Obedience to the gospel of Christ is the result of the heart that loves Christ (John 14:15). As much as this world needed a moral law because of the blindness to sin, it needed yet more a Savior, who gave both a pardon and a gospel that would prevail over the strength of sin. Sinai needed a Calvary and the moral law needed a gospel. The culmination of history was in the advent of the gospel of Christ, it being the full revelation and completion of what the moral law strove for, but could not attain, without Christ.

1  *Philip Schaff, History of the Christian Church Vol. II p. 320 (1991, WM. B. Eerdmans Publishing Company)*

2  *Ibid p. 324*

3  *Ibid p. 328*

4  *Archko Volume p. 202, 203 (1975 by Keats Publishing Inc.)*

5  *Ibid p. 203, 204*

6  *Flavius Josephus, Antiquities of the Jews, Book III, chapter V, point 4*

7  *Archko Volume p. 176 (1975 by Keats Publishing Inc.)*

8  *Ibid p. 172-174*

9  *Ibid p. 183-185*

10  *Flavius Josephus, Against Apion, Book 1, point 22*

11  *Matthew Henry's Commentary, notes on Matthew 2*

come out of her my people

# chapter two

# The Abrogation of the Civil and Ceremonial Laws by the Gospel of Christ

The coming of Christ to this earth changed the course of history forever. Gentile kings would come to the brightness of His rising (Isa. 60:3), their pagan superstitions dispelled by the light of truth. The religious establishment of the Jews was exposed as hypocrisy, and the very foundation of their beliefs was shaken by the gospel of Christ.

Herod the Great knew that according to Daniel's prophecy of seventy weeks the coming of the Messiah was at hand, so he offered to build the Jews a temple like Solomon's, thereby possessing the public genealogies of Zerubbabel's temple, so that no professed Messiah could prove Himself the Son of David. This was his attempt to thwart the prophecy of the Scriptures concerning the root of Jesse who would come to reign and smite the earth with the rod of His mouth and slay the wicked (Isa. 11:1-4). He thought the mere confiscation of lineages would confuse God's plan, and allow him to continue his reign over the Jews in Palestine.

Yet he was to have a great surprise when the Magi came to worship the KING OF THE JEWS (Matt. 2:2).

His reaction to the news is typical of all wicked men when confronted with the gospel; there are vacillations between curiosity, fear, and fits of rage.

What is there about the Child in the manger that causes such strong reaction in the palace?

It is but twelve years until this child is in the temple bringing amazement to doctors of the law by His profound questions and answers (Luke 2:46,47). What is there about the Child's understanding and knowledge that will challenge established opinions and question even the basis of their faith?

Had not their laws been handed down by God to Moses? Did they not survive heathen criticism? As Josephus relates, many Greek philosophers such as Aristotle and Pythagoras could not lightly dismiss the antiquity and authority of the Jewish Sriptures, and incorporated some aspects of Jewish thought into their own philosophy, especially in the realm of morality.[1]

During the time of Daniel, had not even world rulers made decrees that were directly influenced by interaction with the Jewish faith and laws? How then could this Nazarene, a mere carpenter's son, baffle and confound a system of religion that had survived the most eloquent onslaughts by some of the world's wisest men?

The religious authorities feared His truth, while the political powers were apprehensive of His person. And yet the Man sought no political office but merely preached the gospel, and mostly to the common people.

What was there about the person of Christ that evoked such controversy, and the teachings of Christ that provoked such antagonism?

The religious establishment courted the political powers to terminate the ministry of Christ. The charges against Him were both religious and political, ranging from blasphemy to sedition. Here then was the combination of the greatest earthly powers and the most venerable of all religious traditions bringing Jesus to trial for the teachings of His gospel. Even Herod, the enemy of Pilate, collaborated in the judgment of Christ (Luke 23:12).

One of the chief disputes that the Pharisees had with Christ was between His teachings and Moses' law. They could not accept that their ceremonial and civil ordinances could be replaced by His teachings. They represented their very national identity. Were they not divinely inspired? Did they not separate themselves from the heathen nations around them? It was not just the Talmuds (rabbinical teachings) that were being questioned, but whole sections of the Torah (Moses' law).

This man Jesus gathered food on the Sabbath (Matt. 12:1,2) when Moses had expressly forbidden the gathering of manna on the Sabbath (Ex. 16:26-30). When Israelites went out looking for manna on the Sabbath, the Lord said, "How long refuse ye to keep my commandments and my laws?"

Who then was Jesus to transgress God's law? Jesus responded with other examples of David and the priests showing how they also violated the letter of the civil ordinance and yet never profaned the holiness of the Sabbath (Matt. 12:3-8). Although in the letter of the ordinance He was a transgressor, yet in the principle of holiness He was Lord of the Sabbath.

What Christ was establishing was the transitory nature of the provisional ordinances of the ceremonial and judicial systems without absolving the eternal principles of the moral law; that a man should keep every seventh day holy to the Lord. He still affirmed that the Sabbath was made for man (Mark 2:27).

The Jews, though, insisted on the continuance of all their ordinances.

Jesus' teachings represented a threat to their dreams of the reestablishment of the Jewish state based on Moses' law.

It may be argued by some that Jesus' life did not contradict the law, only the traditions of the rabbis; but this is a vain assertion. Jesus never disputed whether God instituted a law against gathering food on the Sabbath, He only showed that there were other precedents for breaking these laws, thus showing that God Himself never intended their absolute continuance or perfection. He not only contradicted the traditions of the elders but also the civil and ceremonial laws, as will be shown.

The arguments that were made against Christ as a lawbreaker were also made against Stephen and Paul (Acts 6:11-14, 21:28, 25:7,8).

Their laws, they argued, maintained their identity; if they were superseded by this man's teachings, all hope of a Jewish state would be gone.

They apprehended and tried Him. They demanded that Pilate also commit to His death. The charges that were initially religious were now changed to political ones. Calling Himself the Son of God was first blasphemy, and then became the charge of political insurrection because He made Himself a King. Away with such a Man!

In the fury of their religious fervor their sentiments completely changed. Initially they wanted to kill Him to maintain their Jewish ideals, but in uniting with the Roman powers to crucify Him, they said, "We have no king but Caesar."

But they could not stamp out the truth of His words. He had prophesied that the Gentile armies would destroy the temple, their center of Jewish faith. Without the temple they could not fully keep the ceremonial law, and without independent sovereignty they could not enact Moses' civil law.

God had been preparing His people for this moment. They had lost their temple and independence before and yet they could still worship God in Babylon. The moral precepts of the law remained unchanged and were still relevant even though they could not practice all their ordinances. But the Jew would not give up his hope for a return of the full practice of Mosaic law.

While God was trying to wean them from the ordinances of the law in preparation for the gospel, they were yearning for the reinstatement of God's laws under which formerly they had continuously rebelled. The law, though, was to serve, not as an end in itself, but as a schoolmaster to bring men to Christ, who was the way, the truth, and the life.

In the destruction of the temple and the Jewish state, God abolished their ability to observe those practices that were to only be temporary until the fullness of time brought Christ.

Thus the gospel of Christ superseded those initial laws. It is comparable to the training of a child, who in early stages hears continually the "laws" of restraint, then the "principles" of restraint, and finally matures into a "love" for righteousness. So the gospel transcends Moses' laws. It is the full revelation of God's love to man, the typification of sacrificial ordinances,and the complete order of conduct for him who patterns his life after the precepts of the Lord.

There comes a time when the lame man must rid himself of crutches if he is to learn to truly walk.

The Jews had Jerusalem for their center of faith so much so that Daniel in Babylon would pray toward Jerusalem, for in it was the temple, the focus of their worship at that time. But when Stephen preached to the Jews that the Most High dwelleth not in temples made with hands" (Acts 7:48,49), they were cut to the heart. How could God ever abandon such a venerable institution? Had He not directed its building?

Would He destroy His own house according to the prophecy of Christ?

If the temple were destroyed, so also their sacrificial system would cease. If their ceremonial ordinances would end, of what value would the civil sanctions be that were meant to enforce them?

The Jews lost not only their temple, but also their land, thus ending for them any ability to *fully* observe either their ceremonial or civil law.

Hillel III, a Jew, cries for an explanation: *"Oh, these sacred ordinances! How can the world do without them? It seems that the world could do as well without the light of the sun, as well without food to eat or water to drink, as to do without these doctrines and teachings of the Jews. But they are all gone. The city, the temple, the doctrine, the priest, the law, and the nation are all gone. Is it so that God has become tired of His own appointments? or does He see a defect in His own ways, or has He become dissatisfied with His own covenant made to our fathers and to their children?*

*I write you these letters, my beloved countrymen, asking you to look at these things, and find out the cause of our abandonment."*[2]

During the destruction of Jerusalem, Josephus records a number of supernatural events that clearly indicated that God was both judging His people and abandoning former institutions, one of which is as follows: *"Besides these, a few days after that feast, on the one and twentieth day of the month Artemisius (Jyar), a certain prodigious and incredible phenomenon appeared; I suppose the account of it would seem to be a fable, were it not related by those who saw it, and were not the events that followed it so considerable a nature as to deserve such signals; for, before sun-setting, chariots and troops of soldiers in their armor were seen running about among the clouds, and surrounding of cities. Moreover at that feast which we call Pentecost, as the priests were going by night into the inner (court of the) temple, as their custom was, to perform their sacred ministrations, they heard a sound as of a great multitude, saying, 'Let us remove hence.'"[3]* (emphasis mine)

The meaning of those last words was that God was leaving the temple, letting it be destroyed by the Roman army. God, though, was not leaving behind a vacuum after this terrible destruction, for He had already provided a new and living way in His Son, Jesus Christ.

Although Christ was crucified, the truth of His teachings would be the most powerful force upon this earth.

They would create a mighty army of saints that would overthrow the paganism of the Roman world. They would succeed Judaism as the religion with the most credible evidence to substantiate its truth.

What then is the gospel of Christ and what is it of Moses' law that has been abrogated by it?

In defining the gospel of Christ we mean simply all truth comprehended in the New Testament, and all that is in the Old Testament, that is in harmony with the New, being given its fullest meaning by being interpreted through Christ.

This statement is substantiated by the Scripture itself.

"For all the prophets and the law prophesied until John." (Matt. 11:13).

"The law and the prophets were until John: since that time the kingdom of God is preached..." (Luke 16:16).

"For the law was given by Moses, but grace and truth came by Jesus Christ" (John 1:17).

These verses indicate at what point in history the gospel was preached. It began with John the Baptist proclaiming, "The kingdom of heaven is at hand."

Christ inaugurated "grace" and "truth" as compared to "law" that was given by Moses.

This does not mean that the law was not true but rather that it was superseded by a blend of both truth and grace. Only in Christ does grace and truth come together. The law works "wrath" or condemnation by truth, but is not able to reconcile men to truth as the gospel does (Rom. 3:19,20; 4:15; II Cor. 5:18-20).

The gospel is not just comprehended in the gospels as some have maintained but is also contained in all the epistles. Christ Himself said that He was withholding truth until the Spirit came, for without the Spirit they could not bear all truth. This is a significant statement for two reasons. It validates the incompleteness of the law as a knowledge of truth, for it was given to men who did not have the indwelling Spirit. Secondly, it makes obvious that the apostles would bring the remainder of the gospel.

Note the following verses: "I have yet many things to say to you, but ye cannot bear them now. Howbeit when he, the Spirit of truth is come, he will guide you into all truth: for he shall not speak of himself; but whatsoever he shall hear, that shall he speak: and he will show you things to come. he shall glorify me: for he shall receive of mine, and show it unto you. All things that the Father hath are mine: therefore said I, that he shall take of mine, and show it unto you" (John 16:12-15).

"For I have received of the Lord that which also I delivered unto you" (I Cor. 11:23).

"If any man think himself to be a prophet, or spiritual, let him acknowledge that the things that I write unto you are the commandments of the Lord" (I Cor. 14:37).

The teachings of the apostles are represented here as the commandments of the Lord, thus they also become part of the gospel of Christ. The gospel, though, was not given through the apostles till after the coming of the Spirit. Before the Spirit came they could have dialogued on the law, as they understood it, but after the Spirit illuminated their minds they perceived the law in a new light, and were able to comprehend the gospel, it previously being very vague to them, as their questions to Jesus often reflect.

These verses thus far illustrate the gospel of Christ as being separate from the law. It will be discussed later in more detail how it is superior to the law. It is necessary first, though, to substantiate how the Old Testament, *if interpreted through Christ, is part of the gospel.* Notice Peter's words: "Of which salvation the prophets have inquired and searched diligently, who prophesied of the grace that should come unto you, searching what, or what manner of time the Spirit of Christ which was in them did signify, when it testified beforehand of the sufferings of Christ, and the glory that should follow. Unto whom it was revealed, THAT NOT UNTO THEMSELVES, BUT UNTO US they did minister the things which are NOW reported unto you BY THEM THAT HAVE PREACHED THE GOSPEL UNTO YOU with the Holy Ghost sent down from heaven;" (I Peter 1:10-12).

Peter says that the prophets themselves did not understand their own prophecies. But the prophecies were written for the time of the Spirit and are now reported by them that preach the gospel. The prophecies, *if interpreted through Christ,* become part of the gospel.

Peter illustrates this again in I Peter 1:24,25, where he quotes Isaiah: "For all flesh is as grass, and all the glory of man as the flower of grass. The grass withereth, and the flower thereof falleth away: but the word of the Lord endureth forever. AND THIS IS THE WORD WHICH BY THE GOSPEL IS PREACHED UNTO YOU."

Isaiah's prophecy has now become gospel for the Church age. What this illustrates is that prophecy must be interpreted by Christ, because without Christ it is hidden. The Old Testament is never to be used as a rule to interpret the New Testament but rather the New

Testament is the Key that unlocks the Old Testament.

Christ Himself alludes to this on the Emmaus road as He explained Moses and the prophets and how they related to Himself. Outside of Christ, the law and the prophets are incomplete (Luke 24:27). Later, when Jesus again appeared to His disciples, He opened their understanding as He spoke to them about the prophecies concerning Himself in the law and the prophets (Luke 24:44,45).

The disciples had long been familiar with these Scriptures, but outside of Christ their understanding of them was limited. Christ, then, is the key to unlocking the Old Testament. As someone has said, "The New is in the Old contained, the Old is in the New explained."

Jesus continually used the Old Testament to reveal truth that without Him would have been hidden (John 7:22, 23, 10:34-36, Luke 20:41-44).

This concept is perhaps most clearly expressed in II Cor. 3:14-16 "...but their minds were blinded: for until this day remaineth the same veil untaken away in the reading of the Old Testament; which veil is done away in Christ. But even unto this day, when Moses is read, the veil is upon their heart. Nevertheless, when it shall turn to the Lord, the veil shall be taken away."

How many absurdities have been advanced from the Old Testament when people did not interpret it through Christ! How many times has the Old Testament been used to force and twist Christ and His gospel into gross caricatures of truth! Men have used the law to condone all sorts of devious schemes. It has been used as an engine of war many times against the followers of Christ, under the guise of maintaining Biblical law in a nation. Satan, from the crucifixion of Christ onward has trained his henchmen to be well versed in the law, so that as angels of light they might wreak havoc on the true Church of Christ. These hypocrites have adorned the tombs of the prophets, whom their fathers killed, and have thought to raise up true religion by killing all dissenters in God's name (John 16:2), thinking to establish Christianity by the Old Testament civil law, being totally deluded by their understanding of Scripture because they see it not through the eyes of Christ. Their actions have paralleled Paul when he was extremely zealous for the law and persecuted the followers of the gospel. It then is extremely important how we understand the relationship of the civil and ceremonial laws to the gospel.

For sake of clarity, the law of the Old Testament has been divided into three general categories, as is often done, to better focus our discussion.

They are as follows:

*Moral Law* - Refers to the Ten Commandments, Decalogue. Its focus: it "defines" sin and morality.

*Ceremonial Law* - Refers to those ordinances that regulate the sacrificial and dietary spheres of Jewish life. This includes all practices for worship and a separate lifestyle. Its focus: it is the Old Testament method to "pardon" sin.

*Civil Law* - Refers to the legal ordinances that determine how Israel as a nation was governed. This also includes sanctions for disobedience of the ceremonial law, which illustrates how inextricably entwined these latter two categories are. Its focus: it "punishes" sin and "preserves" morality.

The moral law has already been defined previously, and explained how it is distinct from both the civil and ceremonial laws. Its precepts are eternal and its principles were strengthened and given spiritual interpretation by the gospel.

The areas yet to be considered are the ceremonial and civil laws.

The first consideration will be:

## THE CEREMONIAL LAW: AN ANTICIPATION AND PORTRAYAL OF CHRIST'S DEATH AND GOSPEL

The ceremonies ordained by God were temporal means whereby a man could be reckoned righteous. The ceremonies, themselves, had no cleansing value, but rather the faith the saints had, that in obeying God's order, God would reckon them righteous and save them. Their faith was not in the unblemished blood of bulls, goats, or lambs, but rather in the covenant that God had made with His people.

If they obeyed Him in the ordinances and believed that God would keep His promises, then there was great value in these ceremonies, for they were the means by which God conferred His blessings and pardon upon them.

God had a covenant of works (Gal. 3:10-12) with His people. Their personal faith and obedience in God's laws could not cleanse them, but it was upon this basis that God *accounted* them righteous.

"Abraham believed God and it was *counted* unto him for righteousness" (Romans 4:3).

"Blessed is the man to whom the Lord will not *impute* sin" (Romans 4:8).

These ceremonies, and their faith in them, anticipated the faith that could be placed in a coming Redeemer, whose sacrifice would taste death for every man. The old saints saw the better promises, from afar off, and embraced them, believing both in what God had ordained for them to obey then, and in the superiority of what would be instituted in the future (Heb. 11:13).

God could only confer righteousness at that point in time based upon obedience to His laws. Even though neither their obedience nor their sacrifices could save them, their strict observance of God's laws was reckoned by God as righteousness, because it was rooted in a *faith* in God's covenant, that He would faithfully pardon according to the means of His ceremonies.

The ceremonial law, then, due to its imperfections, had its greatest value in foreshadowing that which would replace it. The law was the shadow of good things to come (Heb. 10:1).

The high priest was the minister of the law to the people. In Christ the priesthood changed from the order of Aaron to that of Melchisedec, thus calling for a change of law (Heb. 7:12). Our new High Priest offers complete cleansing once and for all, and thus the repetitious rituals of cleansing become void and the need for a new covenant arises that is established upon these better promises (Heb.

7:18,19, 8:6, 7).

The following reasons illustrate why the ceremonial law has been abrogated.

a. Inability to cleanse sin (Heb. 10:1-8). The law offered only a legal pardon but could not give an actual cleansing .

b. It never changed the nature of the offender (Rom. 7:4-6). Paul acknowledges that while under the law he was in the flesh and subject to the motions (workings) of sin. Only a death to the law and union with Christ brings forth true fruit unto God. The priest needed to minister daily sacrifices for the continual sin of the people (Heb. 10:11).

The ceremonial law served as a regular reminder to man of his sin problem (Heb. 10:3). Its daily rituals spoke of its ineffectiveness to deal with the sin problem.

These reminders, though, were necessary, so that when Christ came to truly save His people from their sins, there was already an established institution in place that proclaimed the reality of sin and man's inability to save himself and also foreshadowed the Lamb of God, as a sin offering for the world.

## The Civil Law: An Instrument of God to Preserve a Separated and Holy People Until the Advent of Christ

God needed a nation with civil institutions and statutes that would set it apart from all other nations of the earth. This would create a peculiar nation which would establish and preserve a moral code of righteousness that would call attention to the prophetic oracles of a coming King who would reign in righteousness.

Moses spoke concerning Israel's laws, "Keep therefore and do them; for this is your wisdom and your understanding in the sight of the nations, which shall hear all these statutes, and say, Surely this great nation is a wise and understanding people. For what nation is there so great, who hath God so nigh unto them, as the Lord our God is in all things that we call upon Him for? And what nation is there so great, that hath statutes and judgments so righteous as all this law, which I set before you this day" (Deut. 4:6-8)?

The institution of God's law was to attract all nations to the uniqueness of Israel in God's plan. Their greatness is attributed directly to the observance of God's law.

The equity of God's civil law was superior to all the statutes of the surrounding heathen nations.

They had a moral code (Decalogue) given by God Himself as a constitution, and ceremonial offerings that honored Deity without human sacrifice, and civil laws that preserved both the moral and religious foundations of society. The civil sanctions were a necessary means of preserving both the moral code and the religious practices.

It needs to be understood that since the Holy Spirit was not yet given to the saints, and therefore not serving an active role in restraining sin in the world, the civil sanctions had to be extremely severe in order to maintain a righteous nation. It may be that some will object by saying, "Did not David say, take not thy Holy Spirit from me?" It must be understood that the Spirit, who is God, was surely active in the lives of the Old Testament saints, but He acted primarily as an "influence" upon them, not a "*Personal* Indwelling Presence." The familiar phrase in the Old Testament is "The Spirit of the Lord came *upon*" an individual. Holy men of God came under the Spirit's influence when giving oracles from the Lord and especially when those oracles became divine Scripture (II Peter 1:21). There are instances that speak of the Spirit of God dwelling in certain individuals and equipping them for certain tasks (Gen. 41:38; Ex. 31:3; Num. 27:18).

These individuals were equipped by the Spirit to perform specific tasks. They are looked upon, though, as a *unique* preparation of specific individuals to fulfill certain roles ordained by God. These special occurrences were by no means representative of the whole body of Israel. In fact, it was these special effusions of the Spirit that set prophets and leaders apart from the main body of the congregation. They did not, though, in even these special instances, have the Spirit as a personal indwelling presence in the manner that a born-again believer does today. They had never experienced the washing of regeneration and "renewing" of the Holy Ghost.

We read in Numbers 11:25-29 that the Spirit of God that was in Moses was transferred to the seventy elders. Two of the elders prophesied, under the Spirit's influence, in the people's camp, having left the tabernacle where the anointing occurred. Joshua was alarmed and asked Moses to reprimand these two. Moses' response indicates that the Spirit was only given to unique individuals. Moses says, "Would God that all the Lord's people were prophets, and that the Lord would put His Spirit upon them!"

There is also reference in the Scripture of the Spirit controlling wicked men sent to apprehend David. The messengers from Saul were controlled by the Spirit and began to prophesy (I Sam. 19:20-24).

What all these instances confirm is that the Spirit was at work during Old Testament times but His influence was far less because He was given discriminatorily and He did not occupy the same relationship to the Jewish saint as He does to the Christian.

His anointing was limited to specific individuals being equipped for special appointments. These individuals were under His "controlling influence" but did not enjoy His personal presence. There are many Old Testament prophecies that anticipate the Spirit's coming to His people, a clear indication of His limited operations in the BC world (Isa. 32:15, Eze. 36:26,27, 39:29, Joel 2:28,29). Jesus expressed this concept very concisely in John 16:7, "Nevertheless I tell you the truth; it is expedient for you that I go away: for if I go not away, the Comforter will not come unto you; but if I depart, I will send Him unto you." The power and presence of the Spirit was not fully realized until Christ's death and resurrection bruised the head of the serpent. He now holds the keys of hell and of death. He opens and no man shutteth, He shutteth and no man opens. All power is given to Him in heaven and in earth, and He has commissioned the Spirit to the believer and to His Church (John 14:26, 15:26, Rom. 8:9). Further, since the prince of this world has been judged, the Spirit's work in the world has greatly expanded; from influencing a select few, to indwelling all believers; from little influence among ungodly to reproving the whole world for their sin (John 16:8).

The previous example given of the Spirit controlling Saul's messengers and then Saul himself was a rarity of that time, but in the days of the Spirit's outpouring when men lied to the Holy Ghost, they could be immediately stricken in death. When this happened, great fear came upon all who heard of this event, showing His expanded ability to reprove the world of sin (Acts 5:3,5,9,11). Perhaps the greatest evidence for the difference between the pre-Pentecost saint and the post-Pentecost saint lies in Jesus' commentary of John the Baptist. Now we know that John the Baptist was filled with the Holy Ghost from his mother's womb (Luke 1:15), and we also know that according to Christ's own words he was the greatest of all the prophets, and yet Christ said that he who is least in the kingdom is greater than he (Matt. 11:11). No man is greater by his own power or accomplishments and yet the least man in the kingdom is greater than he. How else except by being quickened and renewed by the regenerating power of the Spirit (Rom. 8:9-11; John 6:63; Titus 3:5)?

John's baptism did not unite a man into a covenant relationship with the Holy Ghost, but only was an expression of repentance. Christ's baptism immerses us into the Holy Ghost (Matt. 28:19; John 1:33). John says, "I baptize you with water, but He shall baptize you with the Holy Ghost" (Mark 1:8). John also said to Christ, "I have need to be baptized of thee" (Matt. 3:14). John clearly indicated, that although filled with the Spirit from the womb, he had never experienced the regenerating power of being baptized of the Holy Ghost. The Ephesian disciples of John did not receive the Holy Ghost until they were rebaptized into Christ (Acts 19:1-6). The only exception to this order of events was the Gentiles in Cornelius' house; they received the Spirit before baptism to prove to Peter that they were worthy candidates of baptism, for he said upon seeing the evidence of the Spirit, "Can any man forbid water...which have received the Holy Ghost as well as we" (Acts 10:47)?

This is no attempt to establish an order of events between the baptism of the Spirit or water but rather an attempt to show that there is a relationship between Christian water baptism and that administered by the Holy Ghost.

The importance of this whole dialogue on the Spirit is to show that without His personal presence in this world, there had to be strict civil sanctions in Israel to uphold morality, or sin would quickly replace "holiness to the Lord". Without His presence, only a mortal fear of punishment could preserve the sanctity of the nation, the Spirit's power not yet being fully evident. The concept of holiness being preserved by obedience to the law is expressed in the following verses:

"Now therefore, if ye will obey my voice indeed, and *keep my covenant*, then ye shall be a peculiar treasure unto me above all people: for all the earth is mine: and ye shall be unto me a kingdom of priests, and an *holy* nation." (Ex. 19:5,6)

The penalties of the civil law for disobedience were also specifically for the purpose of maintaining a holy society, thus they were very severe, often being capital punishment. Notice this thought in the following passages:

"And the Lord spake unto Moses, saying, Again, thou shalt say to the children of Israel, Whosoever he be of the children of Israel, or of the strangers that sojourn in Israel, that giveth any of his seed unto Molech; he shall surely be put to death: the people of the land shall stone him with stones. And I will set my face against that man, and will cut him off from among his people; because he hath given of his seed unto Molech, TO DEFILE MY SANCTUARY, AND TO PROFANE MY HOLY NAME" (Lev. 20:1-3).

"The hands of the witnesses shall be first upon him to put him to death, and afterwards the hands of all the people. SO THOU SHALT PUT EVIL AWAY FROM AMONG YOU" (Deut. 17:7).

"Then shall ye do unto him, as he had thought to have done unto his brother; SO SHALT THOU PUT EVIL AWAY FROM AMONG YOU" (Deut. 19:19).

"And all the men of his city shall stone him with stones, that he die: SO SHALT THOU PUT EVIL AWAY FROM AMONG YOU; AND ALL ISRAEL SHALL HEAR AND FEAR" (Deut. 21:21).

In all these passages there is a correlation between physical punishment and the preservation of a holy people. Without the ministry of the Spirit in the world, convicting and reproving men of their sin, evil would have gone unchecked, man's heart being given over unto evil continually, except God had provided a system of law to restrain abominable sins with severe discipline. The Spirit strove against sin before Christ (Gen. 6:3) but His work was made more effectual when the prince of this world was cast out and his power broken.

The civil law, then, served as an interim measure by which God could restrain evil and preserve a separated people. It was necessary as a means to enforce both moral precepts and religious ceremonies. But we find in Christ's own words that what was said of "Old Time" is superseded by the bringing in of a "new" and "better" covenant. The phrase "But I say unto you" introduced the gospel of Christ, both by strengthening the unchanging morality of the Ten Commandments, and by abrogating the civil institutes of the Old Testament law.

## THE CIVIL LAW: SUPERSEDED BY THE TEACHINGS OF CHRIST AND THE APOSTLES

It needs to be understood that the civil laws were ordained to not only enforce moral precepts but also the ceremonial ordinances. A person could never clearly catalogue the body of laws that are ceremonial or those that are civil, as the two are inextricably entwined in some of the ordinances. To say the one has passed away and not the other is to propound an illogical and unscriptural fallacy. The whole body of political laws served to regulate the religious ordinances. For example, in Leviticus 19:5-8 a peace offering to the Lord was to be eaten on the same day that it was offered. He that ate it on the third day following was to be cut off from among His people. Now if we delete the sacrifice itself, how can we maintain the civil penalty, seeing that it no longer penalizes anything? So it is seen that the sanctions cannot apply to obsolete ceremonies. So they either stand as a sanction against nothing or they are removed with the religious observance.

These arguments are also admitted in Reformed doctrines, to some degree.

John Calvin writes in his Institutes, *"For there are some who deny that any commonwealth is rightly framed which neglects the law of Moses, and is ruled by the common law of nations. How perilous and seditious these views are, let others see: for me it is enough to demonstrate that they are stupid and false. ....Meanwhile, let no one be moved by the thought that the judicial and ceremonial laws relate to morals."*[4]

These sentiments are also admitted in the Westminster Confession, which is probably used more than all other Reformed Confessions.

*"To them also, as a body politic, he gave sundry judicial laws, which expired together with the state of that people, not obliging any other, now, further than the general equity thereof may require."*[5]

It must then be asked, "Do all the civil sanctions still apply that support the moral law?"

If the answer is "yes," then the civil sanctions must be divided between those that relate to ceremonies and those that relate to the moral precepts. This once again is nothing more than an arbitrary process, as the selection will greatly vary between individuals.

Furthermore, it is confounded by the fact that even the moral precepts are expanded upon by Christ. "Ye have heard that it was said by them of old time, THOU SHALT NOT KILL; and whosoever shall kill shall be in danger of the *judgment:* But I say unto you, That whosoever is angry with his brother without a cause shall be in danger of the *judgment*" (Matt. 5:21,22) Now if the penalty for killing is to be maintained according to Moses' Judicial law, then the teachings of Christ, here, present a dilemma. Let it be noted that both offenses bring the same *judgment*. The sanction in both cases being a call to judgment for the offense. Now if the Judicial law of Moses is still in effect to support the moral law, then Christ would be saying in addition to judgment for killing there must also be judgment for unjustified anger. But there is no penalty in Moses' law that addresses punishment for an attitude towards your brother, nor does Jesus ever offer any civil punishment for this sin. So it is evident that Jesus, here, is not seeking to uphold Moses' penalties for moral transgressions. Moses' law is not adequate for both cases, and if Jesus was adding to it, then it is obvious that He felt it needed to be changed. The "but I say unto you," strongly suggests a change. The change is two-fold, He propounds a spiritual interpretation for the law against murder (anger without cause), and a judgment at the last day when the secrets of men's hearts shall be revealed.

This does two things: it strengthens the moral precept "thou shalt not kill" and renders the civil punishment of Moses' law nonapplicable. This does not mean that murder should not be physically punished, but rather it should no longer receive punishment according to Moses' law.

The second issue Jesus raises, in the Sermon on the Mount, is adultery and divorce and remarriage. "Thou shalt not commit adultery" becomes strengthened by Jesus' words that equate lustful looking with adultery. Here He does not even include the civil penalty for adultery but rather strengthens the moral precept by enjoining moral purity to it. The penalty that He then includes is a whole body that can be cast into hell because of one offending (lustful) member. In these two circumstances the civil law is not the center of focus, but rather a strengthening of the moral commandments to include attitudes of the heart.

Now it might be objected by some that Jesus had stated that He did not come to destroy the law, and promised greatness to the one who would both do and teach the least of these commands (Matt. 5:17-20). Then it is to be supposed that He was not abrogating the judicial law in His following discourse. But one could make the same argument, then, that not one jot or tittle should be removed from the ceremonial law either and thus continue the sacrificial system.

The only proper interpretation of what Jesus meant, by fulfilling the law, and asking us to observe commandments of the law, can be ascertained by His own explanation of His gospel versus the law.

It has been shown thus far that Jesus did not destroy the morality of the law. Now we shall see where He nullifies the civil statutes.

In Matthew 5:31,32 Jesus gives the law's grounds for divorce and then gives His gospel. The law allowed for divorce due to uncleanness, but it needed to be legalized with a writing of divorcement. Yet Jesus says that divorce cannot be proper, except in the case of fornication. The Pharisees questioned Jesus further on His teaching in Matthew 19 and posed the question as to why it was allowable by Moses, if God disapproves of it. Jesus' answer was that Moses allowed it due to the hardness of the human heart, but in God's original plan legalized divorce was not an option. This teaching squarely contradicted Moses' civil ordinance and nullified it.

It should be noted that while Jesus allowed a putting away for fornication, He never permitted a remarriage (whosoever marrieth her that is put away committeth adultery) nor did He condone a writing of divorcement anywhere to legally and finally separate from an unfaithful partner, but rather as Paul explains in I Corinthians 7:11; let the offended one remain unmarried or be reconciled to her husband, so that the covenant may be until death (Rom. 7:1-3).

The main emphasis here, though, is that Jesus changed the civil law's statutes on marriage and still maintained the moral precept "Thou shalt not commit adultery."

Next, Jesus quotes the law on oaths. It should be remembered that every time Jesus says, "It hath been said" He is *not* referring to Jewish traditions but always to Moses' law. Every quotation He makes is from the law itself. He gives the basis for oaths under Moses' law and they are the following:

1. Thou shalt not forswear thyself.
   a. Do not lie under oath. (Lev. 5:1  19:12)
   b. Do not break your oath. (II Sam. 21:7; Mal. 3:5)
2. Perform unto the Lord thine oaths.
   a. Swear only by the Lord. (Deut. 6:13, 29:12,)
   b. Fulfill all your oaths. (Psa. 15:4,  Lev. 6:2-5)

Now it should be observed that all these precepts are contained in the law and precepts of the Old Covenant itself. Therefore Jesus is not merely condemning frivolous oaths, for the law already does that. Jesus says "Swear not at all." James also says, above all things "swear not," not by any oath (James 5:12). The whole law was sworn upon Israel through their judicial system. It was a religious exercise to swear by God to perform one's duty. But Jesus says swear not at all and always be men of truth outside of any oath. Christ is here laying aside more of Israel's civil institutions that were given for that time.

Christ then addressed the issue of "lawful" vengeance. Here again the law itself has always been against a "personal" vengeance, so that is not what Jesus is speaking about. It is a lawful right that one has to seek redress for damages that Christ is speaking of. If any man sue thee at the law and take away thy coat let him have thy cloak also. This does not suppose that you lost your coat due to your own faults or grievances, but rather that the law was used maliciously against you for another's gain. Jesus makes no implication of wrong on the sufferers' part. "For what glory is it, if, when ye be buffeted for your faults, ye shall take it patiently" (I Pet. 2:20)? Jesus is implying that if someone uses the law to get unscrupulous gain of you, do not seek "lawful" revenge (eye for eye) but rather give them even more.

Jesus then strikes at the precepts of the law that preserved them as a nation. They were, under the law, to love their neighbor, or brother if you will, but they could, yea, should, hate all those who were the enemies of their nation and laws.  God Himself had said, "I hated Esau" (Mal. 1:3). David said, "Do not I hate them, O Lord, that hate thee?" God had stated that He would visit wrath upon all those that hate Him (Ex. 20:5; Deut. 7:10,15). Israel, likewise, was to show no mercy on the heathen who inhabited the land sworn by God to Abraham and his seed forever (Deut. 7:2). If God poured His wrath upon His enemies and asked Israel to show them no mercy, then it can be understood why David would say, "Am not I grieved with those that rise up against thee? I hate them with perfect hatred: I count them mine enemies" (Psa. 139:21,22). Now, Jesus is teaching that His disciples should love their enemies. Israel had been taught to love the Lord and their neighbor but to hate both evil and the evildoer. These precepts helped to preserve the purity of their nation. But this self-ordained, pseudo Messiah claims that one must love His enemies. How could He so blithely set aside what came from God to Moses as their complete culture, that they had fought and died for, and now were hoping to once again establish when the Roman yoke was cast away? How could they establish their nation again upon love for one's enemies? It is hatred of oppressors and love of country that inspires men to great exploits when mounting an insurrection against tyranny. Had not God commanded them to utterly destroy the heathen and show them no mercy, either upon their women, children, or cattle when they were possessing Canaan? Should they not be seeking ways to drive out the hated Roman legions from the land sworn unto them, by God, to their fathers, so that they could reestablish Moses' law instead of living under the compromising influence of Sadducees and the rapacious tax collections of the Publicans?

Yet this self-appointed, unschooled rabbi has the audacity to quote Moses; or rather God's law, and then say, "But I say unto you, but I say unto you, but I say unto you...." They yearned for the day of deliverance, when their Latin oppressors could be driven out, perhaps even with the Messiah at the forefront, treading the heathen in the winepress, staining His garments in blood, trampling upon them in His fury, and declaring His vengeance for His redeemed (Isa. 63:1-4), but now this self-professed Christ would have them carry the soldiers' packs the extra mile and bless them and pray for them. Perish the thought! And then Christ even went on to commend the faith of a centurion over that of all Israel (Luke 7:9)!

They needed a way to turn the tide of public opinion against Him, giving them the opportunity to annihilate Him, without risking their own position of respect or authority in the eyes of the common people.

They concocted a scheme whereby they could instrument their plan (John 8:1-11). Did not Jesus clearly imply that their civil law from Moses was being superseded? Yet He seemed to continue His support for the moral law. They would set before Him a case of infraction of the moral law, whom both He and the people would ascribe to, and then ask Him how He would judge the case and the penalty, if Moses' civil statutes were now obsolete. Jesus had already endorsed the law "Thou shalt not commit adultery," and surely also the common people would affirm the eternal value of such a weighty moral precept; but the question to Jesus would be, "How shall she be punished if it be not according to Moses' law?" If He merely pardons her, He will be perceived as diminishing the gravity of an offense that is both against God and detrimental to society. If He condemns her, we shall ask by what law she shall then be punished? If He says by Moses' law, then He has contradicted what He earlier implied was being superseded. We can then ask, "Why retain one portion of it while abrogating other portions?" If He says she shall be executed by Moses' law, then we both have a case of contradiction and the opportunity to approach the Romans with the information that Christ is seeking to establish Mosaic civil law which is at odds with Latin law, which, in effect, constitutes rebellion against Rome. Or shall He establish another judicial law that is contrary to both Jewish and Roman law? Or shall He say, "Punish her according to Roman law;" if so, then we shall expose Him to the public as an agent of Rome who is both sympathetic to their enemies (love them), and seeking to encourage compliance and apathy toward their oppressors. If He makes His own law He can still be exposed as the enemy of Moses and/or a seditious man who is instigating rebellion against Rome.

This case had the potential to both vilify Jesus in the public's eyes or make Him guilty of revolution in Rome's eyes, or possibly even both. It was a brilliant plan, and seemingly infallible, but they were pitting the intellect of men against the wisdom of God.

John's commentary concurs with these sentiments as he says concerning the question posed, "This they said, tempting Him, that they might have to accuse Him" (John 8:6).

They may have been a bit tentative at first, with the question "Now Moses in the law commanded us, that such should be stoned: but what sayest thou?", because Jesus had bested them before in such confrontations. But they had good evidence; she was caught in the very act. They surely had sufficient evidence and witnesses, for Jesus never once disputed the evidence or the witnesses, and acknowledged even the sin by saying, "Go and *sin* no more."

Some have sought to prove that Jesus did not issue a sentence because there were either not enough witnesses or the evidence was insufficient. They have tried to prove this from Jesus' words, "Where are those thine accusers?" But this overlooks the fact that this statement was made after they (accusers) had left, not when they were still present. Nor does Jesus even once insinuate that the case should be dismissed because of lack of witnesses or evidence. As previously stated, He acknowledged the sin by saying, "Go and *sin* no more."

Others have said that Christ did not render a judgment because He was not a civil magistrate. This again overlooks important points. First of all, Christ stated that the Father had committed all judgment to the Son, (John 5:22) and "Christian" magistrates all acknowledge the Lordship of Christ over their office, so if anyone is qualified to judge, it is Christ. Secondly, they were asking for Christ's *opinion* of what the proper judgment should be; and as one who had all things delivered to Him from the Father, He surely would have been qualified to give judicial advice, if He so desired.

But all of these vain conjectures assume that the scribes and Pharisees were quite ignorant. Now if they wanted to trap Jesus they surely would not have made such elementary blunders as to not meet all the requirements of the law in order to gain a conviction. They were well schooled in the law; much better than those who offer these arguments, and so such a mistake being offered as explanation for Jesus' response is too absurd to even imagine.

In the account, after the initial questioning, Jesus merely stooped and wrote on the ground. We have no knowledge of what He wrote, and possibly John does not know either, but what was written, if seen by the Pharisees, did not seem detrimental to their case, for they continued pressing Him for an answer. Most likely they assumed that Jesus' silence was evidence that He was either stalling or was totally confuted by the dilemma and the force of their arguments. They "continued" asking Him, probably feeling more secure in their position with His silence. Undoubtedly, the gleam of victory was in their eyes, like a pack of wolves closing in on their prey.

Jesus lifted Himself up and said, "He that is without sin among you, let him cast the first stone." He clearly referred to Moses' judicial penalty as being applicable in this case were it to be used, and He also acknowledged the woman's guilt. Their conviction of conscience was no doubt the result of Christ's words that "whosoever looketh on a woman to lust after her has committed adultery with her already in his heart." They knew that their carnal desires had been at variance with the spirit of the law, "Thou shalt not commit adultery." They, too, deserved the penalty of death for having hearts that were at enmity with the law in which they professed to believe.

They left from the eldest to the youngest, probably since the older saw the wisdom of His answer first, and better saw the magnitude of their own guilt, having a larger catalogue of sins to review.

The trap was sprung and remained empty. Christ upheld the purity of chastity. He acknowledged the guilt of sin. He was impartial in His verdict, even to His enemies, by admitting her guilt when He said they could stone her if they were innocent. He did not destroy the necessity for civil law. But He did clearly establish that the death penalty of Moses' law was inappropriate for use by those who were also sinners.

This was a most powerful and convincing way of abrogating Moses' sanctions for offenses to the moral law, for it illustrated that the proper penalty for *all* moral sins is death, whether they be committed physically or spiritually, and placed the whole human race under condemnation.

No man has the right to administer such severe punishment any longer when he himself is a sinner. Furthermore, this also demonstrated the Spirit's work in Christ's ministry and the power of truth to convict, for all the accusers left convicted, and the woman was also instructed to sin no more. Jesus was not removing from the magistrate the right to judge or punish, per se, but rather that it could no longer be according to Moses' civil law.

Judgment under Moses' law was without mercy (Heb. 10:28). But Christ said, "Blessed are those that are merciful: for they shall obtain mercy." Judgment without mercy will be meted out by God upon all those who judged unmercifully, for mercy has been elevated by Christ over judgment (James 2:13).

Christ also demonstrated the power of forgiveness of sins. It is the "neither do I condemn thee" that sets a man free to "go and sin no more."

Now if Christ were seeking to uphold both forgiveness and Moses' law, He would have forgiven her then had her executed, so that forgiveness could be demonstrated and Moses' civil law enforced. It was quite clear to the Pharisees that day that Moses' penalty would not be enforced nor endorsed by Christ, and it should be just as clear to us that the mercy and forgiveness of Christ have triumphed over it.

There was another incident that aroused the ire of the Pharisees. Jesus' disciples picked corn on the Sabbath day (Matt. 12:1-8). The Pharisees responded by saying, "Behold, thy disciples do that which in not lawful to do upon the Sabbath day."

They could have pointed to Exodus 16:26-30 for precedence in their indictment. But Jesus never contested whether it were *lawful* or not based upon Moses' law, but rather showed other exceptions to the civil interpretation of the moral command "Remember the Sabbath day to keep it holy." He said neither David nor the priests were strictly lawful in their observance of the Sabbath. This He showed to illustrate the transitory nature of Moses' civil laws.

Some have argued that the Sabbath as a precept cannnot continue unless its observance be the same as it was originally. In other words, the principle and historical observance stand or fall together as a unit. It is all or none. If the strict observance is replaced, then so must also any moral principle that undergirds it. This has already been examined somewhat in the first chapter. But here in this passage we find an additional aspect of thought to include in our Sabbath discussion. It is sometimes remarked that we violate the Sabbath even in our Sunday worship activities, in the work that is involved in teaching the gospel or in the preparation of food for meals that day. Let it be here observed that Jesus, who is Lord of the Sabbath, sanctioned preparation of food upon this day by picking corn for food. He also showed how the priests labored on the Sabbath in the preparation of sacrifices for spiritual worship (Matt. 12:5, Num. 28:9,10). On a hot summer day, standing by the flaming altar, in priestly vestures, this would have been a perspiring duty. So much so that Jesus equated it with profaning (or breaking) the legal requirements of the Sabbath. Not only was the priestly duty much work, but the priests' work was required that they might eat on this day (Lev. 6:14-18, Num. 28:9, 10). Jesus illustrates that even under the law there were exceptions to its strict observance, thus prefiguring a time when its legalities would cease, but Christ Himself would still be Lord of a Sabbath day. If the principle also expired, then He would have affirmed His Lordship over nothing, which, in effect, is to be no Lord at all.

His final argument then was that there was one standing there who was greater than the temple that sanctified the priest's sacrifices. He was Lord also of the Sabbath. He who had spoken the laws into place could also change them. If they would understand that He, as Lord of the Sabbath and its laws, was changing them, instituting the preeminence of mercy over Mosaic ordinances, as prophesied of old

(Hosea 6:6), then they would not condemn the disciples as lawbreakers, when they were guiltless, the law itself having been changed by the lawgiver, standing in their presence.

It is no wonder then that the scribes, Pharisees, and lawyers were so incensed by this man's doctrine; He not only exposed their hypocrisy but also challenged the very basis of their culture by instituting changes both in their civil and religious ordinances, all the while claiming to fulfill the law.

Of what good is a moral constitution unless there be accompanying civil sanctions for disobedience, based not upon this man's philosophy but that which was handed down by God Himself to Moses? Away with such a man; it is not fit for such a man to live. He professes morality and yet changes that body of law that seeks to preserve it. The common people are enamored with His spiritual insights (while some indeed may be good), but they become blinded to the fact that He will destroy all our national aspirations, and as such, is a great enemy of our state and Jewish identity. One can almost feel the intensity of hatred, frustration, and venom in the caustic words, "If we let Him thus alone, all men will believe on Him; and the Romans shall come and take away both our place and nation" (John 11:48).

There is one passage that must be observed that is often used to prove a continuation of the civil law: it is in Matthew 15: 1-6. Jesus in verse 4, quotes the moral law, "Honor thy father and mther" and also the civil law's penalty for cursing them, "Let him die the death." This is supposed by some to mean that because He quoted the civil law, He also was endorsing its continued usage. Now if the mere quotation of it suggests its continuance, regardless of the fact that it is not expounded upon at all in this passage, then a dangerous precedent has been established for Biblical exegesis. By the same logic, then we could suppose that Peter on the day of Pentecost was not only arguing the prophetic basis for the coming of the Spirit that day, but also that he was claiming that this was the day of the Lord also, for he quoted Joel's prophecy the whole way through to the day of the Lord (Acts 2:17-21). Now if Jesus' full quotation meant that the whole of what He quoted was in effect for that time, even though He did not expound upon that portion, then it could be equally stated that Peter said this experience of Pentecost was the "day of the Lord," for he said, "This is that which was spoken of by the prophet Joel" (Acts 2:16). If this is the case, we need no longer look for His return, it being accomplished at Pentecost.

Now why did Peter quote the full prophecy of Joel, including the "day of the Lord" with its accompanying signs, if this was not that event. This day of the Lord spoken of is clearly the last day of the world. Notice the following passages that correlate the cosmic signs with the end: (Matt. 24:29-31; Mark 13:24-27; Luke 21:25-28; II Pet. 3:10-12). Joel is using the term "day of the Lord" in its normal usage, referring to a physical and bodily return of Christ that is preceded by visible and physical signs. Did Peter then quote this portion for no apparent reason if it was not in effect at that time? The answer is an obvious "No," for Peter uses this passage to catalogue all the events that must occur *before* (Acts 2:20) the great and notable "day of the Lord" comes. One of these events is the pouring out of the Spirit. Every Jew yearned for that day of the Lord when the heathen nations would be judged. But as Peter points out, it cannot happen until the Spirit is first given, thus placing it as a very important prophetic event.

Now Jesus in Matthew 15:4 quotes the penalty for a reason also; not to suggest or endorse its continuance, but to illustrate the gravity of the precept to honor thy father and mother. He uses the sanction to show how important the command was, a penalty to which they would have agreed. Now if dishonoring one's parents, such as by cursing, merits a capital punishment, then it is extremely important to observe God's command to honor them. This is the manner in which Jesus presents His arguments. He does not quote the penalty for a discourse on civil law; in fact, there is no mention made by Christ of the use of this law, or an affirmation of its continuance, but rather it is used to show that what God has considered of great value they have set aside in preference for their tradition of "Corban," thus absolving themselves of all responsibility to requite their parents, under the pretext of consecration. This passage can by no means be construed to teach Jesus' affirmation of the continuance of Moses' civil law.

Notice also that this commandment is again affirmed in Ephesians 6:2, 3 with no notice taken to a judicial penalty, but rather to the penalty of a shortened life if one does not actively honor his parents. Who but God could arbitrate in such a matter as to whether one has sufficiently honored his parents to enjoy long life? Further, it should be noted that if Moses' law is to be obeyed, then many sons and daughters in our land should be slain, as they have cursed their parents. If God's law is to be obeyed as an unchanging statute, then let the blood flow. If the magistrate will not do his lawful duty, then let a Jehu be anointed to this office, and God's penalty be incurred, that the fear of God may be in the land, upon all these children who have not honored their parents sufficiently or have cursed them.

I speak after the manner of men, but we have not so learned Christ.

If the civil law were to be instituted in this land or any nation, we could quickly cure any overpopulation problems.

The laws that applied to the Israelite, *and the stranger* sojourning in the land, with capital punishment for disobedience are as follows:

1. blasphemy, Lev. 24:16

2. fornication, bestiality, incest, Lev. 18:1-30

3. Sabbath breaking, Ex. 35:1-3, 20:8-11

4. sexual relations with a menstruating woman, Lev. 20:18 (This was included for a stranger also in Lev. 18:19, 26, 29)

Also any man with wounded or mutilated genitalia was not to enter the congregation of the Lord (Deut. 23:1).

A bastard was to be excluded from the congregation to the tenth generation (Deut. 23:2).

If these laws were established, according to every jot and tittle, in any modern nation, the population of that nation would be greatly reduced and the churches depleted. There should be no hedging on this issue about observing only the general equity of these laws, for that makes them open to human interpretation as to what their equity truly is. This would be a subtle form of autonomy, to profess to believe the whole civil law, but then to qualify it by affirming only the general equity of it. Either one keeps the law as God ordained it, or he has made himself a judge of the law in place of God, by trying to determine just what the principles are and how to arbitrarily establish them.

As James says, either you are a judge of the law or a doer of the law (James 4:11).

This whole issue of whether the Gentile church should observe Moses' law became the occasion of the first church council (Acts 15). The consideration initially was whether a convert needed to be circumcised to be saved (vs. 5). But when the issue came to council, the believing Pharisees expanded the subject to insist that the converts also keep the law of Moses (vs. 5).

The conclusion of the council was not only that Gentiles are saved by grace (vs. 11) but that their only requirements out of the law were to abstain from polluting practices of idol worship, from fornication, from strangled animals, and from consumption of blood (vs. 19, 20, 29).

In the epistle to Antioch, the Judaizing Pharisees are critiqued. They are judged as being "troublesome," causing dissension and schism in the church (vs. 24). It is often to be found that some of the greatest controversies in a church are over issues that have no eternal merit, these often being either directly or indirectly related to the issues of law and not the commands of the gospel. Secondly, the epistle characterizes such men as "subverters of souls." Paul warns the Galatians against the errors of seeking perfection (sanctification) through an observance of the law (Gal. 3:3). One mistake is to assume salvation by works (circumcision), another is to assume perfection or sanctification by living a lawful life. There is a distinction between obedience to the gospel and obedience to the law. The first is the natural result of a loving heart; the second is an act of the will to comply with perceived duty. Paul goes on to warn them that their faith may be in vain, with their penchant for following the law (Gal. 3:4, 4:11, 5:4). Not only are the teachers of the law blinded, but they are subverters of other men's souls, false teachers, to whom the apostles did not give audience; no, not even for an hour (Gal. 2:4, 5), lest the gospel of grace be brought under the regulation of the law.

These examinations of the abrogation of both the civil and ceremonial laws are sufficient for anyone willing to believe, although they are by no means exhaustive. Let it also be understood that much truth and equity can be gleaned from these laws that have passed away in legal form. All Scripture is given by inspiration of God and is profitable for doctrine, correction, and instruction (II Tim. 3:16).

Paul also writes that Israel's history has value even to those at the end of the age (I Cor. 10:11). There is no precept of the law that may not be used to instruct man in righteousness and point him to Christ or give historical understanding, but it is through Christ that they are understood, and they are not now to be used as a smoke screen for a political agenda in the reestablishment of Moses' civil law for a "law of nations".

There are instances in the epistles where the civil case laws from Moses are affirmed in the context of the Church, thus showing that these laws, although voided as civil statutes, still provide instruction in righteousness. In I Corinthians 5:1 Paul upbraids the Corinthian church for countenancing a case of incest. Incest is only dealt with by the law in a specific manner, and Paul here also calls it a sin; even worse than what is acceptable to Gentile morality. In Leviticus 18:7 the civil law forbids such a practice, which is probably the basis of Paul's admonition, a case in point where the man of God may be instructed from earlier principles.

However, the specific letter of the law is not observed and Paul even warns against it. Paul asks that the church turn this man over to Satan, so that when all righteous restraints are removed, this man may indulge in fleshly desires unreservedly, and thus sicken himself with that which he craves, so that in this way he might see the bondage of sin, and the spirit may be saved and restored. Now under the law no mercy was to be granted for such an offense, but rather this man was to be "cut off" or executed for his sin (Lev. 18:29). (There are many references that use "cut off" to mean "execute.") But Paul here seeks restoration in the punishment. This man was brought back into fellowship with the body after sorrowing over his sin. He beseeches the church that they would affirm their love towards the repentant one and not allow him to sorrow overmuch, for his punishment was "sufficient" (II Cor. 2:5-11). Under the law, though, this would not have been adequate punishment. What is evident is that a principle, in part, is continued from the law, but the legal interpretation has been repealed.

Another case shall also be examined that is recorded both in I Timothy 5: 17, 18 and I Corinthians 9:8-11. The law is quoted that states, "Thou shalt not muzzle the ox that treadeth out the corn." This was another case law that dealt with the equitable treatment of animals, so it seemed. But Paul quotes it as proof that ministers of the gospel should be supported. He further argues in Corinthians that the intent of the law, in its fullest sense, was not in allowing oxen to eat while threshing the grain, but rather it was intended for us in the gospel age, as an admonition to provide for those who labor in word and doctrine.

Here again the letter of the law and its legal interpretation is set aside, while a spiritual principle is derived from it for our admonition.

As a side note here, it should be observed that the balance of Scripture teaches that ministers be willing to work and provide for their own needs, (II Thess. 3:7-10, I Cor. 9:15-18, Acts 18:1-3, 20:33-35) and proclaim the gospel free of charge, but the congregation has the responsibility to voluntarily support them in their expenses (I Cor. 9:1-14, I Tim. 5:17, 18, II Cor. 11:7-9, Gal. 6:6). Here then is an avoidance of both a professional, hireling ministry or one that expends the majority of its energy in the cares of this life. Would to God such a balance could be more fully realized in the churches.

The law then in its strict and legal sense has passed away, but in the spirit and principles of it one may continue to find instruction.

## CAN THE OLD TESTAMENT CIVIL LAW ESTABLISH A CHRISTIAN NATION?

The Church in its early years was considered a reproach and threat to a lawful and well ordered society. The Romans and Jews spread many pernicious and libelous tales about the primitive Christians, including participation in cannibalism, (take, eat, this is my body which is broken for you), incest, (salutation of "brother" and "sister"), and sexual orgies (love feasts). They were viewed as the outcasts of society, impoverished, and disconnected from the affairs of this life. Their commitment and zeal for their faith was viewed merely as fanaticism. The persecution at times was very intense, as the incensed Romans sought to obliterate this sect from their empire. As their numbers grew, more people began to realize that the dark rumors that had been spread about the Christians were simply untrue. Some philosophers were converted and became great apologists for the Christian faith. Like the apostle Paul, they brilliantly defended Christian truth in public forums and before emperors. Those who were despised as ignorant and unlearned were dispelling the elaborate myths of heathen philosophies with the force of simple, concise, and absolute truth. Eventually, Christians were not viewed as a threat to society because of unrestrained living, but were considered a threat to the unity of the pagan beliefs that undergirded all of Rome's law.[6] If Rome was to prosper she needed unity, in practice of faith, belief in their laws, and common morality.

All heathen nations had their special deities that they worshiped, upon which beliefs they established their laws. Rome accepted and incorporated other deities into their religion to create a pagan pluralism. However, all pagan religions have a common root in Babel, and trace to beliefs in Nimrod, Semiramis, and Tammuz. Rome was able to accommodate, like the Greeks before them, various styles of worship of diverse deities, since they all had a common source. And although in competition with one another, these various religions were not necessarily antagonistic toward one another.

The origin of paganism, as well as the New Age and occult, has been well documented by both secular and Christian historians as deriving from Babylonia, and so will not be documented here.

But Rome could never accept or incorporate into its society either Jewish or Christian beliefs and practices, as they were diametrically opposed to paganism. Almost every world empire from Babel on was fascinated with the idea of a complete sovereignty in authority and a unity of belief throughout the whole world, in order to create a lasting power. As Jesus, and later Abraham Lincoln, observed, "A house divided against itself cannot stand;" so, too, these world powers realized that only in a common unity would their political dreams be realized.

Now here in Rome these Christians' new religion was challenging the very basis of the unity (paganism) and was succeeding in overthrowing the eloquence and reasoning of their greatest philosophers. As the Christian faith progressed, by spreading of the Word, it became evident that eventually a new moral foundation for Rome would be needed if she hoped to preserve a unity of ethics, and the faith with the greatest empirical evidence, namely, Christianity, was certainly a viable alternative to paganism.

The last three emperors who persecuted Christians died violent deaths, which was viewed by Christians as God's judgment upon their actions. Following this came the edict of toleration, which was an acknowledgment of the weakening of paganism and the enduring strength of the Christian faith.

Constantine arrived on the scene around 313 A.D. and realized that Rome was not only in danger from the barbarians at this time, but was also internally weakened through divisions of faith. He had a great fascination with Christianity after His vision of the cross. He desired and created a "Christian theocracy," which consisted of the two arms of Church and state being united into one divine government, thus bringing into union the ministers of the gospel with the "ministers of God" (Rom. 13:4). He styled himself as *The universal Bishop of the external affairs of the church.*[7]

On the surface this would appear as a grand triumph for the Church, with the opportunity to create a "Christian state" and re-create the Israel of God under Christ in a manner similar to the nation of Israel under Moses. Why not seize this moment and exploit the opportunity to make all subjects Christian, at least externally, and enact such laws as are necessary to construct a Christian society. Surely this opportunity was providential. And in some ways it was. The era of Constantine and its accompanying respite from persecution was surely the providence of God, who works all things according to the counsels of His own will, and sets up such kingdoms as He deems necessary to accomplish His purposes.

It must, however, be recognized that the assumption that it was God's will to betroth the Church, the bride of Christ, to a union with the state, which is spiritual adultery, is not supported by Scripture. This union was really an attempt to duplicate what God had ordained only for the nation of Israel. It has been shown how the civil and ceremonial law of Israel has been repealed by Christ Himself, both in His gospel and His death.

Here, then, we see subtle reenactments of both the ceremonial (a national faith and form of worship) and the civil (a body of Christian legislative statutes) laws.

While Constantine did not always seek to reinstitute the letter of those laws, yet those principles which surely apply to the legal observance only, he condoned.

The whole ceremonial system was intended to be observed by everyone, so that no sin at all remained in the nation to bring them under God's judgment (Lev. 16; Josh. 7).

The civil law, as shown earlier, served as a coercive means to bring the citizen into conformance with Israel's polity as a nation, along with the stranger among them, in order that they might all worship and obey God. This was not a voluntary religion (although God desired it to be so) nor an option to obey, but rather a command to either obey or be punished by either the magistrate or divine judgment (Deut. 30:15-20, 19:15-21, I Sam. 2:25). The capital offenses have already been catalogued, which included those to uphold religious observance such as a stoning for a violation of the Sabbath, (Num. 15:32-36), so there is no need for reiteration.

It is upon the basis of Old Testament national policy that religious persecution of dissenting sects has been advanced by "Christian" nations, under the guise of "putting evil away from among you." The Church defines the heresy and the state punishes it.

Constantine executed his brother-in-law and wartime rival, Lucinius, in spite of a solemn promise of mercy, and then Eusebius, his close Christian friend and Bishop justified it, since he (Lucinius) was an enemy of the Christians.[8]

The adopting of a state religion, by its very nature, suggests that others will either be excluded from certain privileges or suffer outright persecution. Although this may not be fully seen immediately, still the fruit will be inevitably produced. Constantine, although he did alternately ban Arians and the orthodoxy (including Athanasius), did not severely persecute people of other religious persuasions. However, his son, Constantius, in the name of Christianity sought to violently suppress heathenism by destroying and pillaging many temples and prohibiting all heathen worship. He then filled up the coffers of the church with his booty. Athanasius reproved the emperor, illustrating what the true Christian conduct is:

*"Satan, because there is no truth in him, breaks in with ax and sword. But the Saviour is gentle, and forces no one, to whom he comes, but knocks and speaks to the soul: open to me my sister (Song of Sol.5:2). If we open to Him, He enters; but if we will not, He departs. For truth is not preached by sword and dungeon, by the might of an army, but by persuasion and exhortation. How can there be persuasion where fear of the emperor is uppermost? How exhortation, where the contradicter has to expect banishment and death?*[9]

It is evident by these sentiments that the whole church had not been blinded by might and some still understood that Christ never intended for His gospel to be advanced through Mosaic patterns.

However, by the time of Augustine, around 400 AD, the Church in general had assumed that it was to be a dominant force in the empire. It had vanquished heathenism by courting political powers which forcibly mass-converted the remaining people to Christianity. But now a new problem arose, this one from within. A segment of the African church withdrew from the general church at large because she was appointing unconverted men to positions of church leadership. These received their salaries from municipal and imperial treasuries as well as from the Church.

The African Separatists argued for a church that was separate from the world, composed only of regenerated members. They became known as the Donatists.

There have been many attempts by church historians to discredit the Donatists as fanatics or revolutionaries. While it is certainly true that these elements existed among those who called themselves Donatists, it is by no means representative of the movement at large. It is wise to remember that the Donatists were contending for a pure church, one that required a change of life for membership, a concept which militates against unrestrained or ungodly living.

The general or catholic church at large believed, by this time, that the church should encompass all members of society, whether born again or not, and should require external conformity to its standards. Augustine, the catholic champion, also agreed that the main controversy between him and the Donatists was about the following: *"The issue between us and the Donatists is about the question where this body is to be located; that is, what and where is the church?"*[10]

Augustine at first thought he could win over the Donatists to the established church with dialogue. But this failed to produce the desired results, and so he counseled that we must "compel them to come in", borrowing language (though inappropriately) from Jesus' parable of the supper (Luke 14:23). Since they would not come by persuasion, he said, *"Many must often be brought back to their Lord, like wicked servants, by the rod of temporal suffering, before they attain the highest grade of religious development."*[11]

The Donatist clergy was then banished, their laity fined, their churches confiscated, and they were ordered not to assemble upon pain of death—all this in the name of Christ, trying to preserve a unified Christian society through civil force.

Does this follow Moses or Christ?

This illustrates an attempt to establish a unified Christian society based upon civil laws that are "Christian" in foundation, and patterned after the example of the Old Testament Mosaic theocracy.

While the specific letter of Moses' law, to some extent, was not enforced, yet the Augustinian era Church sought to Christianize the world in the same manner that Jehu cleansed Israel of iniquity.

When these methods of Christianizing were first used, some of the Church recoiled in horror at such blatant disregard for the teachings and example of Christ for evangelism. Athanasius has been quoted, but also Hilary reproved the emperor against the destruction of heathenism with the sword and the filling of church coffers with the spoils. He says, *"With the gold of the state thou burdenest the sanctuary of God, and what is torn from the temples, or gained by confiscation, or extorted by punishment, thou obtrudest upon God."*[12]

After such measures were used to quell paganism and convert the heathen, then the Church began to use such measures on all dissenting groups of Christians from the catholic church, provoking a Donatist Bishop, Petilian, to say, *"Think you to serve God by killing us with your own hand? Ye err, ye err, poor mortals, think this; God has not hangmen for priests. Christ teaches us to bear wrong, not to revenge it."*[13]

Yet, the now firmly established catholic church became even more rigid in suppressing diversity from their understanding of what was the orthodox faith.

Theodosius, the "Christian" emperor, decreed *"all peoples over whom our rule extends shall live in that religion which was revealed to St. Peter... We give orders that all these are to adopt the name "Catholic Chris-*

*tians*"; the rest we shall let pass for fools and they will have to bear the *reproach of being called heretics. They must come first under the wrath of God and then also under ours.*"[14]

From primitive faith that endured suffering to an "established" faith that enjoyed privilege and support from the state to finally a repressive and intolerant religion that persecuted other sects, the Christian church may be traced in its descent into corruption. And with such decline, the purity of the catholic (general) church became compromised. That which once was unified in its desire to be betrothed unto Christ, is now adulterously married to civil government, thus conceiving a "Roman Catholic Church" that in the spirit of Christ's disciples will call down fire upon all that oppose them (Luke 9:54). Since God will not honor their requests, they will kindle their own at the stake. In the name of God they will annihilate those that have remained chaste unto Christ (John 16:1-4), calling them both heretics and seditious.

As Christ's rebuke to the disciples indicated, He never intended that the kingdom be advanced in the same manner that the Old Testament saints (Elijah) upheld Moses' law, nor does it need any physical force to either support or advance it, for it possesses the authority which Christ has given to it. He is the Head over all, and upholdeth all things by the Word of His power.

These sentiments are evident in John Chrysostom's thoughts during Theodosius' reign when he says, *"Christians are not to destroy error by force and violence, but should work the salvation of men by persuasion, instruction and love.*"[15]

The beginnings of the Roman Church have been examined, with their doctrine, which increased with vigor down through medieval times, birthing both the Jesuits and the Inquisition, who were experts in every artifice of malicious torture, being instructed of the devil himself how they might destroy those saints who had come out of her (John 8:44; Rev. 17:6).

The Reformers during their great contest with Rome also decried her violence against God's people; those who had not drunk the wine of her fornication.

Martin Luther, initially, in his dispute with Rome, like Augustine in his early life, makes a clear distinction between the realms of the church and the state.

His views on separation of church and state sound almost identical to mainstream Anabaptism.

The following are some extracts from a book on the civil magistrate published in 1523:

*"God has ordained two governments among the children of Adam, — the reign of God under Christ, and the reign of the world under the civil magistrate, each with its own laws and rights. The laws of the reign of the world extend no further than body and goods and the external affairs on earth. But over the soul God can and will allow no one to rule but Himself alone. Therefore where the worldly government dares to give laws to the soul, it invades the reign of God, and only seduces and corrupts the soul.*

*"Faith is a* voluntary *thing which cannot be forced. Yea, it is a divine work in the spirit. Hence it is a common saying which is also found in Augustine: (in his early days) "Faith cannot and should not be forced on anybody."—For heresy can never be kept off by force: another grip is needed for that; this is another quarrel than that of the sword. God's Word must contend here. If this fails, the worldly power is of no avail, though it fill the world with blood. Heresy is a spiritual thing that cannot be hewn down by iron, nor burned by fire, nor drowned by water. But God's Word does it. As Paul says, our weapons are not carnal, but mighty in God."[16]* (emphasis and parenthesis mine)

These sentiments are in harmony with Christ and the Ante-Nicene church and most other groups of persecuted believers from then to Reformation times, such as the Waldenses.

Luther later reneged on these assertions, when proffered protection by German Princes and the opportunity to establish his beliefs in an organized state church. The opportunity, which seemed to him divinely ordained, gave him liberty to reform the Church in a larger way. But with the offer of state protection came civil control over spiritual matters, as he found his protection contingent upon his willingness to cooperate with his benefactors in establishing a church suitable for the acceptance of the whole populace.

After that, many who once walked with him departed, when seeing this compromise of faith and liberty of conscience, and formed what became known as Anabaptism.

This exodus prompted frustration, then outrage, and finally fury from Luther, as his dreams of a unified state church would not be realized. He, like Augustine before him when dealing with the Donatists, changed his position on religious freedom and adopted views of severe repression against all other nonconforming groups.

The following is a statement that reflects this change:

When speaking against unlicensed (by the state) Anabaptist ministers preaching in Lutheran parishes he says: *"They must neither be tolerated or listened to, even though they seek to teach the pure gospel, yes, even if they are angelic and simon-pure Gabriels from heaven —— Therefore let everyone ponder this, that if he wants to preach or teach let him exhibit the call or the commission that drives him to it or else let him keep his mouth shut. If he refuses this then let the magistrate consign the scamp into the hands of his proper master - whose name is Meister Hans* (Hangman)*."*[17] (parenthesis mine)

Luther also commissioned Urbanus Rhegius to respond to the teachings of the Anabaptists on the separation of Church and state. The following is from him:

*"The truth leaves you no choice; you must agree that the magistracy has the authority to coerce his subjects to the gospel. And if you say, 'Yes, but with admonition and well chosen words but not by force," then I answer that to get people to the services with fine words and admonitions is the preacher's duty, but to keep them there with recourse to force if need be and to frighten them away from error is the proper function of the rulers."*[18]

These two quotations could be greatly multiplied with additional Lutheran writings upon the subject. But these two illustrate that the Lutheran intent was to restrict all religion to their own, and hang, execute, or banish all dissidents. The magistrate was to be instrumental in enforcing an attendance upon the Lutheran faith. Melanchthon, the Lutheran theologian, says, *"Now let every devout man consider what disruption would ensure if there should develop among us two categories, the baptized and the unbaptized."*[19]

Here in the Lutheran camp we find an attempt to establish the Christian faith in the same manner the Jewish faith was upheld; by civil law.

They also repeatedly justified their establishment of a state religion and persecution of nonconformists by reverting to the Old Testament Israel as a model for the church in a Christian land. They would not acknowledge the separation Christ made between His gospel and the civil law, and so like Israel they sought to exterminate all the heathen; the heathen being all those who disagreed with their form of religion, thus exhibiting the spirit of the law rather then the spirit of Christ.

Urbanus Rhegius says, *"It follows that our magistrates should punish heretics and faction makers and exterminate them, not with less, but with greater zeal than did the kings in the Old Testament."*[20]

The Reformed Calvinistic stance in this matter was similar to the Lutheran, as shall be demonstrated. In fact, Lutherans accused the Calvinists of being too rigid in enforcing their forms of religion. The Calvinistic confessions of faith called for the magistrate to perform his God-given duty to punish heresy. The Belgic confession in article 36 states concerning Christian magistrates:

*"And their office is, not only to have regard unto and watch for the welfare of the civil state, but also that they* protect *the sacred ministry, and thus may* remove *and* prevent *all idolatry and false worship; — that the kingdom of the antichrist may be thus* destroyed, *and the kingdom of Christ* promoted." (emphasis mine)

The Calvinistic view of civil law here is that it be used to "protect" and "promote" the Church (their sect of it) and to "remove and "prevent" all false worship (anything that is at odds with Calvinism) so that the kingdom of antichrist, by the power and aid of the civil state, be "destroyed."

Earlier Calvin was quoted as saying the judicial laws of Israel had expired with that economy. What is to be understood here in this seeming dichotomy is that the Christian state was not obligated to a Mosaic legal system per se, but rather, in the Reformed Calvinistic view, it was to be used as a model for the state both in principle and practice, and wheresoever they deemed expedient, in exact precept. The result of this is, though not enacting always specific Old Testament civil laws as statutes, they tried to follow its example in its rigidity towards maintaining a "one true religion" (Reformed, of course) and in its severe penalties against all heresies (those who were not Reformed).

This was a duplicate of what took place during the times of Constantine and Augustine. Those who dissented from the established church were not only heretics but also seditious and enemies of the state.

The Calvinists' idea of reforming the Church was not to return to the example of Christ and the apostles, but rather to cleanse the Church of Roman Catholic impurities and innovations that had crept in since the days of Constantine. They considered the era of Constantine a culmination of Old Testament prophecy in church history that extended beyond what the apostles realized in their time. This was no attempt to restore the Church to its primitive state by separating it from the government and making it a body of redeemed only, but rather an effort to purify Christendom (church and state) of pagan or unscriptural practices and return it to its glory as realized under the Christian Emperors, rather than the Catholic Popes.

The following is from the Calvinist Bogerman:

*"The service of the magistrate in the matter of the care of religion began in New Testament times with Constantine the Great ...., seeing that the preceding rulers were heathen and hostile to the Church and that Constantine put forth proper zeal to procure for the church outward peace and the true doctrine together with opposition for the teachings which he considered heretical."[21]*

Theodore Beza, Calvin's contemporary and successor writes:

*"After God launched Christianity by unarmed apostles He afterward*

*raised up kings by whose wisdom He intended to protect His Church."* Speaking against the Anabaptists he says, *"They do not like it that civil laws are enacted against their wickedness, saying that the apostles have asked no such thing of kings – but these men do not consider that those were different times and that all things agree with their own times. What emperor had at that time believed in Christ, in the days which Psalm 2 was still in effect: ......When we invoke lawfully and divinely instituted protection against stubborn and incorrigible heretics we only do what the Word of God and the authority of the holy prophets assert."[22]*

What is manifest here is that the Calvinists knew they were in contrast to the example of Christ and the Apostles, but they justified their enactments of "Christian" civil law on the basis of their prophetic interpretations of Psalm 2 and their Old Testament prophecies; namely, they ascribed all millennial passages to an earthly fulfillment under Christian rulers. One must differentiate when dealing with Constantine, Theodosius, Charlemagne, etc. (Christian Emperors) between the Sovereignty of God in world events and the prophetic fulfillment of millennial prophecies. Did God ordain these emperors to power? Yes, as well as all heathen powers, for there is no power but of God (Rom. 13:1). Did they provide unprecedented opportunities for the Church? In some cases, yes. Does this mean they are the fulfillment of Psalm 2? If one says yes to this, then one must ask; why has the civil rule of Christ and His dominion over nations been overthrown? Has Christ failed to subjugate the heathen? Did His rod of iron break? Or was His rod of pottery, and the nation's resistance that of iron?

Either one must acknowledge that the rule of Christ (as a reformed nation) has failed to extend to modern times, because of the collapse of His dominion, or that the Calvinistic system of interpretation of prophecy is fatally flawed. Also, should prophecy be interpreted in a manner that contradicts the example of Christ and the apostles, as well as their teachings? Yet this is the classic Reformed position on the relationship of the Church and the civil law, that the one should "promote" and "protect" the other.

It is not that the Reformers were not exposed to the concept of separation of church and state, for they knew both the Donatist and Anabaptist positions, but rather they rejected it and inveighed against it. They also rejected this concept when it arose from within their ranks. Huibert Duifhuis, a Reformed minister preached the following words in a sermon, *"Let the civil rulers permit no one to mislead them so as to employ force in matters of faith and of conscience, nor to persecute any for such matters, seeing that these things belong to God."* At a meeting in 1578, Reformed leaders read to him from Beza on the necessary suppression of heresy with the use of force. Duifhuis interrupted them and said, *"If those are your sentiments, then my soul may not linger in your council; with such I do not care to be identified,"* whereupon he dismissed himself from the assembly. Hendrik Alting, one of the leaders present, responded that Duifhuis was a "wolf in sheep's clothing, whom men should resist in private and who, that failing, should be brought to the attention of the magistrates." During the process of time he was removed from office.[23]

In Geneva, under Calvin, we find also a severe repression of all nonconformity to Reformed law. There were laws that regulated all types of extravagance or irreligious activity—from the types of singing allowed, down to the number of dishes you could serve at a meal. Parents were not allowed to use the name of any Catholic saint for their children and were asked to use only Old Testament names to avoid the possibility of such an error. The attendance to public worship was enforced by way of a fine, with watchmen appointed to see if all the citizens complied. A man was banished from Geneva three months for remarking that the braying of an ass was the praying of a beautiful psalm. Once three men laughed during church service and were imprisoned three days. A child was whipped for calling his mother a thief and a she-devil. (A whipping here was certainly in order but not by the state). A girl was beheaded for striking her parents, and the action justified under the civil sanction to uphold the fifth commandment. Men and women were burned for witchcraft. The death penalty was used against heresy, idolatry, blasphemy, and the second offense of adultery. Between 1542 and 1546 there were fifty-eight executions and seventy-six banishments. Worse yet, the barbarous practice of torture was retained in manner similar to the devices of the Inquisition.[24]

The most public atrocity was the burning of Servetus for his unorthodox views of the Trinity. A great deal has been argued about this event both for and against Calvin.

One might wonder why Servetus was singled out for publicity when Geneva itself had such a catalogue of repression. The answer lies in the fact that the other instances were merely business as usual and local in nature, whereas Servetus was widely known among all the Reformers and had written books expounding on his false notions about the Godhead. He was considered a plague to all the churches. He frequently badgered Calvin with letters containing his wild fantasies, which he quite brilliantly proposed, sometimes challenging him to public debate on these matters.

When Calvin would not consent to a public forum of discussion, he (Servetus) sought a guaranteed safe conduct to Geneva to meet with him. Calvin wrote to Farel concerning this request on February 13, 1546 *"Servetus lately wrote to me, and coupled with his letter a long volume of his delirious fancies, with the Thrasonic boast, ... He offers to come hither, if it be agreeable to me. But I am unwilling to pledge my word for his safety; for if he does come, and my authority be of any avail, I shall never suffer him to depart alive."*[25]

The impetuous Servetus would not allow himself to be ignored, so to Geneva he came, with no guarantee of safety, but with a determination that Calvin would be forced to give him audience.

Servetus soon found his confines to be a jail cell, compliments of Geneva.

An earnest trial ensued, with Calvin as the lead prosecutor for his conviction and execution, arguing for the *Mosaic civil law* concerning blasphemy to be observed in this case, equating his views of Christ's deity with blasphemy (rightly so) and seeking the death penalty as an appropriate punishment.[26]

The council that judged the case was initially somewhat divided in its views of the case but eventually the intellectual force of Calvin's arguments prevailed upon them and they gave a unanimous decision for his death by fire. Calvin objected to the use of fire and asked for the sword, but the council did not waver.

It is important to understand that Calvin did not seek a relinquishment of the death penalty but rather wished for it by the sword instead of by fire. It will not be dogmatized upon as to why this request was made, but it was probably so it would appear that the offense was civil in nature rather than an orchestration of the Church to bring about his mode of death. The standard treatment of heresy by the Catholics was burning at the stake. Calvin probably wanted to avoid what might appear as an "ecclesiastical" execution. If the sword was used, then it was a "civil" execution.

The Jews sought the same of Pilate, with the initial charge being blasphemy, then by twisting it into sedition against Ceasar, sought a Roman execution of crucifixion, rather than a Jewish penalty of stoning (like Stephen), thus trying to create the look of criminal offense and distancing themselves from its full responsibility. Whatever may be the motive, even if it be mercy, Calvin still sought his apprehension, conviction, and execution, and defended in public writing to the other churches afterwards this course of action, thus proclaiming for all time his confessed responsibility for this execution.

It is but one more example of zeal to establish a Christian society by civil law in a manner similar to Moses; a society that manifests itself contrary to the gospel and the example of Christ or the prophets.

If we leave the Reformation era and move up in time to the period of early settlements here in colonial America we will find that among Reformed peoples this persuasion concerning Mosaic civil law still persisted in both England and America, especially among the Puritans.

The Puritans arrived in the New World to establish the Massachusetts Bay Colony in the year 1630. It was only one year later that a young minister came to the colony with his wife to serve as a pastor in one of the Puritan congregations. His name was Roger Williams.

The Puritans looked at their opportunity to found a Christian society as unprecedented in Church history. Wherever the gospel had been preached before, it had met varying degrees of acceptance or rejection. They had been diligent in trying to reform the Church of England, yet with little success. Many of their number had suffered for their faith in England.

What is definitely true about Puritans is this; they were devout, God-fearing, well educated, and Calvinistic in their theology. Now here they were in a new land, with the opportunity to construct a Christian society that would be comprised wholly of Puritans. In Geneva, Calvin had met opposition from more liberal elements of society. Here in America, they could create a society from a core of people who all had the same theological framework. They could construct a completely Christian society, without trying to reform an existing corrupt institution. They would enact Christian civil law and elect Christian magistrates and governors. There would be one true Church which all would join.

The Bible would be both the polity of the Church and the constitution of the state. In the Church the gospel would be proclaimed and in the state the Christian officers would find guidance from Biblical civil law.

The magnitude of the moment was not lost upon the Puritans; they realized that they were (in their terminology) a "city set upon a hill" that could be an example unto all nations. They labored diligently to utilize this moment in history to create a model Christian society.

But the young minister in their midst was having growing convictions against the use of civil law to create a Christian society. If all men in the society were in the Church, then where was the world? The concept of the world becomes nonexistent in a society in which all profess Christ—a society in which everyone has been baptized into the Church as infants, attends church for worship, and everyone receives the sacraments of bread and wine as a token of the new birth. These were not always individual decisions but rather mandatory requirements of the commonwealth.

Was someone a Christian because the Church baptized them as an infant and declared them Christian? Could the state enforce the worship of God, or was worship a voluntary attitude of the heart?

As Roger Williams' convictions strengthened, so did also the opposition against his views. He saw how religion became used as a tool of the state to create a Christendom that was a formal and political faith which became the vehicle for all manner of atrocities to be committed under the guise of advancing the cause of Christ. A national church may create a Christendom but it could never create Christianity.

Although history was replete with coercion of faith, yet Williams argued, *"But so did never the Lord Jesus bring any unto His most pure worship."*[27]

In 1635, the Bay Colony required all male inhabitants to take an oath of fealty to the governor and all other elected or appointed officials. The oath ended with the quite familiar words "so help me God." Wiliams declared, *"A magistrate ought not to tender an oath to an unregenerate man"*, for that would cause him in reality *"to take the name of God in vain."*[28] Could someone who did not walk with God call God as his witness for the truth?

The Puritans undoubtedly would have argued they either did all have faith, or that these forms of faith could lead someone to true faith.

Williams argued that the magistrate ought to attend to his civil duties and not convolute the Church with the sphere of the state.

The Puritan community was only five years old and still under the scrutiny of the religious world, watching to see the success of this fledgling Reformed society.

Roger Williams posed a threat to their ideals for their "city set on a hill"; he must needs be banished before the pernicious views of this minister undermined the authority of their civil and ecclesiastical institutions. The Puritan Court and ministers were aghast at Williams' talk of a *"wall of separation between the garden of the Church and the wilderness of the world."* Such ideas were diametrically opposed to all their understandings of a "Christian commonwealth."

A ship was secretly prepared to export him back to England, but being warned by friends, and even by John Winthrop, the Bay Colony Governor, Roger Williams fled the colony in the middle of winter. Were it not for his previous friendship with the Indians and their willingness to requite his kindness, he most likely would have perished.

He would eventually establish Providence and then form the colony of Rhode Island, which became a haven from all those Protestant colonies that had an established church with mandatory attendance, enforced with heavy sanctions.

It might appear that this should have been the end of the dispute between him and the Puritans, but rather this was only the beginning, for the battle between established state churches and the philosophy of separation of church and state would heat up in print between Roger Williams and John Cotton, the most prominent Bay Colony minister.

Williams went to England to obtain there a charter for his new colony. It was there that he published a writing called, "Queries."

In his conclusion he directly assaults the Reformed view of government in six points.

*1. The ancient nation of Israel is no pattern for any modern nation, since the shadows of Moses "vanished at the coming of the Lord Jesus."*

*2. Religious persecution is a violation of the Christian Spirit and, beyond that, "opposite to the very tender bowels of humanity."*

*3. State-required conformity hinders the conversion of the Jews, since it does not allow them "a civil life or being."*

*4. Religious warfare is the chief disturber of civil peace, the chief murderer of men, women, and children.*

*5. The soul is violated, "ravished into a dissembled worship, which their hearts embrace not."*

*6. Although leaders profess to seek more light, in fact they persecute and suppress those from whom new light might come. After sixteen hundred years of bloodshed, it was time for the Christian churches to forsake Moses and follow Christ.*[29]

In mid 1644 his next work became public, for which he is most known by, "The Bloudy Tenent of Persecution, for the Cause of Conscience." John Cotton responded to this work with his own work entitled "The Bloudy Tenent, Washed and Made White in the bloud of the Lambe." In 1652 Williams responded to Cotton with "The Bloudy Tenent Yet More Bloudy: By Mr. Cottons Endeavor to Wash It White In The Bloud of the Lambe."

The following are some extracts that illustrate some of the differences between Williams and Cotton on the issues of church and state.

Williams writes:

*"All magistrates are God's ministers ... bounded to a civil work.*[30]

The purpose that God has ordained for them is*: "the preservation of mankind in civil order and peace (the world, otherwise, would be like the sea, wherein men, like fishes, would hunt and devour each other and the greater devour the lesser.)"*

Again he writes:

*"Now what kind of magistrate soever the people shall agree to set up, whether he receive Christianity before he be set in office, or whether he receive Christianity after, he receives no more power of magistracy than a magistrate that has received no Christianity. For neither of them both can receive more than the commonwealth, the body of people and civil state, as men, communicate unto them and betrust them with."*[31]

These statements are quite representative of Williams' view that the magistrates' office pertains unto civil affairs only, and is no arm or extension of the Church, the magistrate himself being or not being Christian, is of no consequence, his obligations being only to civil duty.

Now to Cotton these sentiments were horrific and tantamount to creating an atheistic state and promoting an unrestrained society. His response was in the classic, Reformed, Calvinistic approach, that God had ordained civil rulers for the care and protection of His Church and it was the magistrates' duty to punish all offenders of the pure religion in the same manner as the Old Testament kings cleansed the land of idolatry.

Moses' law was to be the guide for civil law.

He writes in an exposition of Revelation 16, published in London 1642:

*"In old time, if a man played the false prophet, and suggested such devices as these (i.e. Roman Catholicism), the Lord judgeth him to death; this was His manner. And so in the New Testament (here in Revelation 16) as in the Old, He condemns all such to death, and He is most righteous in so doing. This is the sum. Therefore, by the ancient laws of that unchangeable God that thought it insufferable in those days, He thinks it insufferable now that priests and Jesuits should bring in other altars, other meditations and mediators, as prayers of saints and angels; the Lord looks at it as deeply meritorious of a bloody death, as in former times. He is the same God, and His zeal and jealousy is deeply provoked against the like kind of viciousness now as it ever was then ...."*

Again he writes:

*"For since God laid this charge upon magistrates in the Old Testament to punish seducers and the Lord Jesus never took this charge off in the New Testament, who is this Discusser* (Williams*) that he should leave this charge still upon magistrates which God laid on and Christ never took off? .... For Christ came not to destroy the law of Moses (Matt. 5:17) ..."*[32]

Cotton's arguments follow the traditional Reformed view, which causes them to be flawed. He equates a civil punishment in the Old Testament with God pouring out vials of wrath upon the Antichrist in Revelation 16. If they are one and the same, then one could argue against all civil government, saying that it is all in God's hands and He shall judge all civil affairs as He sees fit, since it is His judgment in Revelation 16, and not civil government's. Or one could argue from this system of interpretation that everything that God punishes man may also punish (and to the same degree), as if when He said, "Vengeance is mine; I will repay" could not have any relevance to the saints here on earth. Nor is God in Revelation 16 using civil government to punish a criminal offender for civil disobedience, but rather bringing His own Divine judgment upon a wicked world.

The equation between the two is purely imaginary.

This is a classic proof text.

Then he argues that since Jesus did not destroy Moses' law (Matt. 5:17) all the same duties lie upon the Christian magistrate as on those that were in Israel, one of their obligations being to punish seducers. Cotton overlooks the fact that Christ can fulfill the civil law just as He fulfilled the ceremonial law; through His death He became both the sacrifice for sin and bore the curse or penalty of sin (Gal. 3:13).

If the "Christian" magistrate is to uphold the law in the same manner as the "Jewish" one in the area of punishment of heretics, then he would also have to uphold the same ecclesiastical system to be consistent, namely Judaism. If Jesus did not continue the ceremonial law in Matthew 5:17 then He could just as well have not continued Moses' civil law. It is only in Jesus' following discussion that one can determine which laws He was upholding and which He repealed. But this has already been seen. Further, there is no case in the New Testament of Christ or the apostles taking a heretic to a civil judge for punishment, or instructing anyone else to do so. But we do have the case of Christ being tried first by an ecclesiatical court and then turned over to a civil (Roman) court to be punished capitally for blasphemy and sedition.

Which example is the "Christian" magistrate going to emulate; that of the Jews, by condemning blasphemers to death, or that of the apostles, who treated heresy with spiritual censure and excommunication?

Cotton, while acknowledging a certain amount of separation between Church and state, merely viewed them as two institutions that are joined together in one theocracy, and not as independent of each other.

In 1636 he writes to Lord Say and Sele:

*"God's institutions (such as the government of church and of common-*

*wealth be) may be close and compact, and co ordinate one to another, and yet not confounded. God hath so framed the state of church government and ordinances, that they may be compatible to any commonwealth, though never so much disordered in his frame. ... It is better that the commonwealth be fashioned to the setting forth of God's house, which is his church, than to accommodate the church to the civil state. Democracy I do not conceyve that ever God did ordeyne as a fitt government eyther for church or commonwealth."*

The reasoning presented here by Cotton is reformed, that is, unable to conceive of any state existing without endorsing a state religion. In his view, following the Old Testament pattern, the state's civil laws should reflect the ordinances and polity of the Church. He could not imagine the two coexisting in the same geographical area as independent entities. Now on the surface this concept appears quite appealing, having a state that enacts such ecclesiastical laws as will honor God and be conducive to the work of the Church. The reality of this in *every* case has *always* been that one denomination is declared the only true Church and all others are declared heretical. The state enacts laws in support of one sect and against all others. The state is called upon by the Church to punish all those whom the Church deems pernicious, and civil law is used to enforce ecclesiastical law, thus duplicating a Mosaic society. The Church also is limited by what the state is willing to adopt, and thus the state corrupts and influences the doctrine and practice of the Church.

The Church is corrupted by the state and the state becomes the discipline of the Church.

It should be remembered that God did ordain this method of government for the Old Testament times when "all" His law was enforced. Every attempt, though, to marry Moses and Christ has produced a spiritual mutation of the gospel. Whenever Jesus sets aside a law, Christ's teachings are readjusted (by Reformed reasoning) to make them out to be nothing more than a commentary of Moses.

No Reformer would take all of Moses' law nor would they bind themselves to its exact precepts, but in their effort to combine its equity to Christ's teachings they both change Moses' law and politicize the gospel, thus creating a hybrid that does not correlate to either Moses or Christ but merely their own arbitrary opinions.

If a person is to argue for Moses' civil law, then he could justifiably argue for the complete genocide of any heathen nation into which Christ's mandate (the Great Commission) sends missionaries, without any moral compunction. Even this is not a good example, for God did not send missionaries to Canaan to give an opportunity for conversion, but rather said "thou shalt smite them, and utterly destroy them; thou shalt make no covenant with them, nor show mercy unto them (Deut. 7:2).

A friend traveled to Ireland and witnessed there this verse on a sign upon which the Ulster Protestants were calling attention to how God would ask them to treat their enemies (the Catholics) in their conflict there; showing how even in modern times these sentiments are still instigating bloodshed.

Roger Williams also saw this theory clearly for what is was, merely a justification for the persecution of many nonconformist groups of Christians, those wishing to establish a church on New Testament principles that were composed only of believing, baptized members.

Williams writes in "A Plea For Religious Liberty":

"....the blood of so many hundred thousand souls of Protestants and Papists, split in the wars of present and former ages, for their respective consciences, is not required nor accepted by Jesus Christ the Prince of Peace.

....the doctrine of persecution for cause of conscience is proved guilty of all the blood of the souls crying for vengeance under the altar.

....the state of the land of Israel, the kings and people thereof in peace and war, is proved figurative and ceremonial, and no pattern nor precedent for any kingdom or civil state in the world to follow."[33]

The Massachusetts Bay Colony would also be put to the test again as to whether they would allow any diversity of Christian faith among them, for after having banished Williams, they were infiltrated by Baptists.

In 1644 the Bay Colony outlawed the Baptist faith. The Baptists had begun their work among the Puritans, calling for a regenerate body of believers to be baptized into the local church, as a completely separate experience from the infant sprinkling into the state church.

Three Baptist preachers visited a blind Baptist church member in the colony and held services and communion in his house. They were apprehended by the state and imprisoned. The three were given the options of a fine or a whipping. Two were released on payment, but the minister, Obadiah Holmes, refused to pay the fine or allow others to pay for him.

The day of reckoning came, with Boston making a public event of it in the marketplace. Holmes' friends besought him to take wine to lessen the pain. But Holmes would refuse all the overtures of mercy, seeking only, as he later wrote, to be sustained by the Spirit of God.

As Holmes was stripped, he uttered to the executioner, *"I am now come to be baptized in afflictions by your hands, that so I may have further fellowship with my Lord. I am not ashamed of His suffering, for by His stripes am I healed."*

Whereupon the executioner laid upon his bare back thirty stripes, as a punishment deemed worthy for a man who had entered a congregational (Puritan) parish and had unlawfully preached the gospel and baptized.[34]

This was not the only opportunity that Cotton and his Puritan cohorts would have to implement the doctrine of physical suppression of all (supposed) heresy; they would not only persecute the Baptists but also the Quakers.

Now the Quakers had arrived in New England and began to spread their doctrine of following the "inner light", which among some groups caused men to grow long hair and caused women to parade naked through the streets, as well as other irrational and unbiblical behavior.

Roger Williams, himself, personally detested their doctrines and their antics. Now it must be noted that not all Quakers carried their teaching of following the "inner light" to such extremes and many were lawful and peaceful citizens.

Williams would debate their doctrines with them, but as long as they were law abiding he would not punish them for holding religious opinions contrary to his own. Not so, though, for Boston. Quaker women were stripped naked and examined for signs of witchcraft and then punished. In 1657 it was decreed that not only were all Quakers to be banished, but any who returned after banishment would have an ear cropped. A second offense would relinquish another ear. A third offense would bring a branding iron upon the tongue until a hole was burned through it.

This still did not stem the tide of Quakerism, and so in 1658 the death penalty was imposed, thus instigating the death of four Quakers by hanging.[35]

John Cotton defended this practice of persecution right up to the end of his life. In his final months he wrote, *"So what if our laws make hypocrites? At least hypocrites give God part of his due - the outer man, but the profane person gives God neither outward nor inward man."*[36]

Again, when defending their actions against the Baptist, Holmes, he states (somewhat cynically), *"I am sure (he) had not been so well clad for many years"* referring to the plush accommodations and clothing provided to Holmes during his stay at the Boston jail by the Puritans.[37]

All these incidents trace to the belief system that retains in practice or principle Moses' civil law as still binding for the Church and nation; with Israel under the old covenant being a model society for Christendom.

Cotton, though, interestingly does admit that a state-regulated religion makes for hypocrites in the Church, although he justifies it as better than an irreligious society.

This completely contradicts the words of Jesus when He said that the hypocrites, when making heathen proselytes, do not better them by converting them to their faith but make them two-fold more the child of hell (Matt. 23:15).

It seems as though Cotton could not distinguish between a moral society and a Christian one. It is understood that society must have a moral foundation, but that is completely different from Christianizing or hypocritizing society.

And then there is the old ploy of endeavoring to wash persecution white in the "blood of the Lamb" by claiming that it is done for the good of the offender, as if Holmes really needed a Puritanic garb to cover himself or a jail cell to escape the elements.

When once a person imbibes of this doctrine of the continuance of Moses' civil law, there is no end to the means he will use to justify the inevitable persecution that follows, nor is any Scripture beyond the reach of strained proof text or mutilation in order to maintain a continuance of that which was fulfilled in Christ and ended.

It was during this era that the most influential and authoritative Reformed confession of faith was being drafted, known as the Westminster Confession (1646). During the drafting of the confession, a dispute arose as to the position that should be taken in regards to toleration of differing religious sects; whether they should merely be censured by the Church or whether the magistrate also should physically punish and suppress heresy. George Gillepsie took the floor and expounded the three views on religious liberty that were prevalent. The first view was that of the Catholic Church, which believed that it is a good service to God to extirpate by fire and sword all that oppose the Catholic faith. This view, (as a Presbyterian) he rejected as "The *Black Devil* of idolatry and tyranny." The second view was that of the Donatists, Arminians, and primarily Baptists and Anabaptists. Their view was that there must be a complete separation between church and state in that the magistrate must not use any coercive powers upon heretics or sectaries. *"The very same is maintained in some books printed amongst ourselves in this year of confusion: viz The Bloody Tenent (by Roger Williams)..."*

*"The third opinion is that the magistrate may and ought to exercise his coercive power, in suppressing and punishing Heretics and sectaries, less or more, according to the nature and degree of the error, schism, obstinacy, and danger of seducing others, requires."*[38] Gillepsie argued for this third view and buttressed this position from Calvin, Beza, and many other

Reformed Confessions.

Notice carefully that these views are not about punishing civil criminals but whether it be right to use civil laws to defend ecclesiastical ordinances and punish all nonconformists. Gillepsie knows of Williams' views and rejects them. The difference between the Catholic view and the Protestant view is not so much in principle as it is in degree of punishment. Gillepsie intimates that the Papists annihilate heretics indiscriminately, while the Protestants use degrees of punishment against heresy that is commensurate with the gravity of the offense, the penalties varying from fines and imprisonment to capital execution. Gillepsie's arguments for the third opinion were accepted and introduced into the Westminster Confession.

In the confession chapter XX, article IV it states that practices or opinions that are contrary to the known principles of Christianity may be proceeded against by the censures of the Church and by the power of the civil magistrate.

In chapter XXIII, article III it states that the civil magistrate's duty is, *"to take order that unity and peace be preserved in the Church, that the truth of God be kept pure and entire, that all blasphemies and heresies be suppressed."*

While there are later recensions to the original form of the Westminster Confession in regards to the aforementioned language, it is this original that most accurately represents classic Reformed thought on the spiritual duties of the Christian magistrate. These articles were not entered into the confession flippantly, but only after considerable discussion, and a reaffirmation of foundational principles of Reformed doctrine. Here then are embodied the "principles" that sanctioned heretical suppression; more truthfully known as religious intolerance and persecution.

A later article says that the civil magistrate is to grant freedom to all denominations, but this needs to be understood that it refers only to those that the Presbyterians deem a true representation of the Reformed faith. They never granted such liberty to Baptists or Anabaptists of their time. Many of these two groups suffered for the faith in England during the times of the Reformation. Many Catholics also lost their lives when Scotland and England became Protestant.

The Presbyterians had already established a "Solemn League And Covenant" in 1643 and required that all citizens in Scotland swear allegiance to it; it was the third one instituted by them as a national covenant between the Church, state, and the populace. George Gillepsie argued that this covenant be mandatory in the following words (extracted from his works): *"When King Josiah made a solemn covenant (the effect thereof was a thorough Reformation, the taking away of the ancient and long continued high places, the destroying of Baal's vessels, altars, priests, II Kings 23, throughout), he did not leave his covenant arbitrary; but he caused all that were present in Jerusalem and Benjamin to stand to it; II Chron. 34:32. In all which he is set forth as a* precedent to Christian Reformers, *that they may know their duty in like cases."* (emphasis mine)

Is this denominational freedom, as pretended to in the Westminster Confession? They define freedom only as the privilege to obey their form of church and state. This is confirmed by the fact that Scotland went to war with England over this covenant, in an attempt to overthrow Anglicanism.

And so when the Reformed tradition in America trumpets that they have always espoused religious freedom and were instrumental in establishing it in America, this is false. For not only were the Presbyterians, Puritans, etc. exposed to these concepts through Williams, but when hearing of them they not only utterly rejected them but inveighed against them. The reformed traditions, as Gillepsie intimates, always looked to Israel as the model for Christian Reformers, which did not allow diversity of faith and used civil law to uphold their religious faith. Williams' concepts to them were so heretical that he was banished.

Samuel Rutherford is known for his classic work "Lex Rex", wherein he establishes the "Biblical" criteria for revolution against tyranny. This is taught by some to be the germ of the American Revolution.

But the principles espoused in his work are not identical or consistent with separation of church and state. Rutherford also was a contemporary of Williams, who was acquainted with "The Bloudy Tenent." He also was part of the Westminster Assembly, which adopted the suppressive language against heresy. Greater evidence still is seen in that he wrote in direct opposition to Williams' views on religious liberty. He wrote a "Free Disputation Against Pretended Liberty of Conscience."

He writes, *"We conclude there is a law against toleration of many Religions, not any repealing of that Law in the New Testament, but divers Religions expressly forbidden as contrary to peace, and foretold to fall out as sad judgments."*

Again, *'....there is but one Lord, one faith, one baptism, and one Religion, whether* Presbyteriall *or* Independent*...."* (emphasis mine)

Again, *"....as for Mr. Williams chaldean, and heathenish or American peace, we leave it to himself ... would he have Christians all keeping such an Heathenish unity and peace, as Babylonians and Americans have, and in the meantime tolerate all Religions. Christians who have one God, and one faith, and one hope are to follow more than a Civill and Heathenish peace."*

It is plain that whatever might be agreed on between Rutherford and the American Founding Fathers on "conditions" for revolution, there is little agreement on the "objectives" that the revolution is to accomplish—his being a state religion, the Americans' being religious freedom. Rutherford makes it clear that the only religion to be tolerated is the Presbyterian and Independent (Puritan). Thus is defined for us the extent of religious freedom in the Reformed view. He calls the concepts of religious toleration heathenish, and argues that since the New Testament does not rescind the Mosaic civil law principles, they are still in effect.

It has been shown that the New Testament clearly does abrogate Moses' civil laws, Jesus having demonstrated that as clearly as could be done in the Sermon on the Mount.

Wherever throughout history there is an alliance between the church and the state, and the adoption of a state religion, it is inevitable that in time all dissenters who will not conform to the state interpretation of the true faith will be persecuted in the name of God for the preservation of an orderly and unified society.

This observation was also grasped by our founders as they sought to avoid the pressure from within to officially adopt the Christian faith, especially when most of the colonies had an established religion already. The following statements reveal their disrespect of all attempts to establish an American state church.

Thomas Jefferson said:

*"The Presbyterian clergy are loudest, the most intolerant of all sects, the most tyrannical and ambitious; ready at the word of the lawgiver, if such a word could be now obtained, to put the torch to the pile, and to rekindle in this virgin hemisphere, the flames in which their oracle Calvin consumed the poor Servetus."*[39]

Thomas Jefferson commented on the disestablishing of the congregational (Puritan) church in Connecticut by saying:

*"That this den of priesthood is at length broken up, and that a Protestant popedom is no longer to disgrace American history and character."*[40]

James Madison wrote in 1819:

*"It was the universal opinion ... that civil Government could not stand without the prop of a religious establishment, and that the Christian religion itself would perish if not supported by a legal provision for its clergy. ... In some parts of the country, however, there remains ... a strong bias towards the old error, that without some sort of alliance or coalition between Government and Religion neither can be duly supported. ... Every new and successful example therefore of a perfect separation between ecclesiastical and civil matters, is of importance."*[41]

When Washington was approached in 1789 by Presbyterian elders seeking more specific language in the Constitution to reference "of the only true God and Jesus Christ, whom He hath sent," he replied that *"the path of true piety is so plain as to require but little political direction."*[42]

Jefferson postulates:

*"Only one significant difference can be detected between paganism and Calvinism, paganism is far more intelligible."[43]*

James Madison wrote in his Memorial and Remonstrance Against Religious Assessments in 1785:

*"During almost fifteen centuries has the legal establishment of Christianity been on trial. What have been its fruits? More or less in all places, pride and indolence in the Clergy, ignorance and servility in the laity, in both, superstition, bigotry, and persecution.*

*Enquire of the Teachers of Christianity for the ages in which it appeared in its greatest lustre; those of every sect, point to the ages prior to its incorporation with Civil policy."[44]*

Benjamin Franklin wrote in an essay on "Toleration":

*"If we look back into history for the character of the present sects in Christianity, we shall find few that have not in their turns been persecutors, and complainers of persecution."*

It is evident from these quotations that the founders of our country were quite knowledgeable of church and state history and had a particular distaste for those denominations that formed alliances with the state and suppressed all separatists.

By all the evidence that has been examined we can only conclude in answer to our original question as to whether the civil law of the Old Testament can be used to establish a Christian nation; "Yes" if the following suppositions are allowed:

A. One does not consider that primitive Christianity had no earthly alliance with the state, nor that it was the true identity of the Christian faith.

B. One does not acknowledge that faith cannot be coerced (only works can, which is not the foundation of Christianity).

C. One does not recognize that Jesus clearly abrogated the civil laws of Moses.

D. One does not consider that a union with the state is also a union with the world.

E. One has no qualms of conscience when persecuting nonconformists for following the example of Christ and the Apostles in separating the Church from the world.

F. One does not consider that they will answer to God for bringing, yea forcing, unregenerate men into the Church.

In short, if one is willing to call a nation Christian because they implement Moses' law, and disregard the gospel mandates, then it is evident that the essence of the Christian faith has eluded their grasp, being blinded by the god of this world, not comprehending the spiritual nature of Christ's Kingdom, nor recognizing that anything outside of that Kingdom cannot properly be called Christian.

A nation can never be Christian in the true sense, as it is not the organism or body of Christ and cannot fulfill all His precepts, such as "Love your enemies." It can be Christian in the philosophical sense in that it accepts the "moral" values of the Bible as its foundation for law, as opposed to those of Islam or Hinduism, but this does not constitute true Christianity; it is merely the morality of it. At best, a nation will be founded on God's moral law, but this is not equivalent to being representative of the faith of the gospel.

## CONCLUSION: THE CIVIL AND CEREMONIAL LAWS ARE ABROGATED BY THE GOSPEL'S PREEMINENCE OF LOVE AND GRACE

In the preceding chapter we have maintained that the moral precepts of the moral law are still in effect and that the righteousness of them is fulfilled in those who walk in the Spirit (Rom. 8:4). However, the complete picture was not given, as to the continuance of the moral law, but was reserved for this chapter to better illustrate the extent of its continuation in relation to the abrogation of the rest of the law.

It was established by Paul that the moral law is not voided by faith (Rom. 3:3) but continues as a means of exposing and imputing sin (Rom. 3:19, 20, 4:13, 7:7-12). Paul does not refer to any civil or ceremonial precepts performing this function.

But this still does not answer fully as to whether the Christian is under the moral law, it only establishes the fact that its precepts are not extinct. Here then is the crux of the matter. If the moral law is continued, how shall it be enforced? This is the argument presented by the Reformed view. Shall it not be enforced with the civil laws God gave to Moses specifically for upholding morality?

First, let us remember that concrete, Biblical evidence has already been given for the civil law's discontinuance. To answer the question of how the moral law shall be enforced, the previous foundation must be built upon, not laid aside by a philosophical supposition that Moses' civil laws must continue to preserve the moral law. Also, let us remember there are no distinct categories of laws that are listed as civil or ceremonial but rather the distinctions are general and merely labeled as laws that apply either to the state (civil) or the religious practices (ceremonial). The eternal moral principles are expressed in the Decalogue (Ten Commandments), those only being spoken directly by God and placed in the ark of the covenant. These commands are what is quoted from often to show a man his sin, or the two principles that undergird them, love to God and love to our fellow man.

Perhaps at this point a quote from an early church leader would be helpful to reinforce what is in view here. Ireneaus (125A.D. - 190A.D.) says, *"The Lord Himself did speak in His own person to all alike the Words of the Decalogue; and therefore, in like manner, do they remain permanently with us, and receiving by means of His Advent in the flesh,* extension *and* increase, *but not abrogation." (emphasis mine)* It is the "extension" and "increase," here spoken of by Ireneaus, that is demonstrated in the Sermon on the Mount, where strengthened moral precepts are gospel, while civil laws are contradicted. But are these original moral principles guidelines for the Christian? Do they represent the morality of a Christian or merely a moral man? Paul says to Timothy (I Tim. 1:9), the law is not made for a righteous man, but for the "lawless" and "disobedient". The moral law continues as a system of morality to restrain sin in unconverted (unrighteous) society; for people Paul enumerates as murderers, profane persons, adulterers, and liars  (I Tim.1:9, 10). It is to restrain sin among the ungodly and expose sins in the self-righteous.

But Paul says, "It is not made for the righteous man." In another place Paul says, "Ye are not under the law but under grace." (Rom. 6:14).

Notice also the following:

"For I through the law am dead to the law, that I might live unto God" (Gal. 2:19).

"But after that faith is come, we are no longer under a schoolmaster" (Gal. 3:25).

"But if ye be led of the Spirit, ye are not under the law"  (Gal. 5:18).

"For if that first covenant had been faultless, then should no place have been sought for the second" (Heb. 8:7).

It was initially shown how the moral precepts are continued but now it is clarified that they were continued not for the "believer" but for the "unbeliever". The believer's walk is in the Spirit under the new covenant, one of grace. The unbeliever does not have the Spirit nor the divine nature to motivate him to righteousness; he requires a moral law that his conscience will affirm, to guide him and restrain him from unbridled sin. The moral law continues then as a system of morality for unconverted man until he comes to Christ, so that society at large is not left without a moral compass or absolute ethical standards.

Paul portrays the relationship to Christ as being as exclusive as a marriage relationship, saying that a divorce from the law is required in order to marry Christ  (Rom. 7:4).

This whole concept is summed up in Romans 10:4, where Paul says, "Christ is the end of the law for righteousness to everyone that believeth."

The purpose of this discussion is to show that the Christian is not under any aspect of the law, therefore his conduct is distinct from the moral code implemented by God for the world. Therefore there is no such thing as a Christian nation or society caused by implementing God's moral or civil law, as the law itself does not represent Christianity; only the new covenant does, which replaces the tables of stone (II Cor. 3:3).

The establishment of a "moral" or "just" society, as opposed to a "Christian" one, shall be examined in another chapter. Also, the civil sanctions of Moses have been shown to have been completely fulfilled in the penalty Christ paid for sin and thus abrogated (Gal. 3:13, Rom. 8:3, 15:3, John 12:47, I John 2:2, Isa. 53:4-6, 8, 10), therefore they have no further relationship to the moral law.

It has been shown how Paul gave spiritual interpretations to civil case laws (I Cor. 8:9, 10) but nowhere established their societal relevance. What sanctions in society are to be employed to conserve morality shall be examined in another chapter. The purpose here has been to demonstrate that wherever Moses' civil or ecclesiastical law has been instituted, there has been the abominable, unchristian practice of persecution in the name of Christ. Moses' civil penalties have no more relevance to morality or Christianity than an animal sacrifice does to the forgiveness of sin.

It is the misunderstanding of these concepts that has caused so many religious wars throughout history.

The "Thirty Years' War" in Europe between Protestants and Catholics precipitated the death of one half the population of Germany, along with creating an apathy towards religious issues after that.[45]

We shall presently examine some statements along these lines made by Charles H. Spurgeon(1800s). But first let it be understood that what is being objected to here is the "Reformed World View", whether Lutheran or Calvinist.

In contemporary times to be a Calvinist merely means embracing a certain view of the Sovereignty of God in man's salvation, including Calvin's views on predestination. This is somewhat misleading, as classic Calvinism also included (along with Calvin's view of predestination) a whole world view of Christian government and church polity.

Charles Spurgeon, recognized by most as a Calvinist in soteriology (theology of salvation, specifically here accepting Calvin's view of election to some degree) is not a classic Calvinist in his world view.

Likewise we also affirm and appreciate many truths propounded by the Reformers but are here objecting to their view of Christian government. It is not our intent to falsely characterize anyone in this work, not even the Reformed churches. We have tried only to represent the facts to illustrate the truth of Scripture. This author has found much inspiration in the works of the Puritans. Calvin's commentaries also portray a judicious exposition of many passages of Scripture. We rejoice whenever Christ is preached (even from Moses' seat) and His doctrine manifested, from whatever tradition it comes (Matt. 23:1-3).

How a man can call himself a Christian and then persecute his brother we know not, but we do know that the fire will one day test every man's work and many that have thought to build upon Christ shall see their work suffer loss and be saved only by fire. All men shall here suffer some loss due to personal impurities (I Cor. 3:10-15), but let us not be guilty of persecuting the body of Christ, lest we be guilty of persecuting Christ.

At the last day many shall profess mighty works in Christ's name, but Christ shall not even acknowledge them (Matt. 7:21-23).

It is our intent to expose false doctrine and its fruit, especially in these times of immorality when some Christians have been deceived into thinking that the old Reformed doctrines shall answer all the woes of our present society.

We equally want to protest against all sin, whether physical persecution or murderous hatred (I John 3:15).

It is our intent to warn against a rising evil that is seeking to rebuild old foundations—an evil that rests its credibility in the tradition of the Reformers rather than the truth of Scripture. Spurgeon's comments are here most appropriate.

Spurgeon has been greatly appreciated by both Reformed denominations and Anabaptist denominations for his scriptural insights on many subjects. He is probably the most quoted and most read preacher of all time since the apostles. This does not put him on a pedestal, but rather means he can speak to many audiences, he being a Particular (Calvinistic, though he more moderately) Baptist.

From a sermon entitled the "Independence of Christianity" we provide this extract:

"... *All swords that have ever flashed from scabbards have not aided Christ a single grain. Mohommedans' religion might be sustained by Scimitars, but Christians' religion must be sustained by love. The great crime of war can never promote the religion of peace. The battle, and the garment rolled in blood, are not a fitting prelude to "peace on earth, good will to men." And I do firmly hold, that the slaughter of men, that bayonets, and swords, and guns, have never yet been, and never can be, promoters of the gospel. The gospel will proceed without them, but never through them. ... Hush thy trump, O war; put away thy gaudy trappings and thy blood-stained drapery, if thou thinkest that the cannon with the cross upon it is really sanctified, and if thou imaginest that thy banner hath become holy, thou dreamest of a lie, God wanteth not thee to help His cause. "It is not by armies, nor by power, but by my Spirit, saith the Lord."*

From a sermon entitled "Fire, Fire, Fire" we provide the following:
*"All the Roman Emperors, with but a few exceptions were persecutors; and the Christian Emperors were as bad as the Pagan, for the Christian emperors were not Christians, nor were they members, as I believe, of a Christian Church. The Christian Church, and especially that Church of which we are still members, which has never defiled its garments, but which, never having had any alliance with the Church of Rome, has never needed to be reformed, – that Church under its different names, Paulitians, Novatians, Albigenses, Lollards, Wyckliffites, Anabaptists, Baptists, has always suffered. It matters not what state, what church, may have been dominant, whether it has been Christian or anti-Christian, the pure Church of Christ has always been the victim of persecution, and though she has persecuted never, but has always maintained inviolate, disunion from the state, and an utter hatred of all laws which would bind the conscience of man, yet she has been especially destitute, afflicted, tormented,*

*and if she hath today a little breathing time, perhaps it is rather owing to the timidity which has made us keep back our sentiments, than to any charity towards ourselves."*

These sentiments are completely agreed with and cannot be much more clearly or eloquently expressed. Every attempt by the Church to form an alliance with secular powers has produced both religious intolerance and Christian hypocrisy, confusing both their spheres of influence, creating a hierarchical clergy and an oppressive government wherein corruption commonly abides, thus denigrating the witness of the Church to the ungodly and giving false hope to the self-righteous members in it.

Spurgeon also laments the fact that religious intolerance should plague the American colonies when Christian peoples had settled America in order to find freedom of worship and conscience.

In the same sermon "Fire, Fire, Fire" he states: *"When our Baptist forefathers, persecuted in England, went over to America to find shelter, they imagined that among the Puritans they would have a perfect rest, but Puritan liberty of conscience meant, "The right and liberty to think as they did, but no toleration to those who differed," The Puritans of New England, as soon as ever a Baptist made his appearance amongst them, persecuted him with as little compunction as the Episcopalians had the Puritans. No sooner was there a Baptist, than he was hunted up and brought before his own Christian brethren. Mark you, he was brought up for fine, for imprisonment, confiscation, and banishment before the very men who had themselves suffered persecution."*

This introduces an important point. The fact that men are willing to suffer persecution does not necessarily mean that they represent the true faith of Christianity. Almost all world religions can produce examples of their martyrs, so martyrdom alone does not establish truth. The real test of faith for a religion is whether, when given the opportunity, will it persecute those that oppose it? "If I give my body to be burned and have not charity, it profiteth me nothing." It is the love of Christ for our enemies that separates the true Church from all other imitations of piety, whether while being persecuted or whether refusing to use a lawful opportunity for revenge upon our enemies. It is sheathing the sword when it could be lawfully drawn. It is this unconditional love of Christ that testifies of the true disciples.

To those who persecute, in the name of God, the Christian brethren, Jesus says, "Why persecutest thou me? Inasmuch as ye have done it unto one of the least of these my brethren, ye have done it unto me."

Paul says that it is the children of the flesh (the law, as the bondwoman typifies) that persecute those born after the Spirit (Gal. 4:29), and so we find it in Paul's life, when he is blameless in the law and profiting in his religion above his equals, he persecutes and makes waste of the Church, but after coming to Christ, he then glories in his tribulations.

The ceremonial law never did cleanse a man from sin, therefore it was supplanted by the death of Christ, who bore our sins in His own body on the tree.

The civil law of Moses also was temporary; for it was ineffective to guarantee true holiness in a nation. Jesus said, "Moses gave you the law, yet none of you keep it." James said, "If any man offend in one point He is guilty of all." Paul said, "That whatsoever the law saith, it saith to them who are under the law: that every mouth may be stopped and *all* the world may become guilty before God." Stephen said the Jews "have received the law by the disposition of angels, and have not kept it."

There is one man, Christ Jesus, who destroyed the strength of sin by fulfilling the law fully in its intent, and satisfied the justice of God's death penalty for every man, and is made unto us our righteousness, sanctification, and redemption (I John 2:2   I Cor. 1:2 Rom. 8:3   Gal. 3:13   I Cor. 1:30). But those who never did fully obey nor were perfect in obedience (Paul, although blameless in the law outwardly, says it convicts him of sin) had come to trust in it as their righteousness, therefore they would not relinquish it.

God needed to completely destroy the temple and scatter the Jews to bring an end to that which was completed, as they had come to wholly trust in their ordinances. Let us not be guilty of building again that which has passed away, lest we also be found as transgressors (Gal. 2:18-21).

It is the testimony of the pure gospel that where sin does abound, grace does much more abound. It is the grace and love of God, wrought in the heart and exemplified in the life, that produces the true Christian witness.

Those who strive to find God at Sinai will find that His threatenings and thunders are terrible and prevent them from nearing the mount with those being thrust through who are so foolhardy as to attempt that ascent into His presence by the lawful path, their moral rags of self-righteousness being their own condemnation. But those who come through the blood of the everlasting covenant shall find an entrance administered abundantly into the everlasting kingdom of our Lord and Savior Jesus Christ. Those redeemed lives shall represent the grace that saved them and the love wherewith they have been loved.

The curse of the law that has bound them to death has been broken by Him that was cursed upon the tree; they then shall not venture to bind upon others what they have been fully delivered from, but shall exhibit that which overcame their own sentence, the grace that is greater than all their sin.

Just as Stephen and Christ met their death by men who were zealous for Moses' law, so also in the ages that followed many Christians would give their lives for elevating the gospel of Christ over the ordinances of the Mosaic dispensation.

1  Flavius Josephus, Against Apion, Book 1

2  Archko Volume p 211, 212 (1975 Keats Publishing Inc.)

3  Flavius Josephus, The Wars of the Jews, Book VI, ch V, point 3

4  John Calvin, Institutes of the Christian Religion, Book 4, ch 20

5  Westminster Confession, ch19, article 4

6  Leonard Verduin, The Reformers and Their Stepchildren, p 29 (1991 The Christian Hymnary Publishers)

7  Philip Schaff, History of the Christian Church, Vol. III, p13 (1991 WM. B. Eerdmans Publishing Company)

8  Ibid. Vol. III, p 16

9  Ibid. Vol. III, p 39, parenthesis mine

10  Leonard Verduin, The Reformers and Their Stepchildren, p 33 (1991 The Christian Hymnary Publishers)

11  Philip Schaff, History of the Christian Church, Vol III, p 144, 145 (1991 WM. B. Eerdmans Publishing Company)

12  Ibid Vol. III, p 39

13  Ibid. Vol. III p 146

14  Leonard Verduin, The Reformers and Their Stepchildren, p 34 (1991 The Christian Hymnary Publishers)

15  Philip Schaff, History of the Christian Church, Vol. III, p 66 (1991 WM. B. Eerdmans Publishing Company)

16  Ibid Vol. VII, p 543, 544, parenthesis mine

17  Leonard Verduin, The Reformers and Their Stepchildren, p 75, (1991 The Christian Hymnary Publishers)

18  Ibid. p185

19  Ibid. p 209

20  Ibid. p 78

21  Ibid. p 60

22  Ibid. p 83

23  Ibid. p 90, 91

24  Philip Schaff, History of the Christian Church, Vol. VIII, p 489-494 (1991 WM. B. Eerdmans Publishing Company)

25  Ibid. p. 692

26  Ibid. p 691, 692

27  Edwin S. Gaustad, Liberty of Conscience, p 31(1999 Judson Press)

28  Ibid. p 35

29  Ibid. p 68

30  The Writings of Roger Williams, 6 vols. (Providence RI: Narrangansett Club Publications, 1866-74) Vol 111 pp 161-162 Taken from Williams' "Bloudy Tenent of Persecution, for cause of Conscience" (1644)

31  Ibid Vol. 111, p 398-399

32  John Cotton, The Bloudy Tenent, Washed (1647) (Arno Press: NY, 1972, reprint edition) pp 450-451

33  The Bloudy Tenent of Persecution, (Publication of Narrangansett Club, Providence RI Vol 111 (1867)

34  Edwin S. Gaustad, Liberty Of Conscience p 115 (1999 Judson Press)

35  Ibid p 177

36  Ibid p 120

37  Ibid 121

38  Philip Schaff, History of the Christian Church, Vol V11, p75-77, (1991 WM. B. Eerdmans

*Publishing Company)*

39  *Edwin S. Gaustad, Neither King nor Prelate p 48 (1993 WM. B. Eerdmans Publishing*
    *Company)*

40  *Ibid p 49*

41  *Ibid p 56*

42  *Ibid p 78*

43  *Ibid p 106*

44  *Ibid p 145*

45  *Funk and Wagnell's New Encyclopedia, 1971, "Thirty Years' War"*

come out of her my people

# chapter three

# The Kingdom of Christ and Those of This World

G od, the Creator of mankind, knows best how man will function within His design parameters and so has kindly given His laws throughout history as a guide to feet that are prone to wander, and as wisdom to the human mind, which is susceptible to self-deception and error. Yet God's law was only designed to instruct the mind and speak to the heart and never intended to regenerate man or give him a new heart, but rather to expose and restrain the evil inclinations of his heart.

The course of the universe is not dependent upon the will or choice of man to either right or wrong. The earth, though, is a battleground, a great contest between the forces of righteousness and evil for God's prized creation, the soul and the mind of man. The outcome of this conflict does not originate in man himself, but in the omnipotence of Him who upholdeth all things by the Word of His power, with whom is neither any variableness nor shadow of turning. Were not God the Author of all truth and right, thus bestowing upon them immortal qualities, the will of man alone would be insufficient to guarantee their victory, and evil would ultimately triumph, for to will is present with us, but how to perform that which is good is not found in us (Romans 7:18). For truth and right to prevail there must be an aid to the will of man that is transcendent over his human faculties and capabilities. There must be both empowerment for the right and sovereign restraint against the wicked heart's capacity to unbridled evil.

In the Scripture the kingdom of God is spoken of as that which ruleth over all (Psalm 103:19). It is God's sovereignty over all that orders the course of this world to accomplish all divine purposes, fulfilling to the letter that which is predicted by the Spirit of prophecy, by Him who works all things according to the counsels of His own will.

His kingdom is that which governs the affairs of this life. He is not the author of sinful action, which is rooted in both Satan and the depraved heart of man, yet His will both guides and governs the thought patterns of even the wicked, so that while they may on their own live in selfishness and rebellion, their desires to please themselves will be directed in the manner that fulfills divine will in the material course of this world (Proverbs 21:1).

The existence of God's absolute sovereignty and the rule of His kingdom are irrefutable truths of Scripture. The following passages speak of the realm of God's kingdom:

"Thy throne, O God, is for ever and ever: the sceptre of thy kingdom is a right sceptre" (Psalm 45:6).

"He shall have dominion also from sea to sea, and from the river unto the ends of the earth. They that dwell in the wilderness shall bow before him; and his enemies shall lick the dust" (Psalm 72:8, 9).

"Thy kingdom is an everlasting kingdom, and thy dominion endureth throughout all generations" (Psalm 145:13).

These verses are a few of the many that establish the fact that God had a universal, sovereign kingdom outside of the scope of the nation of Israel. In fact, the kingdom of God was completely independent of the confines of Mosaic law. It is when Israel is in exile and politically powerless that some of the most profound statements are made by world powers concerning the universal rule of the kingdom of God.

It is in the chronicles of Daniel that we learn how God uses His people, Israel, to introduce to Nebuchadnezzar the rule of God over the world power of Babylon.

The three Hebrew faithfuls explained to Nebuchadnezzar that they are not careful (tentative) to proclaim their allegiance to a God who is able to deliver them from the great inferno. The miraculous deliverance of the three by the hand of the "Fourth" provoked a most startling proclamation of the rule of another kingdom over Babylon. Nebuchadnezzar proclaimed to all people, nations, and languages in the earth, "How great are his signs, and how mighty are his wonders! His kingdom is an everlasting kingdom, and his dominion is from generation to generation" (Daniel 4:3).

How quickly, though, he would forget that utterance and was driven by God from among men to eat grass as an ox, till he would learn that the Most High ruleth in the kingdom of men, and giveth it to whomever He will (Daniel 4:25).

Surely, the skeptic reasons, this account must be a mere Jewish fable. Over the years, it became a focal point of Daniel's credibility to the infidel and skeptic, who thought for sure that they had found a weak link in divine inspiration. But an old tablet has been unearthed from the ruins of Babylon, inscribed by the king's secretary and signed by Nebuchadnezzar himself. The translation by Rawlinson is: "For four years the seat of my kingdom did not rejoice my heart. In all my dominions I did not build a high place of power. The precious treasures of my kingdom I did not lay up. In Babylon, buildings for myself and the honor of my kingdom I did not lay out. In the worship of Merodach, my Lord, the joy of my heart, in Babylon the city of his sovereignty, and the seat of his empire, I did not sing his praises. I did not furnish his altars with victims, nor did I clear his canals." Rawlinson then adds, "We can scarcely imagine anything that would account for this record but some extraordinary malady as that recorded by Daniel."

D. L. Miller reported that in the valley of Euphrates there is a peculiar grass that is eaten by the natives that is called *"Nebuchadnezzar grass."*[1]

Nebuchadnezzar regained his understanding after seven times (possibly an indefinite period, defined by seven as a complete duration of judgment) and utters these words concerning the Most High: "I praised and honored him that liveth forever and ever, whose dominion is an everlasting dominion, and his kingdom is from generation to generation..."

The most powerful man in the world at that time is brought low under the hand of God and acknowledges that it is His kingdom that rules over all and that "he doeth according to his will in the army of heaven, and among the inhabitants of the earth: and none can stay his hand...," (Daniel 4:34, 35).

The next world empire was the Medo-Persian, which also was forced to acknowledge the rule of the heavenly kingdom over the affairs of men. The event leading to this acknowledgment is the familiar account of Daniel being thrown into the lions' den because of a law that is enacted, being irrevocable according to the Medo-Persian statutory tradition. Here then is the rule of law binding even Darius to its precepts and bringing death to any transgressor of it.

Yet the rule and will of Jehovah will not be infringed upon nor thwarted by any law of man. The men may plot the consignment of Daniel to the lions but they cannot open the mouths which God's angel has shut, nor could they shut the mouths of the lions when their sins returned upon their own heads.

Israel had no great military to demonstrate the power of God upon their enemies; in fact, they had been vanquished by their foes. Yet God chose at this time to demonstrate His omnipotence, when it could not be tainted with any human or earthly glory or assigned to any heroic effort of man, by ordering an angel to shut the lions' mouths.

Darius first wondered if Daniel's God was *able* to deliver. Upon seeing the demonstration of His power, Darius decreed to all peoples, nations, and languages, "That in every dominion of my kingdom men tremble and fear before the God of Daniel: for he is the living God, and steadfast forever, and his kingdom that which shall not be destroyed, and his dominion shall be even unto the end" (Daniel 6:25, 26).

This is a most marvelous proclamation, and an affirmation of heathen powers to the sovereignty of God at a time when His own people appear to be utterly helpless.

As someone has said, "Man's extremity is God's opportunity."

The empire that would supplant the Medo-Persian was the Grecian under Alexander the Great. Alexander was involved in the siege of Tyre when he sent a message to the Jewish high priest at Jerusalem that he should send Jewish auxiliaries to supply his army with provisions. The high priest answered that he could not aid Alexander, as he had sworn an oath of fealty to Darius, who was then still reigning as a Persian Monarch, and would not break his word.

When this message was delivered unto Alexander, he was very angry and declared that after the siege of Tyre was complete he would lead his troops against this Jewish high priest and make an example of him to all men, to teach them unto whom they should fulfill their oaths.

Alexander marched against Jerusalem in great haste, whereupon Jaddua, the high priest, upon hearing the news besought the whole nation to make supplication and sacrifice unto God for His protection. God spoke unto Jaddua in a dream that Jerusalem was under His care and that they should open her gates, have all the populace put on white garments and the priests their vestments, and walk out in procession to meet Alexander upon his arrival. Jaddua led the procession out to meet Alexander, with his mitre upon his head, clad in purple and scarlet, and bearing the golden plate upon which the name of God was engraved. Alexander, upon seeing this spectacle, left his army and came to meet the high priest alone, saluting him, and then adoring the name upon the golden plate. Alexander's men supposed him to have become disordered in his mind, whereupon one, Parmenio, came up to Alexander and asked him why he would adore the high priest when all other men adored him (Alexander).

Alexander replied, *"I did not adore him, but that God who hath honored him with that high priesthood; for I saw this very person in a dream, in this very habit, when I was at Dios, in Macedonia, who, when I was considering with myself how I might obtain the dominion of Asia, exhorted me to make no delay, but boldly to pass over the sea thither, for that he would conduct my army, and would give me the dominion over the Persians; whence it is, that having seen no other in that habit, and now seeing this person in it, and remembering that vision and the exhortation which I had in my dream, I believe that I bring this army under the divine conduct, and shall therewith conquer Darius, and destroy the power of the Persians, and that all things will succeed according to what is in my own mind."*

Next he offered a sacrifice to God under the direction of the high priest.

The book of Daniel was then brought to him and in it there was shown unto him those Scriptures that spoke of a Grecian destroying Persia. Alexander supposed himself to be that man. He then granted unto the Jews a great latitude in the observance of their laws and customs.[2]

This is again a most marvelous account of the third world empire acknowledging the dominion of the Most High.

The fourth and greatest world empire would come face to face with the Son of God, upon whom was bestowed all power in heaven and in earth.

There was 400 years of prophetic silence between Malachi and John the Baptist, but the 69 weeks of Daniel indicated that Messiah the Prince should soon be appearing and His coming was to be preceded by the messenger, Elijah.

Israel lay under the rule of the most powerful of all world empires, the fourth one of Daniel, having the iron teeth that broke in pieces the residue of all the former powers. She was granted a measure of liberty but not the independence she desired.

Into this atmosphere that was charged with seething rebellion and unrest under Rome, and with an expectant Messianic hope, came John the Baptist as the herald of the Anointed One. The mighty kingdom of God who ruled over all the former world powers and brought Nebuchadnezzar, Darius, and Alexander to obeisance was now being proclaimed as imminent.

John's message was, "Repent, for the kingdom of heaven is at hand" (Matthew 3:2).

Messiah would fill the office also of Priest after the order of Melchizedek (Psalm 110:4), so it was reasonable to expect a national repentance before the Priest was anointed Prince. Multitudes were baptized when John warned that every tree that is unfruitful would be hewn down and cast into the fire. All Judea and the region about Jordan came to the river to confess their sins and be baptized. The anticipation was great that there was one coming after John who would baptize with the Holy Ghost and with fire, insomuch that the self-righteous Pharisees came for the baptism of repentance and the skeptical Sadducees supposed that possibly God had inspired this man John.

When Jesus began His ministry, the theme was reiterated, "Repent, for the kingdom of heaven is at hand" (Matthew 4:17). He then commissioned His disciples, "Go, preach that the kingdom of heaven is at hand."

The devils were cast out of people, showing the submission of the powers of darkness unto Christ, who then said, "If I cast out devils by the Spirit of God, then the kingdom of God is come unto you" (Matthew 12:28).

The Jewish anticipation was for the establishment of a glorious kingdom that would subjugate the kings of all the earth (Psalm 2:8). It was the coming Messiah who was prophesied to rule this coming kingdom.

Notice the following passages:

"I have set my king upon my holy hill of Zion" (Psalm 2:6).

"...the government shall be upon his shoulder" (Isaiah 9:6).

"Behold, the days come, saith the Lord, that I will raise unto David a righteous Branch, and a King shall reign and prosper, and shall execute judgment and justice in the earth" (Jer. 23:5).

The New Testament scriptures unequivocally ascribe this office to Jesus Christ.

"...he shall reign over the house of Jacob forever; and of his kingdom there shall be no end" (Luke 1:33).

"Now unto the King eternal...." (I Timothy 1:17)

"...the prince of the kings of the earth...." (Rev. 1:5)

"...to him be glory and dominion for ever and ever..." (Rev. 1:6)

"For he must reign until he hath put all enemies under his feet" (I Cor. 15:25)

The Son, in His ministry here on earth, claimed that the Father had bestowed upon Him the authority to rule in the realm of His Father. The heavenly kingdom that ruled over all earthly kingdoms was now inherited by the Son. The Hebrew writer says, "But unto the Son he saith, Thy throne, O God, is for ever and ever: a sceptre of righteousness is the sceptre of thy kingdom." (Heb. 1:8; see also Heb. 1:9, John 5:22, 23, Matthew 22:44)

The Apostles affirmed that, "Him hath God exalted to be Prince and Saviour" (Acts 5:31).

The Apostle Paul teaches that, "God also hath highly exalted him, and given him a name which is above every name: that at the name of Jesus every knee should bow, of things in heaven, and things in earth, and things under the earth; and that every tongue should confess that Jesus Christ is Lord."

The Jews were enamored with the thought of God's kingdom coming to earth and destroying the heathen powers, but they could not accept that this kingdom would be merely a spiritual one and entered into by a new birth, as opposed to being a physical reality.

How could God's kingdom be established without a sovereignty over civil affairs enacted?

Christ's teachings illustrated that the greatest enemy to be destroyed was sin and its author. To merely gain world power without overthrowing the god of this world's rule in the hearts of men is to be a ruler of the basest sort, having the physical power but not the willing allegiance of the subjects. It is the same as a father declaring his supremacy over his family because he is physically stronger than they, and can force them into submission, as opposed to the father who demonstrates his headship by both command and the willing obedience of his wife and children.

Christ's first mission is to "destroy him that had the power of death, that is, the devil; and deliver them, who through fear of death were all their lifetime subject to bondage" (Heb. 2:14, 15).

The Apostle John also affirms this truth in saying, "For this purpose the Son of God was manifested, that he might destroy the works of the devil" (I John 3:8).

This is one of the reasons that Christ cast out the devils; to show that as Prince and Savior the demons must be subject unto Him. He makes clear to the Jews the relationship between the coming of His kingdom and the expulsion of demons in Matthew 12:28, where He says, "If I cast out devils by the Spirit of God, then the kingdom of God is come unto you."

Concerning His crucifixion, Jesus reiterates this truth, "Now is the judgment of this world: now shall the prince of this world be cast out."

God's kingdom had ruled over all the world from the beginning of creation, overruling all the designs of wicked men, but now in Christ, men may willingly enter that spiritual kingdom and acknowledge both His worldly dominion and His spiritual dominion over their hearts, to prepare for the day when they shall rule in Christ's kingdom as joint-heirs, in that which is still appointed to His saints (Dan. 7:22, Rom. 7:17, II Tim. 2:12, Rev. 20:4).

The kingdom then that Christ has initially established here is spiritual in nature, destroying the power of sin and bringing its subjects into obedience to Christ.

The Jews demanded that Jesus explain His kingship by asking Him to define His kingdom (Luke 17:20). How can you be a king without a kingdom? Or if you are a king show us your kingdom. It is one thing to aspire to have dominion; it is another to say you already are a king if you cannot physically demonstrate your kingdom. Jesus' response was that it does not come with observation or corporeal substance but rather it is within you. All His subjects are willing. All have bowed their wills to His Lordship, and given their hearts to His dominion. This kingdom is available to all those who will receive it. "Fear not, little flock; for it is your Father's good pleasure to give you the kingdom" (Luke 12:32). It comes as a gift to the willing heart. It does not occupy the civil institutions of this world nor derive any power from them, nor even use them to physically advance it. Yet it remains the only unshaken kingdom, that shall stand for eternity, received by the saints as a kingdom that cannot be moved, while the earth shall tremble and quake with the woes that are yet to come upon it (Heb. 12:26-29), causing great fear to grip the kingdoms of this earth (Rev. 6:12-17).

Pilate was also perplexed, as the Jews were, by this man who claimed to be a king, yet seemingly had no kingdom.

"Art thou the king of the Jews?" he asked. "How is it that your own subjects deliver you unto me for trial when you are their king?"

Jesus replied, "My kingdom is not of this world; if it resided in physical power on this earth there would be none that could deliver me unto death, as my servants would prevent it." He had at immediate disposal the legions of angels who could set Him free; but He laid down His own life willingly to establish the foundation of an everlasting kingdom that would possess the earthly kingdoms of this world.

"Art thou a king then?" asks Pilate. "To this end was I born and for this cause came I into the world," replied Christ.

Pilate's confidence was shaken. Who was this king that provoked such rebellion from His own people who were to be His subjects, and yet calmly assured the truth and strength of His kingdom?

What was it that caused his wife to tremble that he sat in judgment of this man?

What king would tolerate his subjects to accuse and abuse him, while never answering them a word?

As Pilate sought His release, the accusations became not only more vehement but threatening against his own person. "If thou let this man go, thou art not Caesar's friend." Those devious Jews would force his hand against Christ by making him co-conspirator to Jesus' kingship.

The man had plainly declared that His kingdom was not earthly and so was no threat to Caesar's realm; why then did He not answer the charges against Him? If the accused would but cooperate with his defense, maybe the case could be overthrown for lack of evidence. The Jewish witnesses had presented contradictory allegations and were lacking in criminal evidence (Matt. 26:59-62, 65-66), and yet this man does not take advantage of this to defend himself, even when he (Pilate) intimates that there is no fault in Him.

Pilate asks Jesus, "What is your origin anyway?" (Whence art thou?) A king with a spiritual or other worldly kingdom is somewhat intriguing when considered alone, outside of this trial, but now it is of grave importance as it bears on the foundation of the allegations. Yet this man does not respond, so composed is He, so assured of the truth of His statements, having the ability to overthrow these arguments, yet remaining now silent before Pilate. He has been mocked and beaten to physical disfigurement, yet that regal composure remains so evident. It seems as if the fury of the accusers knows no limit, as they demand the release of a convicted felon in place of the man. Surely, Pilate doubtless thought, if this man would but understand that His life hangs in the balance He would not ignore my attempts to help Him. Perhaps I can jolt Him out of His reverie by threatening Him myself, with death. "Knowest thou not that I have power to crucify thee, and have power to release thee?"

Ah, mere mortal, though man has invested you with earthly power, what presumption is it to assume that you hold the fate of this man in your hands, when it is He that upholdeth all things by the Word of His power. "Thou couldest have no power at all against me, except it were given thee from above."

Pilate could not prevail upon the Jews to release Christ. So he taunted them with, "Behold your king" and "Shall I crucify your king?"

Those deceitful and hypocritical Jews, who longed for political freedom from Rome retorted, "We have no king but Caesar."

Thus Pilate's hand was forced, as he knew that the Jews would discredit his loyalty to Rome unless he granted the death penalty of crucifixion to portray Christ as a political criminal rather than a religious martyr (for blasphemy).

His last attempt to vent his frustrations against the Jews was in the insignia that he put on the cross, "Jesus of Nazareth, the king of the Jews." He remained firm in spite of their protests against it by saying, "What I have written, I have written."

Till the end of that crucifixion day, all knew that the death of this man was unusual; the sun became dark at a time when no eclipse could occur (it being full moon at the fourteeth of Nissan, and lasted for three hours, as no solar eclipse does). The earth quaked and the rocks rent, the graves were opened, and the Roman centurion who had probably witnessed many crucifixions along with his soldiers, cried, "Truly this man was the Son of God."

The crowd that had mocked the kingship of the man on the middle cross grew strangely silent as they realized they had partaken in the death of an unusual man. Their fury gave way to trepidation and foreboding as this man who bore all the physical suffering so patiently, now poured out the anguish of His soul, as He waged conflict alone with unseen foes, crying out to His Father, "My God, My God, why hast thou forsaken Me?" Who could look upon this sight and not wonder at what anguish this man must face that would make Him so oblivious to His own human suffering, for the travail of His soul.

As He rose up to fill His lungs, He cried with a loud voice, "It is finished." Some great battle had been fought and this was the cry of the victor. He had fought alone in the flesh, treading the winepress, staining His garments with the blood of His foes, and purchasing the redemption of His own, and mortally wounding the head of His enemy (Isa. 63:1-6, Gen. 3:15).

In that struggle with sin, He bore its full penalty as He gave His soul as an offering for it. He became the sin offering, thus incurring the separation from the Father that He might destroy death (eternal separation from God). In that separation and travail He still remained the Lamb without blemish and retained His full Divinity, for though separated from the Father, yet God was in Him, reconciling the world unto Himself (II Cor. 5:19).

When that great work was finished, He committed His spirit into the hands of His Father, thus portraying the union and fellowship available to him that will overcome by the blood of the Lamb and be crucified with Christ and unto the world.

While the world poured forth its venom upon Him, He became their propitiation. Who but the Son of God Himself would be able to bear the full wrath of God's justice and make a way of escape, and open an entrance into the mercyseat?

This crowd that had been excited to a frenzy of demonic fervor was now subdued as they witnessed this King lay down His life so willingly and so abruptly when He committed His spirit into His Father's hands. They felt the guilt of their crimes as they smote their breasts and departed (Luke 23:48).

The effect of His death upon Jerusalem was significant, but the impact of His resurrection upon the world was profound. It was in this event that Christ was highly exalted, and heralded by the angels; "Lift up your heads, oh ye gates, and the KING OF GLORY shall come in."

Christ now sits at the right hand of the majesty on high (Heb. 1:3). He came meek and lowly, yet possessing the lineage of a king. He established a kingdom that shall never be destroyed but shall ever increase until the earth is full of the knowledge of the Lord (Dan. 2:35, 44, Isa. 11:9).

The first phase of this kingdom, though, is only spiritual. The King is calling forth His willing subjects to enter into it. It does not possess political characteristics, though it will shake all nations. It dwells in the hearts of men (within you) and is righteousness, and peace, and joy in the Holy Ghost (Rom. 14:17).

# THE SCOPE OF CHRIST'S KINGDOM

In seeking to define Christ's kingdom we must consider to whom it does pertain. How does one enter into it? What are the requirements for citizenship? What then are the duties enjoined upon the subjects?

Nicodemus came to Christ one night to discuss with Him His teachings. At the very outset of this conversation, Jesus affirms the spirituality of His kingdom by saying, "Except a man be born again, he cannot 'see' the kingdom of God." It is not identifiable to the men who have been blinded by the god of this world. Jesus builds upon the thought of the new birth. A man cannot be merely assumed into this kingdom or forced into it, but rather must be "birthed" into it. "How shall this man be birthed?" asks Nicodemus. "Can he re-enter his mother's womb?" Is not conversion merely accepting a different belief system? If a man gives mental assent to Christ's doctrine, believes it from the heart, and is willing to obey it, would not this be sufficient to be a member of Christ's kingdom? This would have been the rational conclusion of any Jew.

Jesus' answer totally mystifies Nicodemus: "Except a man be born of water and of the Spirit, he cannot enter into the kingdom of God." That which is born of flesh (or natural birth) only, can only inherit a physical realm, for it does not have the spiritual perception (cannot see, John 3:3) to comprehend anything else. But what is born of the Spirit is able to comprehend spirituality, for its spiritual awareness is awakened, thus it can enter into a spiritual kingdom.

So what is "birthed" by flesh perceives fleshly or tangible things. What is "birthed" of the Spirit embraces spiritual things. Without the "spiritual birth" (born again) one can not "see" Christ's kingdom any more than the baby in the womb can see the material world until it is birthed into this world.

The water spoken of here can hardly logically refer to a natural birth as some have assumed. It seems somewhat plausible at first glance, as Nicodemus is questioning whether a man can enter the second time into his mother's womb, and Jesus responds by saying,

"That which is born of the flesh is flesh." But if it is examined more closely, it is evident that Jesus is defining His first statement in that He explains how a man can be born again. Jesus first says, "Ye must be born again", with Nicodemus postulating "How?"; and He then responds with, "By water and by the Spirit." That which is born of the flesh can only perceive fleshly or tangible things, but that which is born of the Spirit can see the kingdom of God.

While it is true that no one is born again who does not first experience natural birth, yet the equating of water to natural birth does not coincide with Jesus' arguments. He first says, "Ye *must* be born again", thus giving a command, a specific duty, to an already living person, who can not possibly enter again into the mother's womb.

In defining the new birth, Jesus places conditions upon it that must be met in order to enter into the kingdom. One of those conditions is not to go and seek a natural birth, or one would have to assume that Jesus' dialogue was to pre-existent souls and not to already living people. He would not require what any audience would already naturally have as a condition to enter into a spiritual kingdom.

Let us notice some other passages that will help define what Jesus had in view with the water referred to here in this passage.

In the Scripture, there is a close relationship between the symbolism of water and the Spirit. Jesus cried out on the last day of the feast of tabernacles, when a golden vessel of water was fetched from Siloam and poured before the altar, "He that believeth on me, as the Scripture hath said, out of his belly shall flow rivers of living water" (John 7:37, 38). John, the narrator, explains that this utterance was prophetic to the coming of the Spirit (John 7:39). Here, then, Jesus used water to symbolize the Spirit as it was often used in the Old Testament prophecies (See Joel 2:23, 28 Isa. 44:3 Eze. 36:25-27).

There is a close relationship to the symbolism of water in religious ordinances with the cleansing work of the Spirit. John records in his epistle that one of the three witnesses of our faith here on earth is also water, along with the Spirit and the blood (I John 5:8). Water, then, is used as an ordinance of the church to bear witness to our faith. Is it not reasonable to believe that being born of water is to enter into an act that unites us with the kingdom in a visible manner that is a witness to an unbelieving world that cannot see the kingdom, nor understand the new birth, (not comprehending whence it cometh or whither it goeth, John 3:8), but yet will be able to identify that this public confession clearly portrays a new spiritual life? What happens inwardly of the Spirit must be outwardly conveyed as a witness to a spiritually dead world. The water does not create the new life but bears testimony visibly unto it. Just as the water in the mother's womb does not create life (the mother does) when the child passes through it, for it is already living, yet it is necessary for that living child to pass through the water as a part of being born into this world. So it is in the new birth; it is the Spirit that gives the life, but when it births it into the kingdom, it causes the subject to pass through the water as a visible sign of its birth.

There are some that believe that the water spoken of here is the Word, which we do not deny is also sometimes symbolized by water; but we do not believe that this is what is in view here, as there is nothing in the context to suggest this. Rather, the relationship between water and the Spirit seems to be an analogy between a spiritual and visible relationship, such as when someone is water baptized into the name of the Spirit in order to visibly join the kingdom that he has been engrafted into spiritually (new birth), similar to the relationship between water and natural birth.

The Great Commission commands that all disciples be baptized into the name of the Spirit. Here, then, is the clear connection between water baptism and union with the Spirit.

The Gentile believers in Cornelius' house received the Spirit before baptism so that the Jews could not forbid them water to be baptized. Here the Spirit's visible signs (speaking in tongues) convinced the Jews that water baptism could not be refused to him that was born of the Spirit.

The order in Samaria was reversed, in that water baptism was first administered and then the Holy Spirit was bestowed by the hands of the apostles.

It is not the intent here to establish a particular order of events between Spirit baptism and water baptism, as many have spent volumes doing, but rather to illustrate that the two are *always* joined together in close relationship in the new birth experience.

Notice the following verses that unequivocally demonstrate that *every* born-again, baptized believer does receive the Spirit, regardless of the order of events you may prefer:

"Repent and be baptized every one of you in the name of Jesus Christ for the remission of sins, and ye shall receive the gift of the Holy Ghost. For the promise is unto you, and to your children, and to all that are afar off, EVEN AS MANY AS THE LORD OUR GOD SHALL CALL (Acts 2:38, 39).

"...how much more shall your heavenly Father give the Holy Spirit to them that ask him" (Luke 11:13)?

"And we are his witnesses of these things; and so is also the Holy Ghost, whom God hath given to them that obey him" (Acts 5:32).

"Now if any man have not the Spirit of Christ, he is none of his" (Rom. 8:9).

"For by one Spirit are we 'all' baptized into one body" (I Cor. 12:13).

The truth of these verses show us that every born-again, baptized believer shall receive the Spirit. There is no such thing as a child of God who has not the Spirit, for he that has not the Spirit of Christ is none of His.

The Scriptures presented here show that the truths Jesus was teaching to Nicodemus are everywhere affirmed throughout the Scripture. To be a part of the kingdom, a person must be born of the Spirit. If someone is born of the Spirit, he will also be born of water as an outward testimony to the saving work of spiritual regeneration. Water baptism is inseparably linked to the spiritual new birth experience. This does not mean that the water alone saves a man, but rather he who will be born of the Spirit must also be willing to be born of water. "He that believeth and is baptized shall be saved." "Repent and be baptized for the remission of sins." Water is not for baptismal regeneration, as many have used this practice to Christianize the pagans, but rather the truth of the Scriptures is that it is associated with the new birth experience.

Romans 6:1-5 presents a close union between being baptized into Christ with the death of the old man and the resurrection of the new man. It is through this spiritual act of faith that Christ performs His work in the heart of man, by slaying the body of sin and imparting a new spiritual life. A thousand baptisms of water alone could not join a man to Christ, but he who in faith believes that when he has been baptized into Christ, has put on Christ (Gal. 3:27), he shall by *faith* be dead unto sin and alive unto God (Rom. 6:11).

Peter expounds upon this concept by comparing baptism to Noah's ark ( I Peter 3:20-21). He explains that the ark was built (by faith, Heb. 11:7) as a means of salvation. It not only delivered him from God's judgment but also separated him from an ungodly world, thus being a visible testament of his faith. Would Noah have been saved if he had merely believed and trusted God's grace but refused to build the ark? The Scripture is emphatic that he built the ark to the saving of his house.

The faith chapter chronicles only the men of faith who acted in obedience, and this is saving faith.

Now if Noah would have been warned of a flood but been prohibited from building a flotation device, no ark could have saved him. The salvation rested solely in the fact that it was God's ordained means of salvation through the obedience of faith.

As the storms buffeted the ark, do you suppose Noah's faith was in the Lord, or his own workmanship? So also baptism, the like figure, shall also save us, not the external washing, but the answer of a good conscience to accept the means of salvation that God has ordained. Our faith is not in the water or the act, but in God, who will keep His Word and save all those who repent, believe, and obey Him.

The words of Ananias to Paul follow this same train of thought,

"Arise, and be baptized, and wash away thy sins, calling on the name of the Lord" (Acts 22:16). The "washing" would have been to no avail had it not been coupled with the "calling," but with the "calling" must come the "washing".

By now some would surely be clamoring that the thief on the cross was promised paradise and yet was without baptism. We answer that if you are nailed to a cross and physically crucified so that you cannot be baptized, your faith shall surely save you; but if you are not nailed to a cross you have no excuse to refuse or procrastinate baptism when it is expressly commanded, if you desire salvation. There is no salvation promised for those that hold God's ordinance in contempt, or are unwilling to obey it. That would be the same as assuming that Noah could have been saved without building an ark, although God had commanded him to. The case of the thief on the cross establishes beyond a doubt that salvation is wrought through faith by Christ alone, who is able to save even to the uttermost. But faith must act in obedience if it be able, or it is not saving faith at all. Shall you (like the thief) wait till this point in time to believe? Sinner, remember that this was likely the first salvation message this man ever heard and it was given graciously, but if you scheme to wait, remember that you have no promise of grace in the future, for "today" is the day of salvation. To procrastinate is to grieve away the Spirit that is your only means of salvation and to presume upon the grace of God, which is necessary to draw you to Christ. You cannot come only of your own will, but only when God chooses to draw you (John 6:44, 15:16). While you may be scheming to come at a more convenient season, the Lord may say, "Thou fool, this night thy soul shall be required of thee."

The message of the gospel is this, "Repent and be baptized," and "He that believeth and is baptized shall be saved." This was the message that Jesus gave Nicodemus, "Except a man be born of water and of the Spirit he cannot enter into the kingdom of God." A mother may talk to her child in the womb about the world beyond its comprehension, but it will never enter this world unless it is birthed into it. So it is with Christ's kingdom, unless a man is born again he can never be included in that realm.

It is the kingdom that is inherited by the born-again saints which constitutes the true Church of Christ. Down through the years as men have sought to Christianize nations, they have developed false concepts of Christ's kingdom and have sought to proof text them from Scripture. They developed the idea of a Christian society and national churches which have been responsible for creating gross distortions of the Christian faith. A national faith that includes all men in the kingdom will not insist that men can only enter it by the new birth alone, by being born of the Spirit before they enter into water baptism.

Augustine was the first person to formulate a theology of the kingdom of Christ that comprehended all of society. His arguments were largely espoused also by the Reformers as they instituted their national churches. One of the favorite passages Augustine, and then the Reformers, used was the parable of the wheat and the tares (Matthew 13:24-30, 36-43).

Their arguments were thus:
The kingdom of heaven comprehends both the wheat and the tares in the same field; both are to remain together until the final harvest of the angels, which is the end of the world. Therefore the kingdom comprehends all of society, both wheat and tares, converted and unconverted, and should not be separated until the final judgment, when it is done by the angels. The church may then include unbelievers, hypocrites, and believers. The ordinances of baptism and communion were considered open to all of society, and became mandatory for all of society.

Following are some quotations that illustrate Augustinian and Reformed theology.

Luther says,

*"From the beginning of the Church, heretics have maintained that the Church must be holy and without sin. Because they saw that some in the Church were the servants of sin they denied forthwith that the Church*

*was the Church, and organized sects... This is the origin of the Donatists and the Cathars... and of the Anabaptists of our times. All these cry out in angry chorus that the true Church is not the Church because they see that sinners and godless folk are mixed in her and they have separated from her... It is the part of wisdom not to be offended at it when evil men go in and out of the Church... The greatest comfort of all is the knowledge that they do no harm but that we must ALLOW THE TARES TO BE MIXED IN... The Schwarmer [Anabaptists], who do not allow tares among them, really bring about that there is no wheat among themselves – by this zeal for only wheat and a pure church they bring about, by this too great holiness, that they are not even a Church but just a sect of the devil."[3]* (emphasis and parenthesis mine)*

Luther argues that only heretics strive for a pure Church, and he that has wisdom understands that wherever there is wheat there must also be tares, or the supposed wheat is not really wheat.

First of all, this argument destroys any reason that Luther could give for separating from Rome because of its abominations. In fact, his attempts to cleanse and reform the church only prove that the Lutherans really are not wheat at all, for the more error that they expel the closer they come to being heretics, and by his own argument against Anabaptism he confounds his own position with Rome.

Secondly, Luther's reasoning suggests that there can be no wheat or godliness without the admixture of tares or ungodliness; that is to say that ungodliness must be present for godliness to be established; which is to say that godliness cannot exist alone; which in effect is to say that ungodliness is a vital component of godliness. The true Church, he argues, must have tares in it to prove that it is true. So error must be a necessary ingredient of truth. By including error a church becomes true, but by excluding error a church becomes a sect of the devil.

These were also the classic arguments of the Pharisees when they said Jesus cast out devils by Beelzebub, prince of the devils. They were saying Jesus' expulsion of devils proved that he was demon possessed. Jesus' response was that a kingdom divided against itself cannot stand. "If I cast out devils by Beelzebub, by whom do your children cast them out?"

In other words, Jesus said, "How can I build Satan's kingdom by destroying his works? Or if the expulsion of evil is Satan's work, how do you justify your son's exorcism?"

How can the Anabaptists become a sect of the devil by destroying the ungodly works of the devil? Or how then does Luther justify the reforming of Rome's corruptions; is it also the work of the devil?

But if the devil's works are cast out, then says Jesus, the kingdom of God is come unto you (Matthew 12:28). But Luther says Christ cannot establish His kingdom unless He allows a portion of the devil to remain. Is this not calling evil good, and good evil (Isa. 5:20)? Is evil a necessary component of righteousness?

John Calvin also speaks similarly along these lines of thought.

He says, *"But as they (the elect) are a small and despised number, concealed in an immense crowd, like a few grains of wheat buried among a heap of chaff, to God alone must be left the knowledge of his Church, of which his secret election forms the foundation."*[4]

Again, *"Such in the present day are some of the Anabaptists, who would be thought to have made superior progress. ...They allege that the Church of God is holy. But that they may at the same time understand that it contains a mixture of good and bad, let them hear from the lips of our Saviour that parable in which he compares the church to a net in which all kinds of fishes are taken, but not separated until they are brought ashore. Let them hear it, compared to a field which, planted with good seed, is by fraud of an enemy mingled with tares, and is not freed of them until the harvest is brought into the barn."*[5]

Calvin's arguments lie foundationally in his views of a secret election that is both exclusive to God and inscrutable to man. The visible church, says he, is not just comprised of the elect, but merely contains the elect, which is an indefinite and indeterminate number of grains of wheat among a huge body of tares, which is the full composition of the kingdom.

These arguments are diametrically opposed to Christ's clear teaching to Nicodemus, "Except a man be born again, he cannot see the kingdom of God," and "Except a man be born of water and of the Spirit, he cannot enter into the kingdom of God."

The fallacy lies not in the fact that imperfect people enter the visible church but rather that people are permitted to enter who cannot testify to having been born again. The visible church is also to be comprised of only those who give diligence to make their calling and election sure. The book of I John has a prevailing theme that identifies the proper witnesses to be used for evidences of salvation, both for the individual in self-examination and for the body to identify the spirit of antichrist and the children of the devil, who neither follow righteousness nor love their brother. (I John 1:6, 2:4, 9,15-17, 22, 23, 3:7-10, 14-17, 24, 4:1-6, 13, 20, 5:4, 5,18, 19)

Christ plainly said, "YE SHALL KNOW THEM BY THEIR FRUITS."

The Church does not have the authority to cast men into hell, for that is reserved for Him that knoweth the secrets of men's hearts, but they do have the obligation to discipline visible and externally identifiable practices of sin and to exclude them from the fellowship, if the sinner remains unrepentant (Matthew 18:17,18, I Cor. 5, II Cor. 6:14-18).

The Church is to be comprised only of the elect, for all the epistles that are written to the local churches address the elect, never the elect among the vast body of reprobates that are all in your church. The carnality of the church of Corinth was also used by Calvin to justify his position that the church of Christ could be composed of tares. But Calvin makes an erroneous supposition; that is, that Corinth allowed members who were unregenerate into the body, but rather the Scripture asserts to the contrary that the letter is addressed to them that are sanctified in Christ Jesus and called to be saints and who have the testimony of Christ CONFIRMED (I Cor. 1:2, 6). The apostle also affirms that by one Spirit we ALL have been baptized into one body and have ALL been made to drink into one Spirit (I Cor. 12:13). Paul was not censuring Corinth because of the tares in the church (which are the children of the wicked one, Matthew 13:38), but because they as born-again believers were still being nourished on milk and were not yet digesting meat, and thus were exhibiting a childish behavior (carnality), though he still called them brethren (I Cor. 3:1). They were rebuked for allowing believers to sin in the church.

The Church is kept pure by not allowing openly unconverted men into her but is finally purged by God Himself, who looks not on the outward appearance but searcheth the reins and hearts (Rev. 2:23).

It is the responsibility of every church to limit its members to born-again believers, those professing Christ both in word and deed, and remove those things that offend, lest the church itself lose its candlestick (Rev. 2:5).

The arguments of the Reformers from the parables of the wheat and tares did not originate with them but rather with Augustine centuries before in his disputes with the Donatists, as to whether the Church should include all members of society or only those who were saved.[6] The Reformers were pressed to adopt the same reasoning in order to justify their national churches in the face of Anabaptist rebuke for mingling the church and the world.

Let us examine the parable itself to see whether there is any justification here for an inclusive church comprised of all the members of a society.

The primary argument for an inclusive church is made from the parable itself, being a reference to the kingdom of heaven (Matthew 13:24), that in the Reformed view encompasses both the wheat and the tares. It relies solely on its own interpretation of the parable and ignores the explanation that Jesus gives to it. What Jesus clarifies is that the kingdom of heaven exists among the tares in the same field, which is the world (Matthew 13:38). The world and the church are never synonymous terms in the Scriptures, although the church is in the world, it is not of the world (I Cor. 5:9-10, John 15:19, 17:9,14,15).

Jesus also reveals to His disciples that the tares are children of the wicked one, while the good seed is represented by children of the KINGDOM. Nowhere are the tares represented as part of the kingdom but as part of the world, among which the kingdom exists.

To the disciples, who had a Jewish faith, the idea of tares existing alongside the wheat would have been completely novel, as they were reared under the old dispensation that asked evil to be put away from among them upon pain of capital punishment. But Christ says they must exist side by side until the end and only the angels and the Son of Man shall determine who are the tares that are meet for final destruction. This was a clear change between the Old Testament law of coercion to faith, and the teachings of Christ, of a purely voluntary faith. No man is worthy to judge another man worthy of death for his faith alone, but rather it is the angels that shall separate the wheat and tares.

It is interesting to note that on one hand the Reformers argue that the church should include tares so as to never risk excluding wheat, but then judged all Anabaptists as worse than tares (an alleged third category) and exterminated them by fire and sword, which is to be judgment reserved only for the angels.

They represented tares as part of the kingdom and represented those who strive for wheat only (children of the Kingdom, as Jesus said), as a sect of the devil, whom they cannot allow to grow together until the harvest, but must uproot and destroy, in order to preserve the true Church of Christ; thus demonstrating in their view that the true Church of Christ is preserved by destroying wheat and mingling in the tares. What an abomination this is of the pure doctrine of Christ, and the very subtilty of the devil himself.

The second parable that is often used as a proof text to justify a national and inclusive church is the one that likens the kingdom of heaven unto a net that captures both good and bad fish (Matthew 13:47-50).

The previous quotation from Calvin alludes to this parable.

One additional quotation from Urbanus Rhegius is given to establish the Reformed view. In it he is rebutting the views of the

Anabaptist Bernhard Knipperdollinck. He retorts against Bernhard's call for a believer's church:

*"Aha, there Bernhard resorts to a genuinely Donatist trick. They condemned and abandoned Christendom on account of some evil and false Christians... Nevertheless there have always been some true and devout Christians in the masses, and we hope they are present also with us. Moreover the fact that wicked rascals are present with us...does not concern us;...We don't want to rend the net because there are some bad fish in it, as the super saintly Anabaptist Bernhard is doing. He gives himself away at this point and shows that he has the Anabaptist devil in him which blinded also the Donatists in Africa. ...for he is a neo-Donatist who has taken offense at the evil lives and has ... tried to raise up a holy and unspotted Church, one in which there are only saints, a pure net without a foul fish, he and his company, cut loose from Christendom... I would forsooth prefer to be a coarse publican in the Christian Church, or a patent sinner, rather than be the most holy Pharisee of all in Bishop Bernhard's spelunck!"[7]*

The Reformed understanding of the parable of the net is manifestly seen; that it represents the church that gathers all fish into it, both saints and sinners.

There are many flaws in their interpretation of this parable. Nowhere in the parable does it state that every fish in the whole sea is caught in the net. But rather, when the net is full it is drawn in to land, whether there are fish left in the sea or not. The Reformed view creates a net that catches every fish, as none are to be outside of the state church.

Also, they say that the net represents Christendom from which no man should be allowed to leave, and the Anabaptists are accused of rending and escaping the net to form another ....what? Net? Church? The parable nowhere speaks of fish jumping out of the net, creating another net, or being caught again. And since when do fish forcibly prohibit other fish from escaping a net? Is not the net controlled by Christ and His angels as to determine when it is full, when it shall be drawn to land, and when the fish shall be separated, the good from the bad? Yet it would seem that Rhegius would argue that

Christendom itself controls the net, which is why they persecuted all who "rent the net" and escaped.

Are not the angels the judges in the parable? Yet Rhegius would forsooth be the angelic reaper and determine the fair and the foul fish. Those who sought to be good he called foul fish and cast them away. The parable also clarifies that the severing of the kinds of fish does not happen until the end of the age, which then shall bring judgment upon the wicked.

The Anabaptists were not casting anyone into the fire for being bad fish, but the Reformers, who argue for inclusiveness in the net which they say embraces all fish, are throwing good fish into the fire, before the end of the world or the coming of the angels, because, they say, they have rent the net, a condition to which the parable gives no allusion at all.

What then does this parable mean?

It follows the parable of the wheat and the tares and builds upon the concepts expressed in the former. The parable of the wheat and tares showed how the "children of the kingdom" and the "children of the wicked one" are both in the same field (the world) until the end of the age. The kingdom is not comprised of tares, but exists among the tares. Christ has established that only the wheat truly constitutes the children of the kingdom. The tares, though detrimental, are not to be uprooted or destroyed.

The question then remains—how does one define wheat? If only the children of the kingdom are wheat or part of the kingdom, how may the children discern between the wheat and tares? As noted previously, Christ said, "Ye shall know them by their fruits. Do men gather grapes of thorns, or figs of thistles? Even so every good tree bringeth forth good fruit, but a corrupt tree bringeth forth evil fruit" (see Matthew 7:16-20).

Christ asked that the wheat and tares be mingled in the world but not in the kingdom. He gives clear teaching on how to exclude tares (Matthew 18:15-17) from the church. The church needs to both comfort the feeble minded and support the weak but yet exclude those who live in open sin and rebellion against righteousness. It discerns, based upon fruit in the individual's life, since all those who believe are to be fruitful (Matthew 7:17, 12:33-35, Luke 8:6-9, John 12:24, 15:1-8,16).

But yet there are some, according to the parable of the sower, who believe the word but after a time become unfruitful (Matthew 13:22). It is classes of men like these that can be in the church as religious professors but are becoming unfruitful. Others lose their first love and need to be exhorted to "repent and do the first works." Some turn the grace of God into lasciviousness and creep in unawares (Jude 4). It is these classes of men that constitute the bad fish that are in the net. They who make a profession of good works but are deceptive to the church, may fool it (the church) and may abide in the net until drawn to shore by the angels, but they shall not escape the judgment of Him that looketh on the heart and is able to reveal its secrets.

This is the class of men of whom Christ speaks; those like Simon, the sorcerer, who believe and are baptized and enter the visible church as hypocrites. Some are excluded later as their fruits betray them; others remain as spots in the feasts of charity until discovered by God Himself. But nowhere does the Scripture teach that men are to be forced into the church in their unconverted state or accepted in such a state of obvious unregeneracy. It is amazing the lengths that they have gone to justify national establishments of religion.

We have seen how parables were used to justify inclusiveness, now we shall examine the primary one used to promote coercion of faith.

The parable of the supper was used by both Augustine and the Reformers to justify compulsory church attendance and membership. They dwelt upon the words, "Compel them to come in, that my house may be filled" (Luke 14:23).

Augustine in a sermon said, *"Whom thou shalt find, wait not until they choose to come, compel them to come in ... 'Let us' say they (Donatists) 'come in of our own volition;' but this is not the Lord's directive. He says, 'Compel them to come in'."*[8]

This passage is so frequently quoted by the Reformers that it is not necessary to provide any further documentation. It is abundantly proved in Leonard Verduin's works.

Here again there is a strained exegesis of this passage.

The following points in the parable are totally overlooked by the previous exposition of Augustine.

1. Those who made excuses for not coming were not compelled to come in. So it is clear that not all are compelled.

2. The house was filled but not by all that were bidden to come.

3. Those who initially refused could not later come, showing that not all are compelled nor should be compelled who are invited. (Luke 14:24)

4. None were compelled to come by the threat of fire and sword.

5. Those who were compelled were those who would have thought themselves unworthy to come. The supper was planned for those that had possessions of their own, but upon their refusal, is extended to those who had little. This is an illustration of Jesus' earlier teaching that a man is blessed when he makes a supper for the poor, the maimed, the lame, and the blind (Luke 14:12-14). These then need to be compelled, for they are reluctant to dine with those whom they feel to be above themselves.

6. Compel does not mean "physically force" but rather "strongly urge or constrain." Nowhere does the passage suggest that men were brought in forcibly, but rather needed to be urged and constrained in spite of all protests. This is how the gospel is presented to the sinner who thinks that God will not accept him.

It was these passages that formed the justification for the establishment of state religions that formed what we know as Christendom. The Kingdom of Christ, a body of born-again believers (born of water and of the Spirit), was reduced to a political and ecclesiastical entity that became a parody of a Judaistic state, which confused the true church of God with the establishments of men, and by hacking and hewing at Jesus' parables were able to deceive many into believing that the Scripture supported such institutions. All the remaining members of society, whether pagan, skeptical, or indifferent to religion at all, were persuaded by the power of the sword to bow to King Jesus by submitting to Christian baptism.

## Gospel Precepts

### BELIEVER'S BAPTISM

The Cornerstone of the gospel of the kingdom is repentance, faith, and "believer's baptism." The necessity for repentance and faith, as foundational precepts, are not argued against by any evangelical body of Christians and so that premise will be the starting point of the following discussion.

The Great Commission as recorded in Matthew's and Mark's accounts reference the necessity of linking baptism to saving faith (belief) and to discipleship. Mark's account reads thus: "He that believeth and is baptized shall be saved." It does not say, "He that believeth is saved and then should be baptized." By this account there are several important factors made plain.

First, belief must precede baptism. There is no record in Scripture of any Christian baptism commanded to be performed upon unbelievers. There are those who may make a "false" profession of faith and are baptized, yet they were baptized upon a confession of faith. Simon, the magician, believed and was baptized although his heart was discovered, by Peter, to be not yet right, but in the gall of bitterness and still in need of repentance. Yet it does say that he believed. By this we can at least conclude that he made a public profession of faith and was baptized. So while a false profession of faith may bring about baptism, this still does not allow for baptism to be performed upon those who make no confession of faith at all. There are those who profess and become a part of us, but in time it is discovered that they are not of us, and therefore they go out from us (I John 2:19). These, then, who do not rightly believe will find no salvation either in their profession or in their baptism. So for baptism to have any significance at all it must be preceded by a true belief and a saving faith. Without this, baptism in the name of Christ is an empty ritual that cannot correlate the symbolism of the visible ordinance to the internal operation of God.

Secondly, baptism must be to one who has believed. This has already been discussed in the examination of the discourse between Jesus and Nicodemus. Never once in all of Scripture is there the least allusion to simply believing, with an allowance made for baptism to be an optional. Faith alone in the operation of God in the heart is what saves a man, but faith cannot be reckoned as saving faith unless it is willing to be obedient. Faith without works is dead and is no faith at all. True faith as illustrated in Hebrews 11 always moves men to an obedient course of action. There is no account given in this chapter of a hero of faith, who by faith refused to obey God.

Faith motivates the action. If the action is not motivated by faith then it is sin, for "whatsoever is not of faith is sin." Manifold immersions shall be of no avail if separated from faith, for without faith it is impossible to please God.

Faith must precede baptism and lay hold upon the finished work of Christ alone for salvation, but then it must visibly typify the death and burial of the old man and the resurrection of the new creature in the baptismal waters. If a man enters the water a sinner he will also emerge a sinner. If he enters by faith he will be planted in the likeness of Christ's death and rise in newness of life. If when baptized, he by faith unites with Christ, then he has put on Christ (Gal. 3:27). Our faith is not in the water for regeneration, but in God who uses this ordinance to unite us with the visible kingdom of Christ.

In the same manner, Communion does not physically impart grace to the communicant, yet Christ says, "Take, eat; this is my body," and "Except ye eat the flesh of the Son of man and drink His blood, ye have no life in you" (Matthew 26:26, John 6:51-58), so that by faith a man may eat the bread, and drink the cup, as means whereby God meaningfully illustrates to us the life that we partake of in the Son, whose body was broken for us, and whose blood was shed for us. Yet the ordinance alone does not guarantee grace to the unworthy communicant; but rather he eats and drinks damnation to himself.

Though the ordinance of baptism, like Communion, may be observed wrongly, yet the man of faith is under obligation to perform it, does so willingly, and receives God's grace upon his life for obedience.

To argue against the necessity of baptism because of false baptisms is the same as discounting faith because some men have made false professions of it.

Thirdly, it must be noted in Mark's account that he that believeth not shall be damned. It is unbelief in the heart that will discount any righteous acts in God's eyes, so that if a man believe not he shall be damned. Unbelief alone is damning and no amount of Biblical ordinances or duties obeyed shall deliver the unbeliever from his perdition. If a man will not believe in Christ, by faith, water baptism is nothing more to him than a ritual that will lead him into self-deception and, like the Pharisaic converts, shall make him two-fold more the child of hell.

Fourthly, it must be observed that this is a universal command that places every creature under the obligation to believe and be baptized (Mark 16:15). There is no contrary mandate by Christ, no exception for different cultures (go into all the world with this gospel), and no individual exceptions (preach it to every creature).

Matthew's account of the commission brings a few more details into view. Baptism is to be into the names of the three Persons of the Trinity. The act typifies being placed into a relationship with the Godhead and coming under the name and authority of Him who has all power in heaven and in earth.

Those that are baptized must also accept discipleship. They must be taught all things that are commanded. Not only are they taught for knowledge, but they are taught to "observe"; that is to obey all things. Being obedient in baptism is the beginning of a life of obedience to the commands of Christ.

Baptism should never be performed upon any that are incapable of faith and belief in the gospel or do not understand the necessity of discipleship.

When the eunuch asked Philip if there is any restriction against him being baptized, Philip laid down the requirement, "If thou believest with all thine heart, thou mayest."

Again, Peter, on the Day of Pentecost, when questioned by the multitude as to what was necessary for salvation, replied, "Repent and be baptized..." Repentance, faith, belief, etc. always are given in Scripture as preceding baptism. Men are not admonished to be baptized and then later urged to confess a newborn faith.

The teachings of all these Scriptures preclude mandatory baptism for a Christian society and the sprinkling of babies as valid Christian baptism. Baptism is to follow faith, which cannot be coerced, and can only be exercised by persons that have the ability to comprehend truth, an ability which infants do not possess.

Infant baptism has been one of the main pillars supporting the concept of a Christian society. National churches or religious establishments cannot survive without compulsory infant baptism. This practice makes society members of the church and subject to its teachings before they are old enough to even consider the matter personally. Thus the church's members are covenanted before they are old enough to protest or make an alternate choice. While this serves to make everyone a nominal Christian, it also deceives them into assuming they are members of the kingdom, when in reality they are still dead in trespasses and sins, or because of self-deception two-fold more the child of hell.

Some of the passages used to substantiate infant sprinkling must be examined to show how they have been twisted and contorted in favor of this invention of men.

The passages Luke 18:15-17, Mark 10:13-16, and Matthew 19:13-15 all speak of infants, or little children, being brought to Christ for blessing. When the disciples observed the children being brought to Christ, they sought to refrain those (probably parents) who were bringing them. But Christ says, "Suffer the little children to come unto me and forbid them not, for of such is the kingdom of God."

From this passage it is reasoned that infants are accepted of Christ into the kingdom and are not to be forbidden; and if therefore they have received the kingdom such as we, can any man then forbid baptism to him that can enter the kingdom?

This reasoning is purely sophistic; while seeming to follow the Scripture's thought it is actually utterly devoid of any scriptural support.

First of all, we do not know if they were brought within eight days of birth as the paedo-baptists (proponents of infant sprinkling) insist upon.

The text also says that they were brought for blessing but does not say for baptism. There is not even the remotest hint in the passage that Jesus' blessing of His words endorsed infant baptism. If they were coming for baptism they would have been given either by Jesus or the parents to the disciples, for it was they who baptized and not Christ (John 4:1,2).

Also, the infant sprinklers maintain that at least one parent of the child to be baptized must be a believer (I Cor. 7:14), yet here neither Jesus nor the disciples ask the parents to confess their faith. Saving faith cannot be implied of the parents merely for coming, for there were many who were blessed by Christ's ministry who did not follow Him. If they were followers of Christ and known as such, it is hard to imagine that the disciples would have rebuked them for bringing their children to Christ.

So in the passage there is no reference to baptism nor a reference to the parents being questioned of their faith so that baptism might be performed. If the coming alone is sufficient faith, then anyone who brings an infant for baptism has faith enough and cannot be denied, which is again contrary to paedo-baptist practice; for they insist that at least one parent must believe and have been baptized.

Paedo-baptists also insist that baptism is necessary for the child to be able to enter the kingdom. Baptism is the visible sign of initiation into the church. John Calvin says, *"Baptism is the initiatory sign by which we are admitted to the fellowship of the Church, that being ingrafted into Christ we may be accounted children of God."*[9]

Now if baptism initiates the infants into the Church, then previous to baptism the infants are outside the Church. If Christ's blessing of infants justifies their baptism because, "of such is the kingdom of God", then here is a contradiction. They are not yet baptized, but yet they are said by Christ to be "of the kingdom of God"; if they are of the kingdom, how does baptism initiate them into it as Calvin supposes? Christ did not say, "Let me bless them that they may be of the kingdom." Rather, they are of the kingdom, so they may be blessed.

Nor can baptism initiate them into the church unless there is regeneration in the water itself. Infants are incapable of faith or belief in God's ability to justify them, and so if baptism initiates them into the Church outside of them exercising faith, then they must be saved by water alone, for there cannot be the answer of a good conscience towards God.

It is by the grace of God, they say, that infants are saved. If God's grace alone has placed them into the kingdom, without any act of faith, then surely water is not needed if faith is not. And this is exactly what Christ is saying, "Of such is the kingdom of God."

How can they be initiated into that which they already are a part of? They are saved by God's grace, though they be conceived in sin. For it is only to him that "knoweth" to do good and doeth it not that it is accounted as sin (James 4:17); that is, damning sin, for the grace of God extends to those who cannot "know" or have an understanding of sin, though they be born in it.

It is spoken of a man, that when he becomes converted he becomes AS A LITTLE CHILD (Matthew 18:3) in order to enter the kingdom. He becomes as a child to enter the kingdom, for the child is of the kingdom already. He, like the child, is not sinless, or incapable of sinning still, but like the child he is held guiltless because of the unmerited grace of God that has been brought to his heart by faith through a knowledge of God, while the other is held in God's grace because he cannot know either God or sin.

God does not hold him accountable to have faith who cannot "hear" the Word of God preached and be able to understand it; "for faith cometh by hearing, by the Word of God." An infant cannot hear the Word and exercise faith, yet Christ says they are of the kingdom. They are of the kingdom not because they are baptized but because Christ has said they are.

If they are of the kingdom and blessed by Christ, to what avail then is the water? It cannot make their salvation more secure. The water does not provide the sign of faith, for faith does not exist in an infant. Baptism into Christ is only for those who have faith in the operation of God (Col. 2:12).

Baptism is to be reserved for later in life when the child can see the work of Christ for him upon Calvary and by faith enter the baptismal waters to be planted in the likeness of Christ's death and be raised in newness of life.

The child is kept safe by God's grace until the time when the Spirit calls upon him to receive Christ by faith. Even paedo-baptists admit that the sprinkled infant must have a confirmation of faith later in life to Christ. Why not then baptize them upon their confession of faith so that the act can have meaning and correlate to the exercise of faith? Nowhere does the Scripture command baptism so that later in life a person may profess faith.

The Reformed understanding of election teaches that God arbitrarily chooses some men unto eternal life while others are left reprobate because God will not give them faith to believe; and yet the parents are supposed to believe that if they sprinkle their babies they will be initiated into the church. How can the parent or the Elder ascertain whether the child is elect or reprobate before the child is able to produce the fruit of election? They cannot, when election is to rest only in the inscrutable will of God. So what then shall they do? Shall they baptize and include in the church someone whom God may have reprobated? Is this not striving against God?

They cannot see the fruit of faith, yet they baptize.

Do they doubt God's ability to save the infant without water, if He may save him without faith? If at this point water, without faith, is still necessary, then it is clear that they believe the water regenerates the infant. They in effect become the Elector of the child to salvation or they become a baptizer of reprobates; either case in which they assume the role that they in theory ascribe only to the sovereignty of God.

Does the grace of God then extend to all infants outside of baptism? Hear the Scriptures; blessed are the children for of such is the kingdom of heaven.

"The grace of God that bringeth salvation hath appeared to all men" (Titus 2:11). (If a contentious one will say the text says men, not infants, then we say also then, that it excludes the women on the same basis.)

"That was the true Light, which lighteth every man that COMETH INTO THE WORLD" (by natural birth) (John 1:9).

"Therefore, as by the offense of one, judgment came upon all men to condemnation: even so by the righteousness of one the FREE GIFT CAME UPON ALL MEN unto justification of life" (Romans 5:18). The sacrifice of Christ is as extensive in justification as original sin is in condemnation. This is not universal salvation to unrepentant men but rather the cancellation of guilt for Adam's sin upon those not able to repent, such as infants. We are still conceived in sin as infants but made of the kingdom by the free gift of Christ till of age when the Spirit shall call us to repent. If the call of the Spirit to new birth is rejected, then we willingly refuse the free gift of grace already given and accept all the penalties for a sinful nature that will enslave us to sin and its consequences. He hath concluded them all in unbelief that He might have mercy upon all (Romans 11:32). God's grace has extended to all those infants who were conceived in iniquity by their mothers, grace reaching fully as far as original sin, and abounding even more.

Most paedo-baptist churches do not allow the baptized infants to partake of Communion because they cannot examine themselves before participating in the service. Yet if they are unfit for Communion how are they fit for baptism? If they are baptized upon the faith of their parents, can they not commune upon the faith of their parents? Paul says, "For we are ALL partakers of that one bread." None in the body are to be excluded except by their own self-examination. Jesus said of the cup, "Drink ye ALL of it." Now if the reference to "all" was only to the disciples and not the whole Church for all time, then the ordinance of the cup also can be reserved for those only who were with Christ, and not for all the Church for all time. In fact, those early church fathers such as Augustine who believed in infant baptism also taught that the infant should also commune; so if infant baptism be argued from antiquity, then infant Communion can be also. But if the infant partake, how shall he examine himself?

What a quandary men make for themselves when they ignore the plain Biblical order for baptism.

Some other arguments for infant baptism need to be examined. The few household baptisms listed in Scripture are often adduced as "reasonable assumptions" that they included infants.

Acts 16:15 records the baptism of Lydia and her household. There is nothing in the text to suggest the age of the household. It is quite certain that she was not married, for it is called "her" household, whereas marriage would have designated it "his." In verse 40 of the same chapter, it is again called the "house of Lydia", when marriage would have made it the house of her husband. Had she been married, he would have believed also as part of the household, and Paul and Silas would have gone to "his" house.

As in the case of the Philippian jailer's wife, she (Lydia) would have been probably the unnamed one, while her husband's name would have been given for the house.

All these facts make it very doubtful that as an unmarried widow she even had small children, let alone have traveled to and from Thyatira and Philippi as a seller of purple with infants. All the facts that we have argue against any infant baptism here.

It is a mere supposition of infant baptism based upon nothing which proves nothing other than that the doctrine itself is based upon the silence of Scriptures, which in effect is to be without scriptural basis.

Another case is the Philippian jailer. Here, though, all the evidence is against infant baptism, for all the house that was baptized (in Acts 16:34) is said also to be "believing" in God, something an infant is incapable of. If the admonition that Paul gave for him to believe was so that the infants could also be saved by their father's faith, then the same could be said for his wife, for she is not once asked separately to believe. Are we to suppose also that the husband believed on behalf of his wife? Nor then should we believe that the jailer believed on behalf of his children, for it says that his whole house believed. Again, all the evidence here is against infant baptism.

The case of Cornelius is also used because the angel told him that Peter would tell him words whereby his whole house would be saved (Acts 11:14). Here again an examination of the facts actually brings arguments against infant baptism. Acts 10:2 makes it clear that his whole house was already fearing God, thus capable of believing in order to be baptized. Furthermore, the Spirit fell on "all" them that heard the Word and they spoke in tongues and magnified God, an impossibility for someone too young to speak a language (Acts 10:44-47).

Another case is the baptism of the household of Stephanas, as recorded in I Cor. 1:16. At the end of the epistle in chapter 16 verse 15 it mentions that this same household had addicted themselves unto the ministry of the saints. I will let the paedo-baptist explain how this sprinkled infant in the household of Stephanas labored in the work of the church.

The time will not be taken to answer every argument that has been advanced in order to find Biblical support for this practice.

One of the chief positive arguments for infant baptism is made from circumcision. It is argued that circumcision, as an iniatory rite into the Old Covenant, is now replaced with infant baptism for the entrance into the New Covenant. Circumcision was performed within eight days of birth for all the males of believing parents, upon the profession of the faith of the parents for the child.

It is further argued that circumcision, based upon Colossians 2:11, typifies the mortification of the sinful flesh, which also baptism does. Therefore baptism represents the same concept as circumcision, so the ordinance may adopt the same practice as the rite for its applicants. The reasoning is quite subtle and appears to carry considerable weight, but it does not follow the train of thought developed in Colossians 2, but rather extracts a few of the principles expressed and uses it to develop a completely different argument than Paul is making in Colossians 2.

The fleshly circumcision of Israel typifies the spiritual circumcision of the heart. Baptism then represents the spiritual circumcision of Christ that is made "without hands." Baptism does not represent or answer to the external Jewish rite but rather the "operation of faith" that is performed in the believer; that is, the death of the old man (or the flesh), and the resurrection of the new creature (Romans 6:1-8, II Cor. 5:17, Gal. 6:15).

Again, baptism is not typified by circumcision, but rather circumcision typifies the "operation of faith" in the heart, which is then typified by baptism. Baptism answers to "spiritual" circumcision and not to "natural" circumcision. Because it answers to "spiritual" circumcision as an "operation of faith", baptism cannot scripturally be performed until faith first operates upon the heart, thus making the baptism of an infant unscriptural, for an infant can neither know sin or the exercise of saving faith.

If baptism be insisted upon for an infant then it is evident that the baptizer expects the water to create faith (an impossibility) and confer grace outside of belief or repentance; or intends to perform a meaningless ritual.

The covenant of circumcision was a recognition of the faith that Abraham already possessed before circumcision (Romans 4:9-11). The succeeding generations of Abraham's seed kept this practice in honor of the covenant between God and Abraham. The covenant was established upon a pre-existing faith. This covenant, though founded upon faith, was a work of the "flesh," and anticipated the New Covenant that would be grounded upon faith for a work in the "heart."

Abraham became the father of us all, (Romans 4:16, 22-24), the father of the faithful, "the father of all them that BELIEVE" (Romans 4:11). This covenant of faith extends only to believers and not to infants, who are kept safe by the grace of God until they can exercise faith.

There is not one word in all of Scripture to suggest that Christian baptism answers to fleshly circumcision. In fact, when this great issue of circumcision was before the Jerusalem council (Acts 15), as to whether it was required for Gentile believers, there is not one word said that intimates the ancient practice was now supplanted by water baptism. If this was the case, the whole circumcision controversy could have been quickly diffused with an explanation of the purpose of the ordinance of Christian baptism.

But the church's silence is so deafening that it speaks volumes to him that hath an ear to hear.

It is admitted, though, that infant baptism does answer quite well to physical circumcision, in that it is a work of the flesh upon the natural person. What is being objected to here, though, is that while "infant baptism" may answer to circumcision of the flesh, "Christian baptism" does not.

It is now exposed that the practice of infant sprinkling does not rest upon any positive command or example from Scripture but merely upon its silence, which is to say that it has no scriptural basis at all.

Many appeal to the antiquity of the practice for support. But the earliest records of Christian doctrine, such as the Didache, reveal only instruction for catechumens for baptism, and are as silent upon infant baptism as the Scripture itself.

If one argues infant baptism from the later church fathers, he could just as well argue infant Communion and chrism also, which shows clearly that it appears in the right class; that is, with all the other traditions of men. For further proof of this assertion one can peruse the Apostolic fathers or read the excellent treatise by John Gill, "Infant Baptism, A Part and Pillar of Popery."

If the Reformed teachers of Scripture would apply the same principles of interpretation of Scripture to infant baptism as they applied to the use of instrumental music in public worship, then the issue would quickly be settled.

R. L. Dabney, a Presbyterian theologian, demonstrates when arguing against instrumental music in the church, that only those ordinances that are "positively" affirmed by Christ and the apostles can lawfully be practiced by the church, when he writes against the defense of instrumental music in public worship:

*"They seem totally blind to the historical fact that it was just thus every damnable corruption which has cursed the church took its beginning; in the* addition *to the modes of worship ordained by Christ for the new dispensation, of human devices, which seemed ever so pretty and appropriate, made by the best of men and women and ministers with the very best of motives, and borrowed mostly from the temple cultus of the Jews. Thus came vestments, pictures in churches, incense, the observance of the martyrs' anniversary days – in a word, that whole apparatus of will – worship and superstition which bloomed  into popery and idolatry."*

John Owens, a Puritan, writing in the same vein of maintaining that the church can practice only what is "positively" affirmed by Christ and the apostles says, *"The principle that the church hath power to institute any thing or ceremony belonging to the worship of God, either as to matter or manner, beyond the observance of such circumstances as necessarily attend such ordinances as Christ Himself hath instituted, lies at the bottom of all horrible superstition and idolatry...."*

The Presbyterian, Larger Catechism of the second commandment explicitly acknowledges that the church may only observe as a practice what God has specifically appointed.

It cannot be proven from Scripture or the early Apostolic history that infant baptism was a church ordinance. The early church is silent upon it, as the Scriptures, thus proving that it is nothing more than a man-made superstitious invention borrowed from the practice of pagan Lustration, justified by the abolished Jewish practice of circumcision, and became a tradition, (supposedly received from the apostles), in the church along with the use of oil, spittle, and devilish exorcism (also pagan) that accompanied its introduction.

The pagan practice of infant Lustration or baptism is well documented, as well as the ceremonies that attended it. The Spanish Catholic missionaries were astonished to find infant baptism here in the New World among the Aztec Indians, that included reference to a revocation of original sin, exorcism of the devil, and the use of holy water. Infant baptism, like most other innovations, was merely an adaptation of a pagan tradition to the Christian religion, and its antiquity has deceived many, for its proponents said it was received as a tradition from the apostles. Of course its advocates would say such, for it cannot be justified from Scripture, and they could not say it was received from the devil or paganism and promote it as Christian, so they say it was "Apostolic Tradition", the same argument the Catholic church uses to justify her many other unscriptural practices. By them saying it was an "Apostolic Tradition" they are admitting that there is no support for it from the Scripture. The practice is as much an "Apostolic Tradition" as that other "Apostolic Tradition" that maintains that Peter was the first Pope. Although infant baptism may have an early date, it has no support among the Apostolic Fathers or the Scripture, therefore it is not ancient enough for us to give it any credence. If someone wishes to find it any earlier than the later church fathers he should look in the heathen archives and there will find abundant evidence.

Let us consider, if infant baptism is credible upon its antiquity alone, then those of the ancients who endorse it must also be given credence as to how it was understood in relation to membership in the Church.

The seventh Council of Carthage, of 87 bishops, moderated by Cyprian (who is often used in support of infant baptism), in 258A.D. is a unanimous referendum against acknowledging the baptism of heretics as Christian baptism. They all agree that he who comes to the Church from the heretics must be rebaptized. They all agree that for baptism to be Christian it must be administered by the Christian Church and a heretic's baptism is no baptism at all, regardless of how sincere the candidate may be.

Now if we accept the antiquity of Cyprian as a good proof for infant baptism outside of Scripture, then the Church's position at this time on a heretic's baptism also carries equal weight as an alleged "Apostolic Tradition".

When the first Reformers, Luther, Zwingli, and Calvin, left Rome they soon claimed that she was either Antichrist or the Babylonian harlot, in which case she was a heretical church. All Reformers received their infant baptism from apostate Rome, and were not rebaptized, or, more truly, baptized at all. Baptism, as Calvin and the other Reformers agreed, was the initiation into the Christian Church, and a person could not be in the Church without it. Therefore by their own reasoning they were outside the Church of Christ, for they never received Christian baptism, but only the Antichrist's, which is no baptism at all, according to the church authorities they cite for historical support of infant baptism. If they had never received Christian baptism it is no wonder they promoted infant sprinkling, which is not Christian baptism either. They argued that they received their baptism from Christ as their head, but yet they would never baptize the child of infidels. Still, though, they maintained that the baptism they received at the hands of apostate Rome was valid. If the baptism administered by Rome to them was valid, then it was also for all the others baptized by Rome. If Rome could baptize people into the Church, then they were leaving a legitimate church when they left Rome and could not justly call her the Harlot.

It is not the intent here to decide whether the Reformers were in or out of the Church of Christ, but merely to show how their own doctrine condemns them when they lean upon antiquity, for the foundation of a man-made tradition.

To their own master they will stand or fall, for personal judgment does not change the decree of God one iota, and the Judge of all the earth shall do right in that day, when the secrets of men's hearts shall be revealed.

Let him that is wise judge in the matter of infant sprinkling and meditate on whether it can be substituted for Christian baptism when there can be no positive proof for one baptized infant in all of Scripture, and the history of its practice is akin to the other pagan innovations that accompanied it. Either we build upon positive Scripture for Christian ordinances or the traditions of men and the silence of Scripture.

## Nonconformity

Another Gospel precept of the kingdom is the doctrine of Nonconformity. Our baptism into the kingdom represents a death to the old man, that the body of sin may be destroyed. It also typifies a union with Christ.

The inevitable result of the mortification of the flesh and the emergence of a new creature, is a nonconformed lifestyle that is separated unto God. The man who has been changed by grace cannot continue to live on in sin, by either willful habits, or by indulging in fleshly desires that war against the soul.

His life is now characterized by an abhorrence and avoidance of sin, and exhibits a transformed mind-set towards its pleasures and allurements. This does not mean that he observes the patterns of the world and then adopts a contrary lifestyle but rather that his affections are rooted in things above and not on things of this earth, and this produces a separation between him and the world. His life demonstrates where his treasure is.

The covenant with God, represented by baptism, brings him out from among the world (II Cor. 6:14-18) into a paternal relationship with God. All that is in the world is representative of enmity against God (I John 2:15-17, James 4:4).

The carnal mind is enmity against God, while the transformed mind presents the whole body as a living sacrifice unto God. Those

who come into the kingdom cannot yoke themselves with unbelievers, for what concord hath Christ with Belial? The kingdom is comprised of those who upon confession of faith and baptism are separated from the world and unto God.

If all of society be baptized, as infants, into the Church, where
then is the world, if it be not in the Church? To unite the Church
with the world, simply baptize babies into the Church and when
they get older tell them that they are already of the kingdom; you will
then have unconverted church members who will bring carnality into
the Church from the world, which is the natural result of an unregenerate heart.

John Wesley was baptized as an infant and was a minister for many
years before he realized that he was not converted.

During the "Great Awakening", Gilbert Tenent preached a stir-
ring sermon on "The Danger of an Unconverted Ministry," which
greatly aroused the ire of his traditional Presbyterian colleagues.
During this time many converted church members formed independent or Baptist congregations and separated themselves from the established Congregational New England Church to form "believers
only" churches that were nonconformed to the religious world.

Even those who are baptized upon confession of faith and born of
the Spirit are engaged in a lifelong warfare against the world's system
of fleshly desires, "for the flesh lusteth against the Spirit, and the
Spirit against the flesh: and these are contrary the one to the other."

Paul says in the Galatian epistle that those who walk in the works
of the flesh shall not inherit the kingdom of God (Galatians 5:19-
21). At the end of the same epistle he portrays the cross of Christ,
which he is one with, as producing a double crucifixion; the world
unto me, and I unto the world. In that crucifixion there is death and
inability to respond to the world, and the world holds us as dead
unto it; beyond its power to stimulate.

This is an ongoing work of faith. Notice the following verses:

"I am (present tense) crucified with Christ" (Galatians 2:20).

"Reckon ye also yourselves (present tense act of the will) to be dead indeed unto sin, but alive unto God through Jesus Christ our Lord" (Romans 6:11).

"If any man will come after me, let him deny himself, and take up his cross DAILY, and follow me" (Luke 9:23).

Nonconformity to the world is essential to membership in the kingdom of Christ.

It is not a reactionary and opposite response to the world's culture, but the natural and inevitable result of being crucified with Christ and living by faith.

It disallows any union or binding allegiance to a worldly power or system.

It is a cardinal doctrine of the kingdom.

## NON-SWEARING OF OATHS

Another doctrine of the kingdom that is often neglected, ignored, or spoken against is the non-swearing of oaths.

The oath was used under the old covenant as a means of binding the law upon Israel (Deut. 29:12). They were to swear by God's name as a means of holding men accountable to agreements between themselves. God's name in swearing was a means to call upon God as a witness to truth (Lev. 6:2-5, Deut. 6:13).

Yet under the law, when swearing oaths as part of covenants, there were stipulations to prevent frivolous and false oaths.

They were not to lie under oath (Ex. 23:1, Lev. 5:1, 6:2-5, 19:12). All of their oaths were to be in God's name alone so that He would be called as a witness against any violations of it (Deut. 6:13, Mal. 3:5). God was always to be the third party of the oath and would hold men accountable to truth. God's name was not to be used in vain (frivolously or falsely), but rather with great solemnity.

The swearing of oaths was a religious ceremony and an integral part of the old covenant relationship between God and His people, to illustrate to them the gravity of speaking the truth. It was also a means of "commanding" fidelity to God's law, so that the citizens of

Israel would not view obedience to it an option, but a requirement. Because it was sworn upon them, the penalties for breaking it equated not only to an infraction of duty, but also to an untruth; the breaking of that which you "swore" to do.

Man in his fallen nature will naturally lie and must be taught and encouraged to tell the truth. The following Scriptures speak of this:

"Their throat is an open sepulchre; with their tongues they have used deceit; the poison of asps is under their lips: whose mouth is full of cursing and bitterness:" (Romans 3:13, 14).

"The wicked are estranged from the womb: they go astray as soon as they be born, speaking lies." (Psalm 58:3)

"...your lips have spoken lies, your tongue hath muttered perverseness" (Isa. 59:3)

"Lie not one to another, seeing that ye have put off the old man with his deeds" (Col. 3:9).

God used oaths to help bind men unto the truth. Many other cultures have likewise realized man's corrupt nature and penchant for lies and also use the oath, with accompanying penalties for perjury in order to enjoin upon men truth and fidelity.

Almost without exception, in the swearing of important oaths, the locally recognized deity is called upon as witness to the act.

Military and political leaders have seen the value of requiring this of soldiers or subjects in order to demand strict obedience, punish insurrection, and deter rebellion. Most ancient and contemporary militaries required/require the soldier to swear an oath of allegiance to their own country or to the national sovereign. Upon these grounds a soldier could be court-martialed for disobeying orders, as well as cowardice or desertion, since it was a violation of their oath of duty.

In ancient times even citizens were required to take an oath of fealty. Starting from the year 1066, every English male took an oath of allegiance to the king of England. When the Protestants had established their power in England in 1688, additional oaths were required denouncing the Pope's authority and the doctrine of transubstantiation.[10]

Oaths to the British crown were imposed on all the early colonists. When the Patriots began to resent the British laws, they adjured some of the magistrates in Massachusetts to renounce the king of England and the laws of Parliament.[11] Not only did the Patriots renounce former oaths that were made under God to the king, but they took new oaths of loyalty to the local colony. Eventually every state required these loyalty oaths.[12] In 1777 George Washington issued a proclamation requiring all Americans to swear an oath of allegiance to the United States.[13]

Thus history illustrates the use of the oath in requiring loyalty to a cause. But it also demonstrates the ineffectiveness of the oath to bind men to the truth. Through civil penalties the oath has some success. But an oath that was sworn under God to the king of England did not prevent even the Puritans from breaking them and revolting against the king they had sworn allegiance unto. These oaths, though solemnly sworn unto God, were taken and then broken by men who were religious and claimed to believe the truth. There were no such conditions in the oaths of the early colonists that provided them the allowance to break their oaths if the king became tyrannical in their perceptions by instituting an unfair tea tax.

The Reformed tradition upheld the use of religious oaths, using primarily Old Testament passages that affirmed the practice. But here in America these Reformed churches broke their oaths made under God when the rule of the king was perceived unjust. Yet God says that those who abide in His tabernacle, though swearing to their own hurt, will change it not (Psa. 15:4).

Matthew Henry, the Puritan commentator says in his notes on this passage:

*"He is one that always prefers a good conscience before any secular interest or advantage whatever: for, if he has promised upon oath to do anything, though afterwards it appear much to his damage and prejudice in his worldly estate, yet he adheres to it and CHANGES NOT. See how weak-sighted and short-sighted even wise and good men may be; they swear to their own hurt, which they were not aware of when they took the*

*oath. But see how strong the obligation of an oath is, that a man must suffer loss to himself and his family, rather than wrong his neighbor by breaking his oath. An oath is a sacred thing, which we must not think to play fast and loose with."*

This is sound hermeneutics and thoroughly condemns those who swore to the king of England and then not only broke the oath but revolted in civil insurrection.

This is not to suggest that God did not ordain the founding of this free country but rather to illustrate the folly and hypocrisy of oaths taken by Christian professors.

"But," say its defenders, "the king was unjust, which gives us the right to break oath." "Where in the oath, we reply, was it stated that your fealty to the king was contingent upon his equity of rule?" If an oath was taken unconditionally (which it was), what right have you to break it? Further what right have you to swear allegiance to anything other than God's law?

The oath to a country pledges unconditional allegiance to an entity that may require a sinful act. If the unconditional oath be broken on moral grounds, then in order to follow morality you are convinced of lying.

It is for these reasons that Christ asks His followers to "swear not at all." For they cannot always guarantee the performance of an oath of loyalty, and the oath in and of itself suggests that this man must be forcibly compelled to tell or walk in the truth. "Let your communication be Yea, yea, and Nay, nay," whether under oath or not. The man who is possessed by the "Spirit of Truth" does not need an oath to compel him to tell the truth.

Many have tried to argue that Jesus was only condemning frivolous oaths; but the law bound men to swear only by God, eliminating frivolous oaths; so while Jesus was condemning oaths by Jerusalem, the head, or heaven; He also was saying "Swear not at all." When men need to strengthen the "Yes" and the "No" with an oath there is the implication of evil, that is, that without the penalties of an oath the truth would not be told.

The Reformed people were fond of using religious oaths to compel men to the Christian faith, but they themselves broke oaths numerous times during the revolts in England and finally also here in America. The law that they used to support oaths convinced them also of transgression.

It is not denied that oaths were proper for the old covenant saints, for they had not the "Spirit of Truth" and some of them lied at times or used deceit, such as Abraham when he told his wife to call herself his sister. It is the converted man that is forbidden by Christ to take an oath.

There are a number of New Testament passages that are used to try to prove that Christ did not mean what He plainly said, when He said, "Swear not at all."

One of the arguments is derived from the fact that God Himself swears. If God swears how can it be a sin? Will you condemn a practice that God Himself performs? This is proven by numerous passages of Scripture that refer to God swearing. The chief passages, though, are Hebrews 6:13-20 and 7:20-28, which speak of God swearing to Abraham the promise of blessing and to Christ for His office of priesthood and the surety of a better testament.

First of all, it is imperative to understand that God may justly prohibit us from performing that which He has reserved for Himself. For My ways are not your ways. He has clearly reserved this a way of right in the area of personal vengeance, for He says, "Dearly beloved, avenge not yourselves" and yet He says, "Vengeance is mine, I will repay." Will we accuse God of sin because He exercises that which He forbids us to do? Or will we say, if He can, then I may also? Is not this a way of man making himself the equal of God? This would be a clear contradiction of what God has stated as a necessary but unequal standard of conduct, one for Him, and one for us. On one hand God has told us not to judge our brother but yet says that to His Master he will stand or fall. The whole argument in favor of swearing an oath is based on the assumption that man has the same prerogatives as God Himself, and is an attempt to make man the equal of God in his ability to choose his actions.

Furthermore, the two main reasons for which God does swear are the same two for which we as Christians should not. God may swear, for unlike us, He knows all truth and He always tells the truth and so will not break His oath. It is He alone that "cannot" lie, and so risks no danger of ever breaking His oath as many professing Christians have done after taking an oath. Secondly, God is able to perform all that He has sworn to do. He has sworn that Christ will be a priest "forever" and He alone can make such a guarantee, for He has sworn and will not repent of it. We, though, however much we swear, can never guarantee a course of actions, therefore we say, "If the Lord will, we shall live, and do this, or that," for we know not what may be on the morrow.

Our yes and no should represent the honest intentions of the heart and will, but above that we risk falling into condemnation (James 5:12) for our inability to perform an oath. Originally the oath was used to commit the will to the proper course of action; now, men that have the Spirit of Truth are to simply affirm it with a "yes" and stand by their word.

The argument for swearing, based upon God's oaths, is shown to be groundless, and merely an attempt to evade the obvious conclusion that must come from the simple words "swear not at all." It uses an argument that when carried to its logical conclusion will nullify a belief in the sovereignty of God to choose a course of action that remains exclusive to Him alone.

Sometimes it is remarked that Jesus replied to the High Priest at His trial after He was adjured (placed under oath by another), thus giving consent to be placed under oath. The argument then is that since Christ spoke after being adjured, it is one and the same as if He had sworn and then spoken. This argument carries more weight than the previous one, for Christ gave us an example, while here in the flesh, to walk as He walked. But this argument is still weak, for the Scriptures do not record that Christ took an oath, but that He responded in a situation that was under the same penalties as if He had taken an oath. If we are to assume that Christ became oath-bound by responding to an adjuration, or that it was the equivalent of Him taking an oath, then we are saying that a man is oath-bound to any course of action unto which a wicked man adjures him.

Therefore when the demon said to Christ, "I adjure thee by God, that thou torment me not", Christ was then bound by an oath to not torment the demon, which is the equivalent of swearing by God to the demon not to hurt him. What utter absurdity is such logic. Jesus both responded and cast out the demon and will one day torment him with the second death eternally.

The moral of this whole account is simply this; a man may respond to an adjuration without being bound by the attempt to foist an oath upon him, and still be in harmony with Christ's words, "Swear not at all."

Some say that the language Paul used in Galatians 1:11, 20, is the equivalent of him taking an oath to certify that the gospel is true. Here again there is no clear reference to an oath being taken, only that Paul is giving his solemn word before God that what he is writing and preaching of the gospel is the truth. This argument is extremely stretched to find support for a legal oath here. No court of law would recognize this as a binding legal oath given to the church of Galatia in absentia.

Are we to assume that this oath of certification is what made the gospel true or believable? If this is such an important element of his letter, why did he not certify all his epistles? Are the others untrue because they are not supposedly sworn in as suitable evidence of truth? Are the other epistles now inadmissible evidence for the truth of the gospel? Do the words of the alleged oath have anything at all to do with the gospel; or is it merely that Paul was saying that before God he guaranteed that the gospel is true and comes not from men or himself but is the direct revelation of Christ to him, therefore it is true, for its source is truth?

I may stand for the truth of the gospel, defend it with all of my personal reputation, and call upon God as my witness, but I cannot add or detract one iota from its credibility by doing so. If Jesus Christ stands a High Priest of the New Testament forever by an immutable oath of God, and is the surety of it, why then should Paul add to it another frivolous oath?

The position presented here is not unique, but rather that which has been affirmed from the primitive Church and many other groups down through the ages.[14] Wherever the nationally established Christian religions have taken root they have tried to use religious oaths as a means to bind the wills and consciences of men to their own expediency and have used various methods to argue that Christ never meant what He plainly said concerning the swearing of oaths. They lay their hand upon the Bible and swear over the words of Christ that forbid oaths, imagining it a religious duty, when in effect it is an act of sacrilege; for it uses a Book that condemns the usage of oaths for the believer as a justification for a Christian to swear.

The non-swearing of oaths is an important doctrine of the kingdom, as it prevents men from binding allegiances that are contrary to the Christian faith.

## The Primacy of Love

Jesus stated the totality of all the law and the prophets were summed up in love to God and love to our fellow man. Love is both vertical (to God) and horizontal (to our fellow man).

The foundation of our love is rooted in God's love for us. "We love Him because He first loved us." God's love for us has enabled us to love Him. We then are able to love our fellow man because of the love of God shed abroad in our hearts by the Holy Ghost.

The first and greatest obligation we have to God is to love Him with all our heart, soul, mind, and strength; that is, with our affections, will, intellect, and physical capabilities. When we are possessed by God's love, we in turn can love Him with all our faculties. But only he that is "born of God" has the ability to love Him in this manner (1 John 4:7), for love is of God.

We by nature are children of wrath and are disobedient, but through God's love, the gift of His Son, are born again into love.

The love of God engages every aspect of our life for the work of His kingdom. The man who is born anew no longer refrains from sin out of fear alone nor lives righteously merely out of duty, but rather God and His Word are the object of his deepest affections.

"If ye love me, keep my commandments."

"This is the love of God, that we keep His commandments."

"He that hath my commandments, and keepeth them, he it is that loveth me."

Obedience is the natural outflow of the love relationship between God and His people. There is an inseparable union between love and obedience when God's laws are written in the fleshly tables of a man's heart. Oh how *love* I thy *law*!

God's people have the mark of love upon their lives, evidenced through careful obedience to Christ from a willing heart.

This love of God, both from Him, and then to Him, flows out also to our fellow man. The love we have for others is a direct and sure result of walking in God's love.

"By this shall all men know that ye are my disciples, if ye have love one to another."

"Love one another as I have loved you."

"If we love one another, God dwelleth in us, and his love is perfected in us."

Christ has asked that the love of God even be shown unto our enemies (Matthew 5:44). Our love is to be as unconditional and indiscriminate as God's love, for He maketh His sun to rise on the evil and on the good, and sendeth rain on the just and on the unjust. Our love to our neighbors is to precede their love for us, for if ye love them which love you, what reward have ye; do not even the publicans the same? Just as God commends His love to us while we are yet sinners, so our love must reach our neighbors and extend even to our enemies, whether they reciprocate or not.

God's love is so sure that where the absence of love is there is also the absence of God, for God is love. If there is no love in the heart toward our brother, then there is also a lack of eternal life in that heart.

"We know that we have passed from death unto life, because we love the brethren. He that loveth not his brother abideth in death. Whosoever hateth his brother is a murderer: and ye know that no murderer hath eternal life abiding in him" (I John 3:14, 15).

There can be no doubt that the Scriptures portray the Christian life as one of unconditional love. This does not mean that we will not speak the truth to our neighbor and possibly offend him, but when we speak the truth it is in love, with his best in our view.

Love can also be a chastening or correcting rod that may be resented by the offender; but yet it is administered for his welfare.

The doctrine of loving our enemies has always stood in contrast to the aim of the martial arts. How can one love his enemy and at the same time take his life? Can he send another unbeliever into eternal hell because his country has declared him the enemy? Or can he take the life of another Christian brother in the opposing army and still love him? The death of the enemy always results in either sending a lost man into eternal damnation or taking the life of a brother; which in the case of a brother, he should not be considered as an enemy.

Many have argued that the Old Testament saints warred against their enemies, which is true; but this has no bearing at all in determining proper conduct for one who is born again and walking in obedience to the new covenant. By the same line of reasoning one could argue for extermination of the enemy, including the women and children, when possession is taken of their land. There is no requirement under the old covenant for a man to love his enemies, but rather as David says, "Do not I hate them, Oh Lord, that hate thee?" (Psalm 139:21). So any argument based upon the conduct of the Old Testament saint alone for Christian conduct is without merit. Just as the basis of redemption has changed with the covenants, so has also the basis of conduct. Jesus illustrated this point to the disciples when they wished to call down fire upon their adversaries like the prophet Elijah. He rebuked them by saying, "Ye know not what manner of spirit ye are of. For the Son of man is not come to destroy men's lives, but to save them" (Luke 9:51-56).

But others say, were not the centurions of the Scripture men of faith? Indeed, they were. This only proves that men from every walk of life may exercise faith. The harlot woman who anointed Jesus' feet with oil was also commended for her great faith (Luke 7:50). Are we to assume from this that Jesus' commendation of saving faith in this woman's life was an endorsement of prostitution? So the only thing that can be proven from the centurions exercising saving faith is that a centurion may also be saved by faith.

But others say, did not soldiers came to John and ask, "What shall we do?" Why did he not answer that they leave off their profession? The answer came with three requirements.

*1. Do violence to no man,*

This statement is complete and categorical. Many would wish it to say, do violence to no just civilian, use discretionary measures only, or do all that your commanding officers require.

*2. Neither accuse any falsely,*

None of the citizenry is to be threatened with false accusation in order to obtain bribes, nor when they are called as witnesses are they to be favorable to their own country over the truth.

*3. Be content with your wages,*

The wages of soldiers were often supplemented by the booty of war. In fact generals would often promise financial reward or honor for any who in combat could be the first to scale the wall, break down the gate, etc. Yet these soldiers are to be governed by principle and not by greed.

John never intimates that they should leave off their profession, for that would be to force the conscience; but at the same time he lays down gospel precepts to activate the conscience against those sins so often indulged in by soldiers. Either they must quit the profession because of the requirements, or pay greater allegiance to them than to their martial oath.

We know not how they chose. We know of no standing military today that holds these principles, as well as the precept to love their enemies, as requirements for their soldiers above their military oath of duty.

It is often the temptation of man to lay down strict guidelines as to what is and is not an acceptable Christian profession, and force people to quit a chosen profession in order to follow Christ. People then can assume that they are following Christ because they have quit a former profession to follow Him, and do so, out of feeling that it is required of them, rather than having Biblical principles presented to them that awaken the conscience, and produce convictions from the Spirit that lead them to evaluate their present station. Either way may lead to a change; but change that is the result of an awakened conscience instead of prescribed duty makes a tremendous difference in the fruit that will come from that decision.

Also, it must be remembered that not all the law was put away at once. The gospel of the kingdom was being preached, opening up the way for the new covenant, but it was not fully in effect until the death of the testator (Christ) of that covenant (Hebrews 9:15-17). It was the death of Christ on the cross that blotted out the handwriting of ordinances against us (Col. 2:13, 14). While Christ was here in the flesh He observed the Jewish festivals and even told the cleansed leper to go show himself to the priest, out of respect to the ceremonial law. Jesus, while He and John were teaching the gospel of the kingdom in preparation for the establishment of the Church, observed the law in order to fulfill it and to complete it.

John, likewise, here does not condemn the soldiers' profession, for the law allowed it, and it was not yet nullified, but rather teaches gospel precepts of conduct that are binding, even upon soldiers.

If John had said, leave off your profession and follow Christ, this would have proved nothing more than already stated; and yet many say that if John had said this then they would abandon the military. By the same reasoning one could conclude that fishing was also unsuitable, for Christ asked the disciples to leave their nets and become fishers of men. Rather, it is the principle that motivates the course of action that is more important than even the action itself. Nor on the other hand did Christ specifically tell any of the adulterous women to quit playing the harlot, but rather, "Thy faith hath saved thee", and "Go, and sin no more."

Are we to suppose that their lifestyles only needed to be reformed and not quit because they were not specifically enumerated and condemned?

Are we to suppose that these soldiers could still observe their martial oaths framed by heathen men, taken in the name of pagan deities, and designed to bind the wills of soldiers to the will of the state, after they had received the baptism of repentance? If they were not already pricked in conscience by the gospel, why did they ask, "What shall we do?" Obviously they anticipated a potential conflict between their occupation and the call to repentance.

John's answer is full of wisdom. If they can fulfill those requirements as a soldier, then let them remain a soldier. If they cannot, then they must choose between their occupation and the kingdom. We also will leave the matter to the conscience of the reader. The only thing we maintain is that this passage cannot be used as an endorsement of military service, but rather as the means by which a soldier will be judged, even if he is under contrary orders and oath. This also does not entertain the thought as to whether a believer may join the military, but rather whether a man who repents while in the military may remain there.

Another passage often cited as proof of Jesus' endorsement of soldiery is Luke 22:35-38. Here they say is Jesus' express command to purchase weaponry. Somehow this passage allegedly substantiates the necessity to kill one's enemies, as if that is the only reason to purchase a sword. But let us examine the context here.

Jesus exhorts them to sell their garment (cloak) in order to buy a sword. This presupposes that all of them do not have swords, and those who had may not have been in the habit of wearing them. Also, the purpose for them buying swords was to fulfill a specific prophecy. Nothing is suggested that they were necessary for self-defense, revolution, or a just war. The presence of swords among them gave the "appearance" of some ability to resist aggression and also created probability of suspicion for being zealous for Christ to establish an earthly kingdom. This was one of the main charges brought against Christ, that He claimed to be the King of the Jews and was a threat to national peace and Caesar's sovereignty. The presence of swords reckoned Him to be among transgressors, making Him a criminal by association.

Now if Christ were preparing for defense He surely would not have declared two swords sufficient. No military commander would ever state that his munitions are adequate when only one in every six soldiers has a weapon.

Later when Peter sought to use one of the swords he was rebuked by Christ who said, "All they that take the sword shall perish with the sword." Some have sought to minimize the import of these words by suggesting that since not all soldiers who draw the sword die violent deaths, then Christ must have had another meaning in view. They say it must mean that all who take the sword either in aggression or revenge will meet the sword of civil justice. But here again this interpretation is not any better than the former, for not every murderer, villain, pirate, or rebel has died by the sword of civil justice. Also, in this case, Peter's sword was used strictly for self-defense, which should be a just cause.

It would seem that any interpretation must recognize that the use of the word "all" suggests completeness. It would seem that Christ was merely saying "all" those that raise the sword shall bring about their own sword of destruction, so that the very instrument they use to kill will awaken within them the spirit of murder, which in turn causes them to perish eternally, as we know that no murderer hath eternal life abiding in him.

However one may interpret Jesus' words, there can be no doubt that they destroy any attempt to interpret Christ's command to buy swords as an endorsement for taking human life.

In trying to reconcile the teachings of Christ on love with the necessity to justify certain wars, the Church down through the years has adopted various means of determining whether a war is just or not. If they can establish the necessity for certain "just wars", then possibly it can be made acceptable for Christians to participate in them. Some of the common arguments have been that a "just war" is either a defensive war or an aggressive war that is fought for a greater good to be realized.

The "defensive war" theory assumes that it is right to defend yourself against an aggressor. The "just cause" theory assumes that war can be initiated against another nation if it is for the greater good of the citizens of that nation, and is in effect a type of crusade.

What these theories do admit is that not all war is good, and seek to provide criteria by which a Christian may lawfully engage in it. While it is true that some wars bring good end results and others bring only misery, the line of demarcation is somewhat blurred.

One country may assert its just cause in initiating a war, which always puts the other nation in the position of either capitulating or using the option of justly defending its borders. In many wars both sides believe their cause for fighting is just.

Who decides whether the war is just or not? If the government does, they will always declare that their cause is just. If the soldier does, then he may put himself at odds with both his nation and oath of loyalty, or he may compromise the principles of just war. Further, he may also compromise the principles John the Baptist gave the soldiers to observe. But if the soldier adheres to the principles of John the Baptist, then he may be guilty of breaking his oath of service to his nation, which is not qualified in any way to be in effect for only just wars; but if the war is unjust, this must surely constitute violence to other men. If the Christian soldier believes in just war only, then he should never take an unconditional oath but rather one that is conditioned only upon "just wars." But then again who decides, the soldier or the government?

Many have tried to evade this dilemma by creating just war criteria from the Old Testament. But wars there usually encompassed the complete destruction of all nations within Caanan, including women, children, and cattle. Outside of Palestine, Israel never engaged in a crusade for good against other heathen nations. They defended themselves against enemies but seldom campaigned to enlarge their borders. Furthermore, God had given them the land and established their boundaries. Today, in border warfare, who may justly define where boundaries of nations ought to be?

God, through the Prophets, Judges, and sometimes the King, told Israel when and when not to engage in war. Who would suppose that God now speaks to nations in the same manner concerning war? If He did, there would be no need for a just war theory but only the determination from God as to whether or not to engage. If the Old Testament does not provide criteria for a just war, surely the New Testament does not either, as it is silent upon the matter.

Christians have never agreed upon what a just cause for war is. In Colonial America, Roger Williams and the Quakers sought friendship with Indians and always sought to avoid bloodshed.

The Puritans, on the other hand, instigated a religious crusade for the destruction of Amalek (American Indians). Cotton Mather called the Indians "a treacherous and barbarous enemy" and called the colonists forth to war against "Amalek annoying this Israel in the wilderness".[15]

When Catholic France employed Indians against the colonists in the French and Indian War, the Puritan pulpits poured out God's wrath upon Popish and Anti-Christian France and her Amalekite allies, and using the illustration of Saul, called upon the colonists to completely destroy Amalek.[16]

While some may argue that the Puritans were only defending themselves, that does not accurately treat the whole matter. They were not merely defending themselves but were seeking to completely annihilate the Indians in the same manner that Saul was to destroy Amalek. Their appeal was to Old Testament criteria to drive out the heathen. If one were to fairly assess the matter, it would be in favor of the native Americans, who were justly defending the land against foreign intrusion.

But, some will argue, God led the Puritans to America for religious freedom and for the spread of the gospel. This we will also admit. But did they spread the gospel to the heathen by using the sword against them and by referring to them as Amalek? Where in Scripture was Saul instructed to convert Amalek to the truth? You cannot argue for the natives' conversion and extinction(as Amalek) both at the same time. Nor does an equation to them as Amalek correlate to a just war, but rather genocide.

Do Christians spread the gospel in a heathen land by extirpating them? The best Reformed commentators will admit that II Cor. 10:3-6 illustrates the spiritual nature of the Christian's warfare. This passage establishes that the cause of Christ is not advanced through carnal weapons, but through spiritual ones. If this be true, which it is, then the Puritan crusade against Amalek did nothing to further the gospel and was purely motivated by other causes.

When Christians take part in military conflicts, they become part of disputes between nations that are not always clear-cut as to right or wrong. Nor can it be assumed that the victor is always in the right, though God allows them to conquer. Because professing Christians have participated in war they often find themselves on opposing sides, as brothers in Christ, and killing one another because they have allowed the state to determine for them what the appropriate action is against a brother in the Lord.

Any candid person, familiar with American history, will acknowledge that during our Revolutionary and Civil wars, professing Christians fought against each other and killed one another because they accepted the government's code of conduct for treatment of the enemy. In fact, ministers on both sides of both conflicts delivered sermons explaining why their side would triumph, since their cause was right and would be blessed by God. Of course God was not for both sides nor beholden in any way to the ministers' sermons on any side, but acted in His own sovereignty.

In fact, it can never be argued that a Christian employed in a nation's military is advancing the cause of Christ by that service. The only work of the kingdom performed in the military is what is done with spiritual weapons, the same as outside the military.

The remaining question that every soldier must ask himself is, how can I, as a soldier, perform spiritual warfare for Christ without being entangled in the affairs of this life by a binding military oath (II Timothy 2:3-6). How can I love my enemies, do good to them that hate me, and be not overcome of evil, but overcome evil with good? God will be the final judge of all those who profess faith, as to whether they have been obedient to their Christian calling or have compromised it to the will of the state. It is every Christian's duty to examine his walk in the light of the Scriptures, which call us to love our fellow man, as Christ has loved us.

We will not pass judgment upon those that engage in the soldier's profession and will let that in God's hands, as John the Baptist also did, hoping they abide by his conditions for service.

The early Church record up to the year 250A.D. is quite clear and consistent upon this matter. As a rule, they refused to take human life. This is admitted by the Protestant historian, Philip Schaff, when he writes, *"But in general the Christians of those days, with their sense of foreignness to this world, and their longing for the heavenly home, or the millennial reign of Christ, were averse to a high office in a heathen state."*[17]

Again he writes, *"Some, on authority of such passages as Matthew 5:39 and 26:52, condemned all war as unchristian and immoral; anticipating the view of the Mennonites and Friends."*[18] There is evidence of some Christian soldiers around 170-180A.D., but the greatest testimony is for the peace position. Some have argued that soldiers as yet had not been converted and so their military presence was unknown. But this totally confutes their arguments of the Biblical centurions, who, after being converted, allegedly kept their military stations. If these soldiers remained in the military there should have been Christian evidence for military service from the earliest times.

Others say they did not join the military until it became christianized in order to avoid oaths taken to pagan deities. Again this argument fails, for if they refused military service because of pagan oaths, how can they presume Cornelius honored his pagan oath and the Christian faith?

The following quotations illustrate why the early Christians refused military service.

*"We who were filled with war and mutual slaughter and every wickedness have each of us in all the world changed our weapons of war...swords into plows and spears into agricultural implements." -Justin Martyr[19]*

*"Christ in disarming Peter ungirt every soldier" -Tertullian[20]*

*"God in prohibiting killing discountenances not only brigandage, which is contrary to human laws, but also that which men regard as legal. Participation in warfare therefore will not be legitimate to a just man whose military service is justice itself." - Lanctantius[21]*

The following are some Early Church Canons:

*"He who is a soldier among the believers, and among the instructed, ...and a magistrate with the sword or chief of praefects, ... let him leave off or be rejected. And a catechumen or believer, if they wish to be a soldier, shall be rejected, because it is far from God."[22]*

*"Let a catechumen or a believer of the people, if he desires to be a soldier, either cease from his intention, or if not let him be rejected. For he hath despised God by his thought, and leaving the things of the Spirit, he hath perfected himself in the flesh, and hath treated the faith with contempt."[23]*

This evidence could be greatly magnified, but it is sufficient for those willing to accept it. For further evidence, one may peruse the Pre-Constantinian writings of the early Church.

The question to consider is, if this is the general testimony of the primitive Church, how can one now call contrary doctrines "Christian" when it was the early Church that defined Christianity? As for us, we will earnestly contend for that primitive faith that was once and for all delivered unto the saints.

If the primary question in one's mind is, "How shall our nation defend its liberties if Christians refuse military service?" then the primitive and Biblical path will be unacceptable; but if the primary question be, "How shall I, as a Christian, best serve my Lord and His kingdom?" then he will be willing, if necessary, to forego earthly liberties for a kingdom not of this world.

We have looked at the main objections against the peace position but we have not examined all the positive evidence for it, as it would require too large a treatment. The foundation of it, though, is the new commandment given by Christ that we would love one another as He has loved us (John 13:34).

The ultimate requirements of the doctrines of the kingdom, when followed, produce a separation from binding allegiances to the kingdoms of this world.

If love of country is greater than the love of Christ and love to our fellow men, then we have rejected Christ's love for earthly affection. The greatest testimony of our faith is in our love one for another. We are to lay down our lives for our friends; but we may fulfill that without taking the lives of our enemies, whom we are also to love.

The kingdoms of this world deserve our obedience and respect, but not our greatest affections, for these earthly powers are influenced by the god of this world.

## The God of This World

We are told in Scripture (II Cor. 4:4) that the god of this world has blinded the minds of those that do not believe the gospel. It is Satan's power and influence over this world's system and governments that causes the people of this world to view the members of Christ's kingdom with hostility.

Jesus makes reference to Satan's fall from heaven in the past tense (Luke 10:18), who having come to earth with his fallen angels inhabits the hearts of men who open themselves to his powers. In Genesis 6:1-5 there is the account of the sons of God coming down and cohabiting with the daughters of men. There are other Scriptures that refer to angels as the sons of God (Job1:6, 2:1, 38:7). The Genesis account is the record of fallen angels coming to the earth to pervert it. This view was held by both Jews and the early Christians. Saints are also called sons of God but it is through adoption and not creation or natural birth. The Genesis account sets the sons of God in contrast to the daughters of men, the difference between angelic beings and humanity. The result of their copulation is the production of a giant race of men of great renown but also of extreme wickedness, which provoked God to destroy the earth.

While it is true that angels in their created state do not reproduce, it is evident from Genesis that the fallen angels had the ability to sexually pervert the human race for a time. Even today the witches at their Sabbats speak of having intercourse with the devil.

Satan works through his fallen angels, known as demons, to blind the men of this world to truth, and uses his power to influence the rulers of the kingdoms of this world. Just as the demon offspring from the Genesis account became great men in the world, so it is Satan's plan to use the powers of earthly kingdoms and their glory to gain control of the lives of men.

In Daniel's visions of world events, Michael spoke to him of Spiritual Powers that sought to prevent God's plan. He is referred to as the "prince of Persia" (Daniel 10:13, 20, 21); that is, the demon that controls the man who is the prince of Persia, probably Cyrus. The demonic powers seek to rule this world by influencing and controlling the world's leaders.

The prophet Ezekiel brings an oracle against the prince of Tyrus, the ruler of a mighty city of that time. But in the oracle Ezekiel addresses none other than Satan himself, as is evident in chapter 28:11-19 by phrases that describe Tyrus as the perfection of creation and containing attributes possessed by no mere mortal. It is Satan and his power that was behind the ruler of Tyre, and therefore Ezekiel speaks to both of the impending judgment for sin.

Satan is continually seeking to control the political powers of this world through demonic influence.

The prophet Isaiah in his oracle against the world power of Babylon specifically also addresses Satan (Isaiah 14:12-14), in the prophecies of coming judgment.

Because of Satan's influence over worldly powers, he felt confident that he could offer the glory of them to Christ, if Christ would but worship him (Matthew 4:8,9).

Satan's influence in the world has become so great that the Apostle John stated, "*All* that is in the world ... is not of the Father, but is of the world," showing the extent of his corruption of worldly things.

One of the chief aims of Satan is to use his political powers to make war upon the saints, the inheritors of the everlasting Kingdom. In Revelation 12:7-17, John speaks of the devil being cast out of heaven and coming down to the earth with great wrath and making war upon those "which keep the commandments of God, and have the testimony of Jesus Christ." There are different prophetic views on who the seed of the woman is, but however it may be interpreted, the point remains that there is enmity between the seed of the woman and the serpent who is bent on their destruction.

The greatest wrath of Satan will be revealed through the coming Antichrist and his war upon the saints. Paul, in II Thessalonians 2:1-9 speaks of this man of sin as one who "opposeth and exalteth himself above all that is called God." He is in *opposition* to *all* that God has ordained and to all His workings among His people. Daniel speaks of this man as the little horn that shall make war with the saints and seek to wear them out by his continual and bloody persecution of them.

This man shall be granted a season of power over all nations of the earth and shall use it to enforce a system of false worship, and put to death all those who resist his rule (Revelation 13:4-10). He uses the world's political institutions to wage war on the saints.

The only thing that is keeping Satan at bay presently is God's restraint upon him until the end of the age (II Thess. 2:6-10), when it will be the time for his revelation.

# Sovereignty of God in Worldly Affairs

We have seen how the Scriptures portray the Satanic influence upon the nations of this world and how the demonic powers control some of them, but yet even those wicked powers are used of God to fulfill His plans in world events.

Psalm 2:2,3 speaks of the rebellion of the kings of the earth against the rule of God and His Anointed One. But yet He that sits in the heavens laughs and has them in derision for their attempts to thwart the purposes of Christ's kingdom.

When Pharaoh attempted to completely subjugate Israel, God merely used that opportunity to have His name declared through all the earth by the use of miracles and plagues through the hand of Moses (Romans 9:17).

In the preceding section we have seen from Daniel that there were demonic powers behind the "prince of Persia" that withstood Michael, but in Isaiah 44:28-45:4 this same prince (Cyrus) is called "God's Shepherd" and will "perform all my pleasure." The Lord refers to Cyrus as His anointed, who will subdue nations so that he would know that God had called him to this office by name, that His elect might glorify Him for His sovereign rule over heathen powers.

The Greek general Xenophon, who was an ally to Cyrus during his conquests, refers to him also in his history as "God's Shepherd." Cyrus was raised as a child by a shepherd in order to avoid a death sentence placed upon him. According to the Jewish historian, Josephus, Cyrus read the Isaiah prophecies concerning him and had a great desire to fulfill them and eventually ordered the rebuilding of the Jewish temple and the city of Jerusalem. Here then was a heathen Persian Monarch, who, though under the influence of a demonic spirit, was fully controlled by God and executed His plan so perfectly that God could say "whose right hand I have holden."

Perhaps some wonder how a generally wise and benevolent king as Cyrus could be under Satanic influence. The answer lies in the fact that he was a practicing idolater and those who sacrifice to gods are worshiping devils ( I Cor. 10:19,20), and thus are under demonic influence. But even the devils and those they inhabit are subject to God's kingdom, who ruleth over all.

In the book of Daniel we are told explicitly that the kingdoms of the earth are set up by God Himself, and He establishes those who will rule, even the basest of men (Daniel 4:17).

Though wicked men may rule over the nations of this earth, God has the heart of those men in His hand and He will turn it to accomplish His own will (Proverbs 21:1).

God's rule over human government is so assured that Paul refers to the political rulers as "ministers of God" attending continually upon His work (Romans 13:4-6). Paul says categorically that the "powers that be are ordained of God." This means that all government rule takes place under the watchful eye of God, and whether or not they rule well, they are there by Divine appointment. There is not one word by Paul to suggest that only "Christian" government is ordained by God, but rather "the powers that be" or that already exist, which at the time of this writing was Emperor Nero, one who surely was not a religious man.

God's desire as laid out in Romans 13 is that civil government reward the good and punish the evil, but above all that His affection lies with the kingdom which was established by Christ while here on earth. All kingdoms of this earth are merely part of the eternal plan that God has for the kingdom of the saints.

Daniel speaks of a kingdom being established during the fourth world empire (Rome) that would grow into a mountain which will fill the whole earth and consume all other earthly kingdoms and stand for eternity (Daniel 2:44). This kingdom was to be ruled by the Son of Man, with its reign extending over the entire earth (Daniel 7:13,14). This kingdom is also to be possessed by the saints who are joint-heirs with Christ (Daniel 7:18).

The kingdom was to begin during the time of Rome's rule, which places it during the first advent of Christ. As we have seen previously, the gospel of the kingdom was preached by John the Baptist and Christ while here on earth and empowered by the Spirit during the ministries of the Apostles. The establishment of the Church was the institution of the kingdom of Christ on this earth. It is not seen by physical observation but is a spiritual kingdom that lies within us, where Christ reigns supreme, and to whom we give our deepest affection. It is "not of this world", as Jesus explained to Pilate, but yet it is a kingdom that will possess and destroy all other kingdoms. Those who have been translated by new birth into the kingdom will also realize the full extent of it when it fills the whole earth and literally breaks in pieces the kingdoms of this world. But we must first walk the path of our Saviour and suffer with Him, that we also might reign with Him.

1  D. L. Miller, Eternal Verifies p. 138, 139 (1915 Brethren Publishing House)

2  Flavius Josephus, Book XI, Chapter VIII, entire account

3  Leonard Verduin, The Reformers and Their Stepchildren p. 107, parenthesis mine (1991 The Christian Hymnary Publishers)

4  John Calvin, Institutes of the Christian Religion, Book IV, Chapter 1, article 2, parenthesis mine

5  Ibid, Book IV, Chapter 1, article 13

6  Philip Schaff, History of the Christian Church Vol. III p. 368, 369 (1991 WM. B. Eerdmans Publishing Company)

7  Leonard Verduin, The Reformers and Their Stepchildren p. 113, 114 (1991 The Christian Hymnary Publishers)

8  Ibid p. 68, footnotes, parenthesis mine

9  John Calvin, Institutes of the Christian Religion, Book IV, Chap XV, Point I

10  David E. Maas, Liberty and Law p. 3 (1987 WM. B. Eerdmans Publishing Company)

11  Ibid p. 5

12  Ibid p. 6

13  Ibid p. 7

14  Homily of John Chrysostom on Matthew 5:33-37

15  Roland H. Bainton, Christian Attitudes Toward War and Peace, p. 168 (1960 Abingdon Press)

16  Ibid p. 169

17  Philip Schaff, History of the Christian Church, Vol. II p. 345 (1991 WM. B. Eerdmans Publishing Company)

18  Ibid p. 344

19  Roland H. Bainton, Christian Attitudes Toward War and Peace p. 72 (1960 Abingdon Press)

20  Ibid p. 73

21  Ibid

22  Guy F. Hershberger, War, Peace, and Nonresistance p. 69( 1953 Herald Press)

23  Ibid

come out of her my people

# chapter four

# The Literal Reign of Christ Upon This Earth

## WHY AN UNDERSTANDING OF THE MILLENNIAL REIGN OF CHRIST IS IMPORTANT

The reader may wonder why a study of, or a belief in, the millennium has any relevance at all to this work. There are a number of prophetic Scriptures that equate the rule and kingdom of Christ to an earthly and civil context. These prophecies are God's inspired Word and must and will be fulfilled. The issue then, is how and when are they fulfilled. To ignore them or attempt to spiritualize them to the point where they have no meaning is not acceptable to any serious and honest student of the Word.

These Scriptures are all brought to fulfillment in Christ. The question then is, are they fulfilled in the first or second advent? Many of the Old Testament prophecies combine the first and second advent together in the same passage. This may cause some confusion as to when they find their fulfillment. The main purpose of the prophets, we believe, for including the advents together in the same passages is to illustrate that the historical man known as Jesus, who fulfilled the prophecies relating to the birth of the Immanuel is the same man who will one day rule all nations with a rod of iron. This style of the prophets helps to prevent the notion that two different individuals could be in view, since some prophecies speak of a suffering Savior while others of a king over all the earth. But when His birth and His government are brought together in one passage such as Isaiah 9:6, 7 the prophet removes all doubt that this individual is man (is born), God (the Mighty God), and king over an earthly realm(upon the throne of David).

God, who performs all His acts with wisdom and foreknowledge, has anticipated the arguments and doubts of men and answered their cavils even before they are raised. The angel who announced His birth to Mary not only proclaimed Him Savior (Matthew 1:21), but also the Son of the highest, who would sit upon the throne of David and reign over the house of Jacob forever (Luke 1:32, 33). The angel dispelled all doubt that these two concepts were irreconcilable.

Some think that the two advents are not clearly identified in the Old Testament prophecies. A cursory overview may make the two advents a bit obscure, but there is explicit Scripture that speaks of them. Micah 5:2 says His "goings (plural) forth have been from of old," an allusion to the fact that there will be more than one.

Jesus' birth, death, resurrection, and ascension (Psalm 68:18) spoken of in Old Testament prophecies all indicate the necessity of a coming again to fulfill the rest of them completely.

There are many prophetic Scriptures in the Old Testament that speak of the "Day of the Lord" as His coming to this earth in a literal manner. This is very explicit in Zechariah 14, that He will stand upon the mount of Olives (vs. 4) and be king over all the earth (vs. 9). If His kingship is taken in a spiritual sense such as the manner in which He now is Governor of the nations, then this passage has no significance at all, for it does not prophesy anything that was not already in effect with God Himself. But the prophet says "the Lord shall be king over all the earth: IN THAT DAY...," identifying a significant change of events. This event begins with the "day of the Lord" spoken of in verse one of the chapter, a still future event (II Peter 3:10).

It cannot honestly be denied then, that the Old Testament does indeed link a Kingship over the earth to the man Jesus in His second advent as the final fulfillment of the Messianic prophecies.

It may be argued that until Christ's death had occurred, the power of sin had not been destroyed; therefore with the commencement of the age of grace, Christ's reign has begun; because all authority has been given Him in heaven and in earth. It is agreed as we have seen previously that Christ has been exalted to the right hand of the Father, far above all principalities and powers and as such is reigning over the affairs of this life. On this premise the Scripture is very clear. His kingdom also is portrayed as, "not of this world" but a spiritual rule in the hearts of men; for it cometh not with observation but is within us (Luke 17:20, 21), which also extends over all the kingdoms of this world. This is the spiritual aspect of the kingdom, which makes it differ from all other earthly kingdoms, in that the rule of Christ not only governs the outward actions but also the thoughts and intents of the heart. The rule of Christ, which orders the affairs of this world to serve eternal purposes, is also outside the kingdom of heaven, which is comprised only of those who have been born of water and of the Spirit.

Christ first rules in the hearts of those who have been born again into His kingdom and then shall rule with His saints after the day of the Lord, when righteousness shall cover the earth. The fourteenth chapter of Zechariah speaks of a rule of Christ that will not be realized until He returns and stands upon the mount of Olives at the day of the Lord. There is certain criteria in this chapter (Zech. 14) that must be met in order for this to be fulfilled, which also illustrates why it must yet be in the future. All the nations of the world must be assembled together against Jerusalem (vs. 2), and then the Lord will go out Himself, and fight against those nations (vs. 3), and bring a great destruction upon them (vs. 12, 13) (Ezekiel 38:18-39:21, Revelation 19:11-21).

There has never been a time in history when "all" nations have been gathered against Jerusalem to battle when the Lord went out against them and slew them with a great slaughter. When Rome came against Jerusalem (in 70A.D.) this was not "all" the nations, nor did the Lord lay waste their armies, for they, in fact, wasted Israel. The battle spoken of here is yet future. The mount of Olives has not cleaved in half (vs. 4) forming a great valley. It is when these events take place that the Lord shall be King over all the earth (vs. 9). This is His second coming as described in Revelation 19:15 when he shall smite the nations and rule them with a rod of iron.

Some have sought to evade the import of this passage by spiritualizing this coming of the Lord. If the graphic descriptions of this passage are merely spiritual illustrations, then upon what basis do we suppose Christ's first coming was a literal revelation of God in the flesh? Was He merely a phantom figure upon whom a divine spirit rested? Shades of Gnosticism! (Gnostics denied that God could become visible flesh). Any attempt to evade the literal events of this passage is the equal hermeneutics of spiritualizing the first advent.

What practical value, then, does an understanding of a literal millennium have? The passages that speak of the rule of Christ in the civil affairs of this earth must either apply to His first or second coming. If they are applied to the first coming, then it must be spiritualized to some degree; either wholly, which then leads us to the same type of interpretation that could spiritualize the whole first advent, or partially (spiritualized), which would understand His rule as a spiritual influence upon the civil powers of this earth. While it is granted that the kingdom of Christ has a spiritual influence now upon earthly powers, this does not fully address how Christ will rule when He comes again, as described in Zechariah 14 and Revelation 19.

The spiritual systems of understanding are known as Amillennialism and Postmillennialism. Amillennialism was never held by any significant number of the early Church leaders, if even any at all, (that we have record of) until the Church united with the state under the rule of Constantine. The earlier Christians all looked forward to the future rule of Christ upon this earth; but when the Church and the state interlocked arms, the Church began spiritualizing the millennial passages and understanding that the reign of Christ would be realized through Christian civil leaders. They saw the triumph of

Christianity over paganism in Rome as a sign of the thousand years of Christ's rule. Augustine was primarily responsible for making this dogma popular in the Church once he fully embraced the concept of a Church state.

This concept was fully embraced by the Reformers also, as they sought to establish "Christian" countries.

But if the rule of Christ was implemented and Satan was bound, why now have the nations of this world become decadent under Christ's civil rule? Has His rule been overthrown? Has it ceased? Why has its prophesied continual increase ceased? How will Christ rule at His second coming over the nations of this earth if those prophecies are already fulfilled? Yet the Scriptures indicate there will be a rule of Christ over the nations at His appearing (Rev. 19:15). There is nothing in Scripture to indicate that Christ's direct civil rule over the nations of this world (even though He now sits at the right hand of God) will occur before He returns as Lord of Lords and King of Kings. He is now calling men into His Kingdom through the gospel, and those who are called and chosen will be joint heirs together with Him when He returns. Those who have suffered with Him will also reign with Him.

We may wonder still what practical bearing the premillennial understanding of prophecy has upon our daily life. A premillennial understanding of prophecy is a major tenet that supports a separation of Church and state as well as religious liberty. If Christ is ruling now, in fulfillment of the millennial prophecies, through civil powers, then they have every right to institute Christian laws, for they themselves are under the rule of Christ, and verily ARE the rule of Christ. It is this understanding that undergirded Reformed thinking of the necessity for having National Covenants and binding religious oaths in order to compel men to accept the true faith, so that the civil rule of Christ might be advanced.

It was the rise of Premillennial thought, largely through the Baptists, that helped to overthrow Postmillennial (and Amillennial to a lesser degree) thinking that all governments of this world should be coerced to embrace the Christian faith. With the spread of their doctrines through the world, religious liberty was again given its proper Christian understanding and the Church was separated from the affairs of the state.

It should be remembered that while we object to the state being a Christian institution, we recognize that it is its duty to uphold and enforce the morality of God's law. This distinction is very important and will be treated more thoroughly later.

What is maintained here is that our view of prophecy can directly influence our relationship to civil authorities. The Reconstructionists of today, who are a branch of Ultra (classical)-Reformed thinking, fully understand this and are working hard to promote Postmillennialism as a major tenet of their doctrines in their attempt to establish Christianity as a national faith here in America.

There is no doctrine of Scripture, when fully understood and firmly believed, that does not impact the manner in which we live, for as a man thinketh in his heart so is he. All Scripture is given by inspiration of God and is profitable for doctrine, reproof, and instruction in righteousness. The doctrines of Scripture are not merely mental understandings but rather also equip the man of God for good works; that is, so that he lives what he believes.

Premillennialism recognizes the prophecies concerning Christ's literal rule on earth, but it also puts them in the proper time frame when they will find their true fulfillment. Christ was the fulfillment of His own prophecies at His first advent and will be again at His second also. He does not need men to try to crown Him with earthly powers, for that will happen when God speaks to the nations of this world and says, "Serve the Lord with fear, and rejoice with trembling. KISS THE SON..."

We will labor in the gospel of the kingdom until the Lord shall see fit to cover the earth with His knowledge as waters cover the sea.

# THE CERTAINTY OF A MILLENNIAL KINGDOM
*Proofs from the Old Testament*

We will not consider every passage that could be examined but will look at some crucial ones that speak of the rule of Christ.

In Micah 5:2 we have one of the most famous and explicit prophecies concerning Christ. The prophecy pinpointed the birthplace of Messiah so that there could be no mistake as to His identity. Yet here He is identified as a ruler in Israel; that is to say that the same one which was birthed in a stable will one day be crowned with power. There are several things in the verses that follow (3-7) that are to be fulfilled by the one born in Bethlehem. He is spoken of as having "goings" (plural) forth, which indicate that this prophecy comprehends events of both of His comings. He is spoken of as waiting for Israel's travail, or the day of "Jacob's trouble" spoken of in Jeremiah 30:1-11, when He shall then appear and bring back the remnant of His brethren, the Jews, to their own land, under His rule. Jeremiah says at the time of their trouble, David (Messianic implication) will be raised up to rule over them. This return of the Jews to their land takes place after the appearance of the King. They return *to* others of the children of Israel, which indicates that some are already returned to Palestine and are now joined by great numbers. The return spoken of here cannot refer to that under Ezra, as that took place BEFORE Christ's advent and this is AFTER.

Micah goes on and speaks of Messiah's rule being great even to the ends of the earth. A rebellion is spoken of under His rule, from Assyria, the land of Nimrod; but He shall go forth and utterly lay waste that land. There has never been a time in all Israel's history where they (Israel) devastated the land of Assyria. The Lord accomplished a great slaughter against Sennacherib when he invaded Judah, but yet they (Israel) only escaped destruction and did not destroy the Assyrian power or lay waste his land. This prophecy must yet be fulfilled under the rule of Christ when He returns to rule the nations with a rod of iron. In that day Christ shall execute vengeance upon the heathen as they have never heard (Micah 5:15).

These prophecies can only be fulfilled in the future by Christ through His literal reign on this earth.

Micah, in chapter 4 verses 1-5, speaks of the peace on earth during this time, as well as the universal knowledge of true worship. Many nations shall come to Jerusalem to be taught of Christ in the ways of the Lord. He will rebuke the nations of military strength so that they will beat their weapons into plowshares, and not learn war anymore. The promise of world peace has never been given to the Church age, but rather that there will be wars and rumors of wars and great tribulation right up until the return of Christ. The only lasting peace this world will know is when it is administered by the Prince of Peace. We may now carry the gospel of peace into all the world and bring it into the hearts of men so that they personally will beat their spears into pruning hooks, but until Christ returns there will not be lasting national or universal peace. For when they say, "peace and safety", sudden destruction shall come upon them. What Micah has in view in this prophecy is yet reserved for the future.

Isaiah is well known as a prophetic book, and chapter 11 contains some specific prophecies that address His birth 2,000 years ago, as well as events that are linked to His second coming. In verses 4-9 a time is spoken of when He will smite the earth with the rod of His mouth and uphold the cause of the poor and meek. During this time even the carnivorous animals shall lose their predatory instincts and will become omnivorous and peaceful. The whole earth will be full of the knowledge of the Lord. When these events are taking place, God shall set His hand upon Israel to return the SECOND TIME to their land. Many try to interpret the passages speaking of the regathering of the Jews to Israel as referring to the return of the Jews to their land during the times of Ezra and Nehemiah. But God has said that there will be a SECOND TIME that they shall return.

The outcasts of Israel will come from the four corners of the earth, not merely from Persia as initially they came. This regathering is spoken of as taking place after Christ's return, and after His rule has been established. There can be no doubt that the regathering under Ezra was not the "second" time.

Some may insist that the return under Ezra was the first, and the second time occurred at Pentecost when Jews gathered there from every nation under heaven and heard the gospel being preached. But this does not meet all the criteria for the second regathering, for when they are brought to Israel this time it is to be scattered no more. Amos 9:15 speaks also of this return and says:

"And I will plant them upon their land, and they shall NO MORE be pulled up out of their land which I have given them, saith the Lord thy God."

The Jews were scattered into all the earth again after Pentecost when Jerusalem was destroyed, so the "second time" spoken of here in Isaiah or Amos cannot yet be fully fulfilled. If the second time refers to their return after the coming of Christ, how then do we account for the Jews' return to Israel as a nation in 1948?

This can be viewed in two ways; either the first time being under Ezra and the second time beginning in 1948 and extending to the return of Christ when there will be a great increase of returning, or it may be viewed as the first time occurring in 1948 and onward with the second time being after the return of Christ. However a person wishes to view this, he must acknowledge that the return under Ezra or at Pentecost does not fulfill this prophecy even remotely; for they must return at a time when they will be no more scattered.

Also, there are prophecies that reveal that the Jews will be already in the land when Christ returns. Zechariah 13:7-14:4 speaks of the day of the Lord occurring after two-thirds of the Jews are cut off at Jerusalem, with the other third being refined in the fire (Jacob's trouble). All nations will be gathered against them at Jerusalem when the Lord returns. This passage illustrates that the Jews must be in their land when the day of the Lord occurs.

Ezekiel 38 and 39 record the account of Gog and Magog coming against Israel, the land brought back from the sword, *a people brought forth out of the nations*, in the latter days (Ezekiel 38:8,16). The battle spoken of here cannot refer to Jerusalem in 70A.D. when Titus besieged the city, for in this account, just like Zechariah 14, the Lord Himself gives the victory to Israel, as opposed to a loss being suffered by Israel. This account also verifies that Israel returns to their land *before* the day of the Lord. In Ezekiel 39:25,27 the Lord speaks of bringing them forth yet again from all the nations where they had been scattered.

It would seem from all these Scriptures that Ezra's return was not in view at all even as the first regathering, but rather that the first time is the gathering we see now, and the second time being that which God Himself shall perform after the return of Christ. These gatherings are all spoken of as being in the "latter days", a time frame which cannot precede the first coming of Christ (Acts 2:17, Hebrews 1:2).

A return of Israel to their land, according to Jeremiah 30:3-7, will take place before the time of Jacob's trouble, which is before the SECOND return at the appearing of Christ.

These passages all speak of a literal return of the Jews to their ancient lands before the return of Christ and after His coming; all of which cannot take place unless the world continues to exist after His return. The return of the Jews to Israel after the coming of Christ speaks of His literal reign on a physical earth. They are called out of the nations from where they were scattered, indicating also the presence of other nations on the earth after Christ's return. The nations of the earth will beseech the Jews for permission to go with them up to Jerusalem to pray and learn the ways of the Lord (Zechariah 8:20-23). The promises such as these to the nation of Israel speak of a millennial period on this earth when Christ shall rule, from Jerusalem, over both the Jews and the Gentiles after He returns.

In Daniel chapter 7 there is given a time line of the nations of this world right up until the Ancient of Days comes with power to establish His own kingdom. The four beasts, representing the four world empires of Babylonia, Persia, Greece, and Rome are described also in chapter two of Daniel in the vision of the Great Image. Daniel indicates that the kingdom of God shall be established in the days of the kings of the fourth kingdom (Daniel 2:44), and that it shall last forever. The time of the fourth kingdom (Rome) directly correlates to the time when John the Baptist preached, "Repent, for the kingdom of heaven is at hand."

That was the purely spiritual phase of the kingdom that we enter by new birth, and which is preached in all the earth by the saints, as well as the invisible sovereign rule of Christ over the visible nations of this world. This kingdom has Christ as its head; the One to whom, after His resurrection, was given all power in heaven and in earth (Matthew 28:18). But yet there is another phase of this kingdom which is both as spiritual and literal as His return will be.

The fourth beast described by Daniel is that same beast of seven heads and ten horns that will be cast into perdition when God's judgment falls upon this world at the end of the age (Revelation 19:19-21). This fourth kingdom is spoken of as the kingdom that is in power at the beginning of Christ's kingdom (as already seen), which also opposes it (II Thess. 2:4, 7), then disappears for a time and reappears at the end of the age to make war with the saints again (Revelation 17:8-14). Daniel illustrates the resurrection of the fourth kingdom in the symbolism of the "Little Horn" who wars against the saints until the Ancient of Days comes and destroys him and sets up His own everlasting kingdom over all people, nations, and languages (Daniel 7:8-27).

Here again is a pattern of events that begins with the fourth kingdom and moves to Christ's kingdom (gospel age), the Little Horn, the great tribulation, the revelation of Christ, and ends with Christ establishing His dominion over all the earth AFTER He returns. Daniel's prophecies portray Christ establishing an earthly dominion when He returns to judge the earth (Daniel 7:9-14).

We have already looked into Zechariah 14 and made some observations concerning Christ's kingdom. This chapter also lays out a clear time line of events. The chapter begins with a universal army laying siege to Jerusalem (vs. 2) which is ended by the appearance of the day of the Lord, in which the Lord decisively engages the besieging troops (vs. 3). The Lord then establishes Himself as King over all the earth in a literal sense (vs. 9) and also establishes a spiritual rule that promotes "holiness unto the Lord" (vs. 17-21). These prophetic passages that were examined are by no means the only evidence of an earthly millennium from the Old Testament but they are strong and sufficient enough to prove the proposition being made.

The case for the millennium, or earthly civil reign of Christ, can be deduced also from New Testament Scriptures.

## Proofs from the New Testament

When examining the Scripture and drawing conclusions it is important that we understand the Old Testament in light of the most recent revelation of God's Word as contained in the New Testament. It is erroneous, though, to assume the Old Testament prophecies do not apply any longer, or can simply be ignored if they do not fit our understanding of eschatology that is derived from the New Testament alone.

What is in view here is that the Old Testament Scriptures cannot be ignored, but rather they must be interpreted in a manner that is consistent with New Testament passages on the same subject. We should understand Old Testament prophecy with the mind and doctrine of Christ (II Cor. 3:12-18). To isolate them from New Testament Scripture can open us up to making grave errors. It is not that the Old Testament is any less inspired than the New, but rather that God gave us a clearer revelation when He spoke through His Son in these latter days.

The examination of New Testament passages on the millennial reign is crucial, so that the unity of Scripture be maintained. Here again, not all the passages in the New Testament will be considered, but some of those that are key to a prophetic understanding of Christ's future kingdom.

The first passage that we shall examine is Luke 22:28-30. The context of the passage was over who should be greatest among them.

It is interesting that this dispute should arise after they have washed one another's feet, as servants to one another, as the Lord Himself gave an example, and have broken bread together as brethren. They then, after Judas has been exposed, are wondering who shall be the greatest. Most likely this discussion was the result of them realizing that Jesus will soon be gone and as yet there is no establishment of prominent leadership among the remaining eleven. If Jesus ever intended for Peter to be a Pope over the whole Christian church, now would have been a perfect time to institute that office, so that the rest of the apostles would recognize his preeminence. But rather Christ exhorts them all to servanthood, as He has given them an example. He also says that these remaining eleven (and the one yet to be added to the number) who have remained faithful to Christ in His temptations (afflictions, trials) would be appointed to thrones in the same kingdom that was appointed to Christ by His Father, judging the twelve tribes of Israel. Christ's premise is this: here in this life leadership is to model servanthood; and for those who are faithful through the tests and trials here (temptations), He will appoint a place of honor and distinction in His coming kingdom. He is illustrating the exact principle that the Apostle Paul lays down to Timothy: "If we suffer, we shall also reign with Him."

Christ further states that they will eat and drink at His table in His kingdom. When instituting the bread and cup, Jesus said He would no more eat and drink of it until He partook of it anew in the kingdom of God. Here then Christ indicates a future time when He again shall literally eat and drink with His disciples in His kingdom, during which time they shall be judges over the twelve tribes of Israel. This promise has not and cannot be fulfilled in the present age. Christ's promise to eat and drink with them is as literal as the actions of eating and drinking He was portraying to them at the time He uttered the words.

He is about to be executed as a "King of the Jews" and as of yet has demonstrated no dominion. But Jesus assures them of a future kingdom and a position in it. He cannot be referring to His spiritual kingdom, for He has already told them that such a kingdom is within you (Luke 17:21). His promise to the apostles to sit upon thrones did not refer to theirs or any other person's heart. That realm is reserved alone for the Trinity, not for the apostles. The kingdom, thrones, and the Lord's table were all future promises to the apostles who would partake of the afflictions of Christ. Israel as a nation has never yet submitted to the authority of twelve apostles; so that part of the promise also remains to be fulfilled.

A very similar promise is given in Matthew 19:27-29 to the apostles. Those that have forsaken all to follow Christ, in the regeneration (the renewal of all things) will be granted a position in judgment of the twelve tribes of Israel. The promise is then extended to believers at large who forsake all to answer the call of Christ, to receive a hundredfold return in the age that is to come. Our reward promised is one that is incorruptible and is not realized in this present age. There is a kingdom yet to come wherein the apostles will be granted authority and the believer his rewards.

Based upon those promises, it is no wonder that the disciples again asked Christ before His ascension if the kingdom was going to be restored to Israel at this time (Acts 1:6, 7). Many Amillennialists deride the apostles for such a question, as if they yet were naive to the fact that the kingdom prophecies only have a spiritual application. This is merely the assesssment of a person who claims more knowledge than the apostles possessed at this time.

There are some truths that must be noticed here. It is quite evident that the apostles were still expecting a literal kingdom of Christ which involved Israel as a nation. After having been with Jesus all these years He had said nothing to make them believe that the Old Testament prophecies concerning the restoration of Israel were in any way nullified. They still expected their fulfillment. Furthermore, there was nothing in Jesus' answer that chided them at all for anticipating a coming kingdom. Jesus was not remiss in rebuking them for lack of understanding (Luke 24:25-27) in matters of comprehending Old Testament prophecies, but rather gave exposition as needed. Yet here Jesus' answer in no way corrects their anticipation, but rather asks that they be patient until its proper time, whereas now they were to be endued with heavenly power to spread the gospel of the kingdom in this present age.

Even after Pentecost, Peter retains this future hope. After having healed the lame man, he commences a sermon to the Jews on Christ, who was crucified through ignorance, but yet needed to die in order that the Scripture might be fulfilled. His Jewish audience would have recoiled at believing Jesus as their Messiah, since He was dead and gone (possibly resurrected) and had instituted no kingdom. Peter knew this was a stumbling block to the Jewish mind, and so in Acts 3:19-21 he explains that Christ (Messiah), after suffering and dying to fulfill prophecy, will return, when sent by God, to usher in the "times of refreshing" and the "restitution of *all* things" (new heaven and new earth) in order to fulfill all the words of the prophets given since the world began. The "times of refreshing" and "restitution of all things" have a direct relationship to the return of Christ and the fulfillment of Old Testament prophecies. Peter explains that the Jewish hope is not nullified but rather will not be implemented until Messiah returns again. The present age, he explains, is when God must fulfill the promise to Abraham, "In thy seed shall all nations of the earth be blessed" (Acts 3:25). Peter's intent is to show that the other prophecies will yet be fulfilled by Christ, but the man Jesus whom they have crucified is He, and His life and death have also been predicted by the prophets and have been fulfilled. Peter's explanation includes both the church age and the Messianic kingdom, giving to the Jew the urgency to come to repentance now, so that they might be worthy to obtain their future inheritance.

The first church council at Jerusalem, when dealing with the subject of circumcision and keeping Moses' law, also established an understanding of the gospel age and the millennial kingdom in order to fully address the issue (Acts 15:13-18). Peter (Simeon - Hebrew name for Simon) had already addressed the assembly, explaining how God had begun His work among the Gentiles, when James, who presided over this council, took the floor and concurred with Peter's observations. James explained that *before* God would rebuild the tabernacle of David, He *first* would visit the Gentiles. The conversions of the Gentiles were a fulfillment of Old Testament prophecies which spoke of Gentiles trusting in Christ. The times of the Gentiles was upon them and was the reason why they could be accepted into the Jewish body of believers without observing Moses' law. James goes on then to paraphrase the Septuagint version of Amos 9:11,12 by saying, "AFTER THIS I WILL RETURN and build AGAIN the tabernacle of David, which is fallen down."

James explains to the assembly that the Gentile church age does not negate God's prophetic promise to Israel but rather, after Christ returns, David's tabernacle, which lies in ruins, will be rebuilt. When Israel is restored to the Lord it will bring many more Gentiles to the Lord. We have already seen that this great return of Israel begins before the return of Christ but greatly increases *after* the return of Christ. James uses the future promises to the Jews to assure them that the Gentile church age does not destroy their hope of Israel's restoration, for it happens AFTER THIS; that is, after the present age. For this reason they could allow the Gentiles into the same body, even if they did not keep the law, without having any fear that this acceptance would negate God's covenant promises to Israel.

It has been examined how Christ has yet promised Israel a restoration and the apostles a position of leadership in that kingdom; a kingdom which shall never be destroyed; a kingdom which occupies a new heaven and a new earth wherein dwells righteousness, as well as lasting for all eternity. The promise of privilege to rule has extended beyond the apostles to those who overcome and persevere to the end. Revelation 2:26, 27 includes a promise to overcomers that they will rule the nations with a rod of iron, even as Christ has received this privilege from His Father. This is a promise that finds fulfillment after the end; that is, the end of time as we presently know it. There is no such promise granted to believers in this age, that if they overcome they shall rule the nations with a rod of iron. It is a promise that finds fulfillment when Christ Himself comes to rule the nations of this world, as recorded in Revelation 19:15. Our reign over the nations of this world is concurrent with Christ's rule and not with man's rule. The rule of Christ over the nations in a literal sense occurs at His physical reappearing, and at this time all those who have suffered with Him shall also reign with Him. This honor is not limited to those who are elected to civil office, as in our times, but rather is extended to *all* His saints (Psalm 149:6-9).

Revelation 19:15 is a direct fulfillment of Psalm 2:7-9. Christ came first as a man-child to this earth and was then caught up to the throne of God (Revelation 12:5), but shall return to fulfill the prophecy to rule all nations with a rod of iron. The first part of Psalm 2 is quoted in Acts 4:25, 26 to show how Christ fulfilled the prophecy made concerning the heathen powers being united together against "the Christ". The latter part of Psalm 2 is quoted in Revelation 19:15 as being fulfilled at Christ's second coming, when he shall destroy the nations of the earth who have gathered together against Him. Both of these passages together teach that the man known as Jesus will also one day rule as Messiah, for He is "the Christ".

Many Amillennialists teach that the only possible New Testament allusion to a literal millennium is the "vague" passage in Revelation 20:1-10, which they say should be interpreted spiritually. In so saying they ignore large bodies of prophecy contained in the Old Testament which speak of the restoration of Israel and Christ's kingdom, which also are supported by the other teachings of the New Testament.

It is necessary for us to answer some of the questions that the Amillennialists raise in regards to Revelation 20:1-10. First of all, the millennium is not established alone by this passage, but rather by the time that this passage is reached in God's unfolding revelation it is already a foregone conclusion. This passage gives us a length of time for Christ's kingdom (1,000 years), as well as some details surrounding it.

The Amillenialist will first try to prove that this passage is merely an analogy of a spiritual and figurative kingdom with 1,000 years being only a relative time line. Typically they will begin by saying that the binding of Satan is a spiritual restraint that was put upon him by Christ, as illustrated by the analogy of the strong man in Matthew 12:29, since the same words (bind) are used in both passages. Then they will use the examples of passages that refer to Satan's work being destroyed by Christ's death upon the cross. And yet the binding they say is merely a figurative restraint. On one hand they argue that the binding is only a restraint but on the other they say it represents his power being destroyed on the cross. The one binding is done before the crucifixion and the other at the crucifixion. Yet the passage here says that the angel actually comes and performs the act at the END of the 1000 years, which they allege is the Church age. This could not then refer to either Jesus' ministry or His death upon the cross, for they both occurred BEFORE the Church age (1000 years).

The previous context is Christ's return, with the capture of the beast and the false prophet when their armies are destroyed. Since there are no chapters in the original text it only makes sense that Satan's binding is a continuance of the previous context; his apprehension being the last act of the elimination of the unholy trinity and their armies.

This binding of Satan is given in a specific sense; that he should *deceive* the nations no more. His loosing in verse 7 is in reference to the start of *deception* again (vs. 8). Therefore the binding is spoken of here in a specific context, and that is his ability to *deceive* nations. It was his work through Antichrist that brought deception to all the nations, and it is his binding that causes deception to cease. Further, we notice that the binding restricts his presence to the pit, while his release again gives him access to the nations of the earth (vs. 7, 8). It is not in any way denied that the binding the Amillennialists speak of is true and scriptural, except to say that it is not the binding specifically spoken of here in this text.

It is inconceivable to assume that Satan does not now, at the present, have access to the earth to deceive the nations (I Peter 5:8, II Timothy 3:13, Revelation 12:9). If they are not deceived then they are all walking in truth, which we know is not true. Such a concept is unscriptural. Of course, we recognize that the light of truth has power to expose deception, but that is completely different from asserting that Satan is bound so that he can deceive the nations no more.

Next, they maintain that Satan is a spiritual being and cannot be bound with a literal chain, therefore if the chain is figurative, as it must be, so this whole passage is figurative. Satan is a spiritual being, as are angels also, but this does not mean they are phantoms and cannot have a definite presence, or that they cannot be confined to a specific sphere. Angels can and have appeared as men. Fallen angels or demons can inhabit specific space and can be cast out of specific people; so this argument against the literal binding of a spiritual being is purely specious.

The issue is not so much what type of chain God may use; but rather, will this chain prohibit his presence on earth and his ability to deceive? If the chain is figurative and makes the whole passage figurative, then we may as well assume that the devil also is a figure of speech, as well as the pit of his confinement. Maybe there is no such thing at all as a literal hell or a personal devil. Such is the logical conclusion of these hermeneutics. The regular and readable sense of this passage does not allow for such interpretations. If such interpretations were applied to Scriptures at large, we could only conjecture as to their real meaning.

The plain sense of this passage demands that there be a time that Satan is bound up in hell during the same time frame in which the saints are ruling with Christ. Are the thousand years a literal period of time? There is nothing in the passage to indicate that God used 1,000 to represent any other number of greater or lesser value. In fact, when Satan is loosed, it is for "a little season", which to us clearly means an indefinite, but short, period of time. Had God wanted the 1,000 years to represent a long, indefinite period of time, He could have said the rule of the saints would be for a "long season". The fact that He said 1,000 years is a good indication that He probably meant just what He very plainly said.

Daniel's sixty-nine weeks of years are an exact count of time to Messiah; but if God's numbers are vague amounts of time, this whole passage loses its value.

When God says a day with Him is as a thousand years and a thousand years as a day, He is not saying they are one and the same but rather that time does not relate to eternity. If they are one and the same, we would not know if the earth was created in six days or six thousand days.

Since God has said His kingdom will last a thousand years, we will believe it and refer to it as the millennium.

The timing of this whole passage is declared by the Amillenialist to be an overview of the Church age. When we understand the binding of Satan and those events involved in Christ's rule, this cannot be considered the sense of the text. Furthermore, this passage is preceded by the return of Christ and followed by the great white throne judgment, which strongly argues for this to be an interval of time to be between those events.

The "first resurrection" here is spoken of by the Amillenialist as the spiritual resurrection that occurs at the new birth. We agree that the Bible uses resurrection terminology to describe the new birth. The question, though, is whether that interpretation is consistent with this context.

The first resurrection is spoken of in connection with those that were martyred by the Antichrist during the tribulation. After they were dead, (spoken of in reference to their physical bodies), they *lived* and reigned with Christ a thousand years, which is the first resurrection. If this is the new birth, then they were not born again until they had physically died, for it says their living was after being beheaded. But if their death was physical, why is not their resurrection also? By the same means of argument one could dispute the bodily resurrection taught in other passages by assigning it merely to the new birth.

Further proof that this is referring to a physical resurrection is found in reference to the time when the rest of the dead came to life. You cannot logically argue that the first resurrection is spiritual and not the second. If the second is spiritual then all men are born again after the thousand years. If the second is a physical event, then why is not the first also, which employs the same terminology?

It is obvious that the wicked dead are raised to go into judgment and the righteous are raised to live and reign with Christ a thousand years. If the thousand years refers to the Church age, then the saints must have immortal bodies on earth, for the new birth does not grant them life for the entire Church age (or 1,000 years), which again points to a physical resurrection.

If the first resurrection is a "living again", as is implied by reference to the second resurrection's terminology (vs.5), when did they spiritually live before their new birth? If the first resurrection is spiritual, when is the physical resurrection of the saved? Their resurrection is given a distinction as "the rest of the dead" and separated by a span of time (1,000 years). The righteous are in the first resurrection *before* the thousand years. If it is spiritual and the thousand years the Church age, then they all are born again before the Church age commences.

Such are the difficulties and inconsistencies of the Amillennial view. If that view can be reconciled with this passage, it is beyond any explanation that this writer has ever heard or read.

A few more points must be addressed that are often urged against the premillennial view. Most Amillennialists will point out that if the *first* resurrection is physical and is a resurrection of tribulation saints, how can premillennialists assert that the first resurrection is before the tribulation actually occurs, when those raised are those that are beheaded during the tribulation? This is not a problem for premillennialism, only for dispensationalists who believe in a pre-tribulational resurrection. If you understand the coming of Christ, the rapture, the resurrection, and the day of the Lord as happening simultaneously after the tribulation the whole difficulty is removed. This is the teaching of historic premillennialism. As for those that espouse a pre-tribulational rapture, it becomes their duty to reconcile how the Church can be resurrected before the tribulation and yet the tribulation saints take part in that first resurrection.

However, to revert back to the Amillennial viewpoint is to create far more difficulties with the passage than what exists for the dispensationalist, to explain his view of the rapture. Often the dispensationalist will try to establish that the first resurrection begins before the rapture and culminates at the end of the tribulation, with it all being one and the same resurrection (except for the fact that it is separated by 7 years). We will let the reader judge as to the sense this explanation makes.

Also, many Amillennialists will question how the devil will be able to raise a large rebellion against Christ at the end of the thousand years, after the whole earth has been under righteous rule. It must be understood that Israel and the saints are given prominence and rule in the millennium, but that they rule over the nations of this world. The saints cannot rule unless there is someone to rule over, which must be people outside of themselves.

The fact that the saints will rule is evident in this passage (they lived and *reigned*) as well as in the others we have examined wherein Christ will rule with His saints. The following is a list of passages that speak of Gentile nations being under the rule of Christ and His saints: Isaiah 2:2-4, 14:1,2, 65:17-66:24 (conditions of new heaven and new earth), Zechariah 14:9,16, Revelation 21:24-26.

The Jews and Gentiles during this time shall have children who will have fleshly bodies (Isaiah 4:1-4, 65:20-23). There will be many children who go into the millennium who have lost their wicked parents in the battle of Armageddon and the judgments following (Isaiah 11:6-8, Jeremiah 3:19).

The Matthew 25:31-46 judgment is largely a determination of which people and nations shall enter into the new earth (millennium), (rather than the personal Great White Throne Judgment as is sometimes assumed), for the following reasons:

1. Saints have already been separated from the nations of this world

when they rise to meet Christ in the air in their immortal bodies in the twinkling of an eye.

2. The saints are neither of the "sheep" or "goat" nations but are a third category of "these my brethren," separate from those being judged (I Cor. 6:1-3).

3. This judgment is based solely upon how "these my brethren" were treated and not upon whether the individuals were saved by the blood of Christ. Nor is it the "Great White Throne" judgment at the end of the thousand years, in which the dead are raised to give account for all their works.

4. The meek are promised an inheritance in the earth. "Blessed are the meek, for they shall inherit the earth", which promise is in addition to heaven for the saints, and extends to all who are meek as an earthly promise. This promise can only be fulfilled in a millennial sense after a determination has been made by a Judge.

5. Those who are on the left enter into everlasting punishment immediately (these shall go away into everlasting punishment) (vs. 46). The "righteous" go into life eternal as "my brethren", for they already have immortal bodies, but the sheep do not have immortal bodies or they would already be with Christ and would not need to be separated from the nations of the world. The term "righteous" is not applied to the sheep nations specifically as the punishment is to those on the left. Rather, those on the right are granted the privilege to "inherit the *kingdom* prepared for them from the foundation of the world" (vs. 34). Even those who give a cup of cold water to a little one shall receive a reward (Matthew 10:40-42). They are not saved by their good works to eternal salvation, but are rewarded for them by inheriting a kingdom.

This concept of judging nations by how they have treated Christ's brethren, whether Israel or the Church, is expressed also in the following Scriptures: Joel 3:12-14, Jeremiah 30:11, 46:28, Zechariah 2:8-12, Luke 18:7, 8.

In spite of the judgment upon the heathen, yet many of the nations will be joined to the Lord in that day (Zechariah 2:11), as the earth repopulates with the sheep nations who wish to be taught of the Lord and walk in His ways.

These nations that have helped the brethren through the great tribulation will be rewarded with life in the millennium, but yet at the end of it Satan shall be loosed for a little that their faith may also be tested. Because many are righteous only because they are under righteous rule, they shall be deceived when Satan is loosed and comes up against the camp of the saints at Jerusalem.

After the destruction of this army, the wicked are raised to stand before the Great White Throne and be rewarded according to their works.

This we believe is the meaning of this passage. It strongly speaks for the rule of Christ over the nations of this earth. All attempts to spiritualize it end in illogical inconsistencies and theological morass.

There may be differences in understanding on some points that have been expressed but the overall premillennial view, we believe, is strong and irrefutable, as well as being consistent with the united testimony of Scripture.

## ISRAEL AND THE CHURCH

Many Amillennialists and some Postmillennialists have sought to prove that the Church will fulfill all the covenant promises to Abraham. God's covenant to Abraham will not be examined thoroughly, but it will be noted that it contained promises regarding land that to date have never been fulfilled but shall be in the millennium. In Genesis 15:18 God's land covenant with Abram extended from the Nile River of Egypt unto the Euphrates River of Mesopotamia. Now God had already made a previous promise to Abram that his seed would possess the land by right forever. The promise then to Abram's seed was eternal (Genesis 17:7, 13, 19, Psalm 105:8-11). But when Abram questioned how God would perform His promise since he was childless, God made a covenant with Abram while he was in a deep sleep (Genesis 15:12-21). The significance of this covenant was that it was executed by God alone while Abram was sleeping. This act of God signified that He alone was the surety of the covenant, that it would not rest upon man's performance but upon God's promise. It would not be contingent in any way upon man but be wholly executed by God. There were no conditions attached to the covenant, nor did God ever remotely intimate in all of Scripture that He would ever revoke the covenant due to the disobedience of Abram's seed. God did warn Israel that they would be severely punished if they broke their covenant relationship with God through disobedience and that the blessings associated with a covenant relationship would be withheld until repentance. God warned Israel that they would go into captivity for their sins, but never once did He indicate that their land would be given to another nation. We have examined many passages that speak of Israel's return to their land both prior to Christ's return and after it occurs. The fact that Israel's sins cannot annul the promises and covenant to Israel is illustrated in the following passages: Isaiah 50:1, 54:4-10, Ezekiel 16 -especially verses 8, 59-63, and Hosea 2:19, 20). Even when God wanted to destroy Israel during Moses' leadership, He still promised to raise up a nation from Moses' loins so that the promise made to Abraham's seed would remain sure.

The covenant included land from the Nile to the Euphrates, which to date has not yet been realized. Although Solomon's kingdom was large it did not possess land to this extent. While Solomon collected tribute from surrounding nations, this in no way is equivalent to an actual possession of the land. Solomon's rule did not comprehend the extent of the promise made to Abraham, therefore Solomon could not have fulfilled the covenant promise of God to Israel. The passages listed earlier, of the prophets who were born *after* Solomon, still speak of the covenant as being yet in effect, and it yet must be for it is everlasting.

Paul describes Abraham's covenant in Romans 4:13-25 as being the grounds for justification by faith in our present dispensation. He speaks quite pointedly "that it was not written for his sake alone, ...

but for us also, to whom it shall be imputed, if we believe on him that raised up Jesus our Lord from the dead;". Paul's argument was that the original covenant of God with Abraham comprehended all those who will believe in Christ also; for through faith we are adopted by Christ into Abraham's seed and become heirs of the promises in the covenant (Gal. 3:15-18, 29). If the covenant would have ceased, we could never have been made heirs of it, nor been blessed in any way through Abraham. But it is said, "In thee (Abraham) shall all nations of the earth be blessed." Abraham's belief in the covenant has made him the father of all who believe, therefore by and through faith making him the father of us all.

Abraham's faith was not in his ability to keep the covenant but rather in God's ability to perform what He had promised (Romans 4:20, 21).

Abraham had a "physical" seed identified by the sign of circumcision and a "spiritual" seed identified by faith in Christ. Abraham had a seed according to the flesh and seed through Christ, who was Abraham's son (after the flesh). Both seeds are brought together into one covenant through the work of Christ (Eph. 2:11-3:6). The two seeds are brought together into one body in Christ.

The covenant had specific promises to Israel and promises also to Gentile believers. The two groups are distinct in the covenant and yet brought together into unity in Christ. This is not only realized presently in the Church, which is comprised of Jew and Gentile, but will also be in the millennium, when Christ's rule over the earth will be extended through the restored Jews and the Gentile saints upon the nations of this world.

God's promises to Israel are both distinct from the Church and yet at the same time comprehend the Church in its blessings and inheritance.

This distinction and union is illustrated in Romans 11. Many Gentiles apparently supposed that the Church would supplant Israel in its covenant relationship, for Paul says, "Hath God cast away his people? God forbid. ... God hath not cast away his people which he foreknew." Paul argues that there is a remnant according to the election of "grace;" that is, in spite of Israel's general unbelief, God is keeping His covenant with those who are called by grace to faith.

"Have they stumbled that they should fall? God forbid." That is, does their unbelief make void the election by God of their race? Are they cast off completely because of their unbelief? God forbid. For if their fall brought riches to the Gentiles, what shall happen when they rise again to the "fullness" of the promise? Shall it not bring a still greater proclamation of truth to this world? "For if the casting away of them be the reconciling of the world, what shall the receiving of them be, but life from the dead?"

If the natural branches (physical seed) can be broken off, do not assume that the wild branches (Gentile church) will supplant Israel. For if God can graft in wild branches (Gentile church) into the tree, He surely can graft the natural branches (Israel) back into their own tree, so that both the wild branches (Gentile church) and natural branches (Israel) can be brought together into one tree.

Paul urges us not to be ignorant of this mystery and warns that the Church should not be arrogant in assuming that God's covenant now lies solely with the Church, the spiritual seed of Abraham. For blindness is happened unto Israel only until the times of the Gentiles (Church age) be fulfilled.

It is after this that "all Israel shall be saved," when the Deliverer comes out of Zion, a time yet future according to Paul, when Christ shall return to set His feet upon the Mount of Olives and Israel shall look on Him whom they have pierced and mourn for Him as an only Son, and turn away from ungodliness. God has declared that this is yet His covenant unto them, to take away their sins.

They may presently be enemies of the gospel and outside the "election of grace" and will perish in their sins if they die in unbelief, yet they as a nation will one day be restored because they are beloved for their father's sake, according to the "election of race." God has promised that they yet shall obtain mercy.

Some will argue that God made a new covenant with Israel as

recorded in Jeremiah 31:31-34 and Hebrews 10:15-18, as though the new covenant is to cancel out the Abrahamic covenant. The new covenant spoken of by Jeremiah is in relation to the covenant made with the whole house of Israel and Judah, which was the covenant made from the law given upon Sinai (Exodus 34:27, 28). The new covenant of grace superseded this covenant of works. The Abrahamic covenant was made before the law was given and will be fulfilled under the new covenant (Gal. 3:15-18), not as a covenant of works, but one of promise.

To confuse the old covenant with the Abrahamic covenant is to confuse Bible terminology. It was God's promise to Abraham that brought an end to the law (old covenant) and ushered in the new.

Jeremiah, after speaking of the new covenant, says that the nation of Israel shall endure as long as sun, moon, and stars perform their functions (31:35, 36). If man could measure the heavens (space) or go to the heart of the earth, then would the Lord cast off Israel for their sins? But the word of the Lord and His covenant with Abraham is eternal and our guarantee of eternal life.

Amillennialists argue for a cessation of God's covenant to Abraham and with the Jews, but Paul and Jeremiah argue for its continuance. Whom will you believe?

Dispensationalists, on the other hand, are sometimes guilty of trying to make the distinction between Israel and the Church so sharp that they fail to see how God intends to bring diversity together into unity through Christ, so that both bodies may be Abraham's seed.

The time that this occurs is after the Gentile age of the Church and is fully fulfilled after the return of Christ, which is in the millennium.

## MILLENNIAL SACRIFICES

When the Amillennialist has been rooted out of all his strongholds, he typically will make one last stand in disputing against the millennium, by asserting that the sacrifices spoken of in millennial passages are incompatible with Christ's sacrifice on the cross, and therefore sufficient evidence to say that the millennial kingdom cannot be in the future.

This argument is based largely upon the assumption that any sacrifice of an animal (for whatever reason) does disgrace to Christ's work on the cross. It is admitting that in THEIR UNDERSTANDING sacrifices are irreconcilable with Christ's work. This is the same as saying if it cannot be understood it must be untrue. It is an argument based upon misunderstanding or lack of understanding.

If the millennium can be proven by Scripture, which it can, then it cannot be disproved merely because we cannot reconcile a seeming dichotomy. If the millennium could be disproved because of this paradox, then could also the mystery of Christ being both God and man. Difficulty in understanding a doctrine is not sufficient grounds for disbelief of it.

Because the evidence for a literal millennium is substantial and convincing we shall proceed to examine why Christ has instituted that certain Jewish festivals and sacrifices be observed.

The most serious charge that Amillennialists make is that sacrifices were for the purpose of absolution from sin under the old covenant and any continuance of that practice is merely an attempt to find forgiveness outside of the blood of Christ.

On the surface it would appear that this argument is indeed a strong and convincing one, since God had commanded blood sacrifices in the Old Testament in connection with receiving forgiveness. There is no doubt that God did require blood sacrifice for those Old Testament saints seeking forgiveness. The question, though, is whether the blood sacrifice actually took away the sin or whether it was a requirement by God of an act that typified something that truly would remove sin.

It is acknowledged that there would be no absolution for those who refused to be obedient to the means that God had ordained for forgiveness, but that is not the same as saying that it was the actual sacrifice that removed the sinner's guilt. If the blood sacrifices fully cleansed from sin there would have been no need for Christ's sacrifice for the Old Testament saints, if they already were saved by animal sacrifice. God never intended that a man be saved by animal sacrifices but rather that they be a reminder to him of his sin and the need to put faith in a coming Redeemer upon whom would be laid the iniquity of us all. Abraham believed God and it was accounted unto him for righteousness.

It was the obedience of faith that saved them; and a faith that embraced the promise from afar off (Hebrews 11:13). Christ's coming was necessary then, so that the faith of the Old Testament saint which embraced His death, would give salvation when Christ had said, "It is finished." It was then that all these just men were made perfect (Hebrews 12:23).

So it is evident then that animal sacrifices never did save a man, nor ever will. This premise is one of the foundational theses of the book of Hebrews.

"For it is not possible that the blood of bulls and of goats should take away sins" (Hebrews 10:4).

So the Amillennial charge that the observance of blood sacrifices presumes seeking absolution from sin by them, is indeed without merit, in that even in Old Testament times it did not remove sin, but rather reminded them of it. If sacrifices did not cleanse from sin during Old Testament times, how can one presume that in the millennium an observation of them indicates a reliance upon them for salvation?

The whole argument is no argument at all unless you believe that blood sacrifices did remove sin in Old Testament times. If it did, Christ need not have come. If it did not remove sin then, you cannot presume that it is intended to in the future either. The whole argument then really has no merit at all, but is only a cavil raised against a literal millennium.

It might then be asked, why did blood sacrifice cease? The answer is that when the substance comes, the shadow is removed. Why then will it be reinstituted, as seen in such passages as Ezekiel 43:18-27, in the millennial temple? We do not know the complete mind of the Lord on this matter but we believe that it most likely will be for the purpose of bringing the Jew to an understanding of what the true meaning of the ancient sacrifices were.

This temple described in Ezekiel is a future one, for one such as this has never yet been built according to those dimensions. It is spoken of as being built after the battle of Gog and Magog is over, which is after Israel has been restored to their land.

Christ participated in the Jewish festivals while knowing that He as God's Son will give His own body for the sin of the world. It is clear that what is spoken of here is instituted by the Lord. It would be wrong for us as men to reinstitute what has vanished away.

If God Himself chooses to reinstitute sacrifices, that is an entirely different matter, and who are we to question His purposes? Jesus ate the Passover with His disciples one day before the normal Jewish time so that He might use that Jewish memorial as a basis for the ordinance of the bread and the cup. He died upon Passover day as the Lamb of God so that the disciples might understand the relationship of the previous evening to His death the following day. Christ said He would no more observe the Passover until IT BE FULFILLED IN THE KINGDOM OF GOD. This then is a clear indication that He intends to observe the Passover again in the future kingdom, most likely to bring understanding to the Jewish mind as to the relationship of His death to that ancient memorial. Although we do not observe the Passover any longer, we will not be so foolish as to deny that right to Christ in the future. Christ has come to fulfill the law and show its true meaning. This yet must be done for the Jewish nation in order that they might understand how He has fulfilled the whole law.

Even in the early Jewish church there is evidence that some of the Jewish sacrifices were observed after Christ's death, even by the Apostle Paul (Acts 21:20-26).

The first Jerusalem council established that the ceremonial law was not obligatory, especially not for the Gentiles, but the ruling in no way indicated that the Jew could not voluntarily continue its observance, as James pointed out to Paul in Acts 21:24, 25. The ability to keep the whole ceremonial law was abolished in 70A.D. when the temple was destroyed. It is not to be observed or reestablished until such time as God institutes it. The ceremonial law answers only to the Jew and not the Gentile church.

Like many other future events, they are not fully understood now, but shall be when the time comes. The premillennialist does not believe that the sacrifices supplant or diminish the work of Christ but rather that they will illustrate it, and be instituted again, only because God has seen fit to do so. To reject the millennium on this basis is to question God's sovereign purposes in doing what He plainly said He would do, and this we do not wish to be guilty of.

## PREMILLENNIALISM PROVIDES A FULL THEOLOGY FOR UNDERSTANDING THE RELATIONSHIP BETWEEN THE CHURCH AND THE STATE

Many of the opponents of premillennial thinking suppose that if they have disproved dispensationalism they have disproved premillennialism. The heart of dispensationalism lies in the teaching of the "imminent return of Christ" (as opposed to watchfulness and expectancy of His return) and a "pre-tribulational rapture." These teachings are not a part of classical premillennial thinking, but rather have dominated premillennial thinking in the last 150 years due to the influence of Darby and Scofield. It is not the intent of this chapter to evaluate dispensationalism or its pre-suppositions, but rather to illustrate that premillennial thinking gives the best and fullest theology to the Scripture, and especially in answering whether certain passages of Scripture are fulfilled or yet prophetic. There is no doubt to any honest student of church history that premillennialism has existed as the prevalent view of eschatology in the early Church until it united with the state under Constantine.

The time will not be taken to fully substantiate this assertion, as the evidence is overwhelming and admitted even by the candid Amillennialists. Philip Schaff writes:

*"The most striking point in the eschatology of the ante-Nicene church age is the prominent chiliasm, or millenarianism, that is the belief of a visible reign of Christ in glory on earth with the risen saints for a thousand years, before the general resurrection and judgment. It was indeed not the doctrine of the church embodied in any creed or form of devotion, but a widely current opinion of distinguished teachers..."[1]*

If the millennial passages are applied to the present church age, then there are some grounds for argument of instituting Christ's rule on earth through civil government. But if these passages have a future application, then they are strong grounds upon which to establish a separation of church and state until such time as Christ returns to establish His own kingdom.

It is the belief of the writer that a premillennial understanding of prophecy gives a complete picture of Christ's kingdom and a clear distinction between it and rulers of this world. It is not indispensable to the other tenets expressed in other portions of this work, but rather is possibly the capstone to them. It is that view of prophecy that complements religious liberty for the church age and militates against the union of church and state.

It is no coincidence that Augustine, the Catholic church, and the later Reformers were ardent Amillennarians, as this view of prophecy strongly buttressed their theology of Christ's rule through civil government for the purpose of smiting all the heathen nations with a rod of iron. The later Puritans expanded the Reformed thinking into agressive Postmillennialism, which made the return of Christ contingent upon making all the nations of the world come under Christian government.

If their rule was Christ's rule, who could oppose them? If they were opposed, could they not smite the heathen? If their rule was Christ's rule, then those who held different beliefs were heretics, for Christ only has one Church. The Amillennial and Postmillennial views of prophecy have been the impetus for nationally established religions and the theological justification for the persecution of all dissenters. If Christ were both head of the government and head of the Church, then these two entities would be united under one head and could enjoy a close relationship. Such is the potential danger of Amillennialism, though many Amillennialists have not followed these beliefs to these logical conclusions, nor will endorse them.

We premillennialists say, we will reign when Christ reigns in person; and until such time we will keep the Church unblemished by the god of this world. Even so come, Lord Jesus.

---

1 *Philip Schaff, History of the Christian Church Vol. II, p. 614 (1991 WM. B. Eerdmans Publishing Company)*

come out of her my people

# chapter five

# The Biblical Basis For Moral Government

We have seen how the gospel has superseded the law with the bringing in of the New Covenant, how the kingdom of Christ is separate from the kingdoms of this world, and the pertinence of the teachings of the Scriptures concerning a literal reign by Christ upon this earth. The question now remains as to whether the Scripture gives any instruction at all for the governments of this world, as to their duties and responsibilities in providing a just form of rule over their citizens. If the Scriptures do not provide any direction at all, then man is left to his own philosophies and speculation as to what the best form of government may be. Man, when left to his own whims, may follow a path that seems right, but the end thereof is certain death, whether it happens quickly or slowly (Proverbs 14:12).

If God has ordained government and rulers over the affairs of this life, then it cannot be said that He is indifferent to earthly government, but rather it must be understood that He has a specific will concerning it. It has never been God's intent to leave man on this earth without any form of direction, especially in those areas that He has ordained institutions for his aid and welfare; yet the realization of man's need for government, and for government to be under God's blessing, has prompted many to assume that the state must be a religious establishment in order to govern according to God's law. This dilemma has caused people to assume that the only good government is a Christian one; that is, one that officially embraces and supports the Christian faith; which then in turn can be instructed by it (the church) in the proper principles of Biblical rule. The next dilemma then is; how can the state implement Christian rule if there are differences of opinion concerning government's role among the Christians themselves? The solution historically has been that a particular form of Christian faith must then be officially adopted. When this occurs, all other forms of religion are now viewed as detrimental to the peace and tranquillity of the society and government, for dissent can breed rebellion, distrust, resentment, or military revolution, and so it is suppressed.

Although nationally established religions cause oppression to dissenters, the only other alternative is often viewed as something totally secular and void of all religious influence, which produces an immortal or even atheistic government and society. Some though, believe that government should be a totally secular entity and should not make any laws that pass a moral judgment upon any issue. Society is left to its own judgment upon moral issues. All things in the government's eyes are strictly legal and secular, not moral. It is this notion that presently grips our nation and has permeated every area of our academia, so that our citizens have come to believe there is no such thing as a moral absolute of right and wrong, and even if there was, it could not be determined by government but only decided by a private person for himself.

This is but an equal and opposite reaction against the other extreme, for it is totally oblivious to the fact that when a nation is founded and its constitution established, that its founders must first know what they believe, in order to develop a constitution upon which laws can be based. The constitution is the expression of what founders believe are irrefutable truths, inalienable rights, and moral absolutes. From these principles the parameters are set for the enactment of statutory and legislative laws. The constitution defines both the freedoms and the limitations for all future law. But the constitution itself is based upon certain beliefs of right and wrong. If the constitution is rejected, then all the statutory laws become null and void. It is an impossibility to found a country's constitution and laws without the founders first determining what they believe. Even if they decide to be completely secular, they have still adopted and believe in secularism. In reality, Atheism and Agnosticism are belief systems, even if it is unbelief; for it represents a choice to believe in relativism (the belief that morals are not absolute but simply agreed upon by society). That to them is their absolute, and if you should challenge their position you will quickly see how "absolutely" necessary they feel it is to believe in relativism.

A country's constitution must give adequate freedom to meet the needs of changing times or it will become eventually a detriment or totally useless to that society. But it must also give appropriate limitations or boundaries or it shall not provide enough constraint against corruption, avarice, and moral decline. The state will then eventually self-destruct because of its own liberties.

If a nation does not adopt a constitution and the "rule of law" for government, then it will invest its power in *people*, whether by direct democracy or tyranny, as opposed to *ideals*. The government then will fluctuate upon the whim of the person/people and be extremely unstable and arbitrary. Emergencies tend to become crises, as there are no laws that are absolute for all times. The only way for any type of government to be good and stable, whether it be a democracy, republic, or a monarchy, is to establish a constitution that transcends the power of any person and holds all men equally accountable in certain areas of conduct. Any form of government that does not operate on transcendant moral values will become tyrannical, regardless of what form of government it adopts; the only difference will be in the degree of tyranny.

Our concern then is upon what basis do we construct a constitution without being totally secular or ecclesiastical? The answer to that question lies chiefly in the ability to define the difference between "morality" and "religion." A good nation will have "freedom of religion" but "established morality." There is no such thing in a stable society as "freedom of morality" or "moral liberty". Our founders never conceived of establishing a society upon arbitrary morality; rather they fought and died for what they believed was a just cause based upon absolute truth. They held that certain truths were "self evident" (thus beyond debate), and as such could not be contradicted even by a king who maintained his divine right to rule; for all men, they said, are created equal, and are equally accountable to acknowledge certain truths. There can be no doubt as to where our founders looked for their understanding of absolute morality. The following are some quotations:

*"The Bible is the Book upon which this republic rests."*

- Andrew Jackson

*"The moral principles and precepts contained in the scriptures ought to form the basis of all our civil constitutions and laws."*

- Noah Webster

*Those people who are not governed by God will be ruled by tyrants."*

- William Penn

*"It is the duty of all nations to acknowledge the Providence of Almighty God, to obey His will, to be grateful for His benefits, and humbly implore His protection and favor."* - George Washington

There were differences among the founders in their personal religion, with Benjamin Franklin being perhaps as agnostic as any, yet even he admitted Jesus had given to the world the best system of morals and religion that the world had ever seen.[1] So while there were differences among them in religious understanding and affiliation, they acknowledged a common and absolute morality proceeding from God to man which was revealed in the Bible. Our founders saw both the need for religious freedom, a separation between the church and the state, as well as the need to establish a rule of law based upon God's moral absolutes. It is important then to recognize, as they did, the . . .

# DISTINCTION BETWEEN MORALITY AND CHRISTIANITY

This distinction in Scripture is derived from a proper understanding of the distinction between the moral law and the gospel. The foundational principles of this separation were developed in the first chapters of this book and will be built upon in order to progress our thoughts in defining the distinction between morality and Christianity.

In order for there to be moral absolutes, there must be a

*Continuance of the moral law.*

Paul affirms that the law can save no one, but rather that salvation comes by faith in the blood of Christ. Yet Paul also affirms that faith does not make void the law but rather establishes it.

"Do we then make void the law through faith? God forbid: yea, we establish the law" (Romans 3:31).

Faith cannot save a man until the law first condemns him as a sinner, therefore faith will not stand upon an arbitrary and shifting foundation. Sin is given a specific definition by the law of God, for sin is the transgression of the law (I John 3:4). If the law were to cease its existence, sin could no longer be defined, for by the law is the knowledge of sin (Romans 3:20).

Neither could men be judged as sinners, for sin is not imputed where there is no law, were men ever so evil (Romans 5:13).

Therefore a moral law is just as much an absolute as salvation is by grace through faith. We know that not all men will come to repentance and live through the exercise of faith, therefore the moral law must remain in effect, for

*The law is for the Unrighteous Man.*

Paul explains in Romans 7:4-6 that a man becomes dead to the law in order to marry Christ. This means that every man is bound by the law until he is released from it by union with Christ. Our union with Christ brings the Holy Spirit into our lives, which frees us from the demands of the law and also teaches us to walk in the Spirit and intent of the law and not merely in the letter of it (Gal. 5:18, Romans

7:6). Through the process of walking in the Spirit we are taught to keep the righteousness of the law in a completely different manner, that is in the power of the Spirit working in us rather than in the strength of the will. This is known as walking in the law of the Spirit of life in Christ Jesus (Romans 8:1-4) or in the perfect law of liberty (James 1:22-25). But yet those who are not in the Spirit must yet be under the requirements of the moral law. This is their eternal restraint against sin that God has provided for the unrighteous man.

Paul expresses this thought succinctly when he states that the law was made for the lawless and disobedient, for a restraint upon those sins that are harmful to society such as murder, immorality, and dishonesty (I Timothy 1:8-10). Without the law as a restraint for sin, man would be left unchecked in pursuing his sinful and harmful tendencies. If the law is implemented as a righteous standard for lawless man, then it is obvious that God intends that even unconverted man keeps His law. While an unconverted man may not escape the sin of spiritual murder because he hates another (in God's eyes), yet he can be restrained by the law from committing physical murder. If a man lives by the external requirements of the law we may count him a moral and just man who will be an asset to the society in which he lives. In spite of his morality, though, we cannot consider him a Christian merely because he externally conforms to God's moral law. Yet in another sense he is a good man, for he is moral and just. The Bible speaks of Cornelius as such a man before his conversion (Acts 10:2). Cornelius feared God and honored His laws devoutly, sensing also a need for Divine assistance through prayers, and as such was a just man, though as yet unconverted (Acts 10:22). Therefore it is necessary to distinguish between

*Moral Righteousness and Spiritual Righteousness.*

Moral righteousness is the result of outwardly and morally seeking to conform to God's law in our life. A moral man will even believe in his way of living and recognize the value of it. The righteousness spoken of in the Old Testament is this form of righteousness in that it is the result of a man's will and life conforming to God's law.

The righteousness that comes as a result of keeping God's law cannot give a man salvation but it can make him a useful and good citizen and a blessing to the nation where he lives.

Paul speaks of his life before conversion as being blameless in conforming to the righteousness of the law (Phil. 3:6). He had externally conformed to the precepts of the law in every way that required a physical action or response. Not only did his life conform but also his will, for he was "exceedingly zealous" for the traditions of his fathers. According to the righteousness that is part of the covenant of works, he was a righteous man. And yet Paul discovered that the law was "spiritual", in that it could discover the thoughts and intents of the heart and show a man who had outwardly conformed to it his inward sins and imperfections (Romans 7:7, 13, 14). The man who on one account is blameless in his obedience to the law is also discovered by the law as having a carnal nature that is sold unto sin. This is the distinction that must be made between Old Testament righteousness under a covenant of works and the righteousness spoken of in the New Testament that is imputed at our time of new birth and lives in us by the power of the Spirit. The one is the result of an act of the will while the other is the result of being born of the Spirit. The one is moral uprightness as a result of right living, while the other righteousness is the result of walking in the Spirit.

The righteousness that is the result of Christ's work in our hearts is the very essence of Christianity. The righteousness that is the result of living by God's moral precepts is the righteousness spoken of commonly in the Old Testament. The rich young ruler who came to Christ was able to say that all the commands of the law he had kept from his youth, but yet he never saw the spiritual implications of the law in its ability to discover his covetousness for money.

The moral law then serves two purposes; one being to provide man in general with an absolute moral standard for right living, and the other being to discover his spiritual sins and carnal nature in order to lead him to Christ. Understanding this distinction between the law and grace is key to understanding the difference between Christianity and godly morality.

It is the business of the Church to not only support and promote morality in society, but specifically to preach the gospel of grace to men to bring them salvation. The Church does not enforce morality in society, it only promotes it. The power of the Church to discipline lies only with those that are within the body; it is God who must judge those that are without for sins of the heart (I Cor. 5:12, 13).

It is the state then, who is spoken of as the

*Minister of God who enforces Morality.*

The law has been established for the unrighteous man, but a law without any administrator or penalties becomes lawlessness. It is in effect the same as having no law at all. For what good is a law unless it be administered and enforced and is used to punish offenders.

Moral absolutes should become the basis of the constitution and statutory law in a nation. Constitutional laws then become binding upon society. The law is then the legal expression of the morality upon which they are based. To assume that morality should not be legislated is the equivalent of saying there should be no law at all, or that law is merely arbitrary and can be changed upon the government's whim. Morality must be enforced through good laws or society will quickly degenerate into uncontrolled corruption and vice. If morality is not legislated, then it is either immorality or personal opinion that is legislated, which is a certain recipe for decline. Even when God invested the supreme powers of the state under a king in Israel, yet the king himself was held accountable to the authority of God's law. The rule of law is a foundational criteria to any good government. What manner of government is chosen may be open to discussion, but no government in any form will be a good government unless it is bound to the same moral precepts as its citizens, and submits itself to the rule of moral law.

It is also important that legislators who enact laws, and the judges who interpret them, have the same moral beliefs as the founders of the constitution, or laws will be passed that are unconstitutional or interpreted in such a manner that is inconsistent with the morality of the constitution. Any government that does not acknowledge the supremacy of the law over its state officials is tyrannical and corrupt.

The government then has the responsibility to create laws that are consistent with morality and then must make them binding upon society. When human civil laws are founded upon God's moral law, they will be equitable and just.

God is the author of the institution of civil government, "for there is no power but of God." It is God's design also that government be a minister of good and a terror to evil. Because God has ordained government, He demands that "*every* soul be subject unto the higher powers." There is no one to be excluded from the realm of civil government.

Further, we notice in Romans 13:1 that "the powers that *be* are ordained of God." The verse does not say that only just powers are ordained of God but rather the powers that are in existence are there by God's decree, as evidence of His sovereign rule. Daniel records "that the Most High ruleth in the kingdom of men, and giveth it to whomsoever he will, and setteth up over it the basest of men" (Daniel 4:17). Therefore sometimes the rulers that God ordains for a land are base men, that is, ones who are evil and corrupt. An example of this kind of ruler would be Nero, who was Emperor at the time that the Apostle Paul penned Romans. Paul exhorts obedience to the ruler who would later take his life. Another example of a corrupt ruler whom God raised up would be Pharaoh. "Even for this same purpose have I raised thee up, that I might show my power in thee, and that my name might be declared throughout all the earth" (Romans 9:17).

Other times God will set up base men to rule, meaning those (base can imply either corrupt and/or lowly) who are of lowly origin either by birth or by privilege. An example of this would be David, the shepherd boy, who was anointed to be king over all Israel.

God not only then establishes government, commands all men to obey it, but also selects the rulers in government. Even though the rulers may be corrupt, they are to be obeyed as long as they do not contradict God's laws in their requirements, in which case then it is better to obey God than man.

"Whosoever therefore resisteth the power, resisteth the ordinance of God: and they that resist shall receive to themselves damnation." God has promised damnation to all those who resist the power of government, for it exists by God's ordinance. Rebellion against the ordinance of government is rebellion against God, who established it.

Are we to assume then that if government is corrupt, or rulers are corrupt, that God will not hold them accountable since He has ordained their rule? Nothing would be further from the truth, for "the wicked shall be turned into hell, and all the nations that forget God" (Psalm 9:17). Even though God has brought them into power, yet will He hold them accountable to rule righteously. Even though God raised up Pharaoh yet, He brought him into severe judgment for his sins.

Are men to confront their rulers if they are corrupt, if they are ordained to office by God? Again the answer is yes. God ordained Moses to confront Pharaoh, Nathan to confront David, John the Baptist to confront Herod, and the Apostle Paul to stand before Felix to reason to him of righteousness, temperance, and judgment to come. God ordained also that Paul would stand and testify before Caesar at Rome (Acts 23:11, 27:24). Jesus also spoke to us all to be ready to stand before kings and rulers, for His name's sake, and for a testimony to them (Luke 12:11,12, 21:12-15). Whenever rulers are not just men, ruling in the fear of God and according to His moral precepts, they are to be confronted (II Samuel 23:3).

Now if men are to be just, ruling in the fear of God, and according to God's law, does it not then naturally follow that they should be or must be Christians? Many have erroneously assumed that the only good ruler or good government must be Christian. This is nowhere stated in all of Scripture. There is no doubt that he must rule according to God's law if he is to be a good ruler. But must a man be a Christian to know and understand God's moral law? The Scripture clearly states that God's law is written upon even the conscience of heathen men who have no knowledge of God's law in its written form (Romans 2:14, 15). The work of the law is written upon the heart and conscience of every man. The issue then is whether he will obey what he implicitly knows. There is no doubt that a specific knowledge of the law is a great asset to guiding man into truth, for otherwise his carnal nature can deceive him. This is the reason why God has given us His law. But as we have shown, it is necessary that Christianity and morality be viewed distinctly, and if so, then a man may be moral, and be a good ruler who guides the nation into righteousness without being a Christian. All the Old Testament kings were not Christian, nor born of the Spirit, and yet some of them ruled righteously.

We also have the account of Cyrus in Isaiah 44:27-45:6 who is called by God as, "My shepherd," who "shall perform all my pleasure." God also refers to him as "His anointed, whose right hand I have holden." God promises to subdue nations before him, for God has girded him. God promises to go before him and prepare the way for military victories and great riches. All this is promised to a heathen king. If God could accomplish all His pleasure through Cyrus, surely He can also through other moral men who may not be Christian.

God has made a special promise of wisdom to all rulers who seek it in Proverbs 8:15-17.

*"By me kings reign, and princes decree justice. By me princes rule, and nobles, even all the judges of the earth. I love them that love me; and those that seek me early shall find me."* When rulers open themselves up for wisdom from God, He will give it, as long as they believe that He is, and that He is a rewarder of them that diligently seek Him. This wisdom is not contingent upon them being Christian but rather upon them recognizing God as the source of wisdom and earnestly seeking it in order to rule well.

There have been many leaders who have never professed saving faith in Christ but yet have earnestly sought God in prayer for wisdom in a crisis and were heard by God Almighty. We have the account in Scripture of Nebuchadnezzar, who humbled himself before God and had his understanding return to him. There are other accounts in Daniel where the heathen leaders sought wisdom from God through Daniel. The records of our own country's history are full of invocations to God for mercy and wisdom, and yet not all of these men had made any type of a Christian profession.

John Adams wrote, *"I feel an irresistible impulse to fall on my knees in Adoration of the Power that moves, the Wisdom that directs, and the Benevolence that sanctifies this wonderful whole,"*[2]

But yet he had a revulsion against orthodox Christianity and commented on John Wesley as *"one of the most remarkable characters that enthusiasm, superstition, fanaticism ever produced."*[3]

Like a number of the American Founders, John Adams believed in God and the morality of the Bible, but yet would not accept the orthodox Christian faith, and was especially anti-Trinitarian. But yet he said, *"The Christian Religion as* I understand *it is the best."*[4] (emphasis mine) John Adams, though, gave significant contributions to the molding of American government, which we believe was a good one, though not embracing the historic Christian faith. Our contention then that good government is possible with unconverted men is proven both by Scripture and history.

God has ordained that government regulate the *works* of men and not their *faith*. They are to be a terror against evil works and a rewarder of the good. The laws that a just government establishes define the differences between good and evil upon the basis of God's moral laws.

The government is required by God also to inflict punishment upon evildoers, for he is not to bear the sword in vain. It is God's instrument of wrath upon evildoers, even to the point of capital punishment. If he does not have the right to capital execution, then he bears the sword in vain. The right to capital execution, is never for political or religious oppression, but only for serious violations of God's moral law, such as when murder has been committed. The punishment is always to be commensurate with the crime, as Paul states when on trial, "If I be an offender, or have committed anything *worthy* of death, I refuse not to die."

Government, then, is ordained by God to enforce morality in a nation and thereby secure a well-ordered society of people that can dwell together in tranquillity. This is God's will for it. If government refuses to follow God's plan, then they bring themselves under the wrath of God. Though government may be unjust, yet it is to be obeyed as long as it does not ask its subjects to commit sin through obedience to its laws.

We are to submit to every ordinance of man in government, for the Lord's sake. Within the same context, we are to submit to the authority over us, whether it be good and gentle, or whether it be perverse (I Peter 2:13-19). Although we submit, we are to reprove the works of darkness, so that while we show a respect for God's institution we show also that we do not tolerate the corruption of it.

While the Church employs ministers for preaching the gospel, the state employs ministers of God to enforce morality.

The difference between the Church and the state lies in the fact that while

*Christianity is Voluntary, Morality is Obligatory.*

Faith by its very nature is both personal and voluntary, otherwise it is known as hypocrisy. Because faith cannot be forced or coerced, it lies outside the realm of the state's dictates. However, morality must be legislated and enforced in a nation. At this point there will be many howls of protest from the liberal quarters, demanding that no one force another morality upon their life. But if there are no moral absolutes, then one man may kill another as long as he believes it is right to do so. His action cannot be called into question unless there is an absolute moral standard by which he may be judged. However the one about to be murdered may object that his own rights will be violated if he is killed. The would-be murderer can respond by say-ing, "You will not impose your morals upon me and restrain my liberty to kill you, for I believe it to be my right, and my morality requires it."

Or another man may slander his fellow man and justify it by saying that his morals permit it. How could it be prevented except by imposing another moral standard upon the fellow that has no scruples about defaming another, especially if it advances his own cause?

Suppose a man was to be tried in a courtroom for an offense and the judge would inform the offender that he was not going to be tried by an absolute standard but rather by the judge's personal opinions and morals. The offender would surely cry foul if the ruling went against him. He would say that he should have been tried by an absolute standard of law and not by the judge's personal morals. An absolute standard of morality is the only fair and equitable means to rule a society. It is the only way to establish any form of justice.

But some people say, "Can we not create our own set of values and laws that will be relevant to our current times and make them absolute?" There are several problems with this thinking. First of all, if they are merely created by opinion of man, they cannot be considered absolute; for if they are created by dialogue they can also be "uncreated" in the same manner. By this reasoning then, truth becomes totally relative to current circumstances and consensus. Once a consensus is reached, it can never be challenged by another group of people upon any absolute basis. This is exactly what took place when the Nazis established their Reich. They developed their own philosophies of life and proceeded to annihilate the Jews and Christians, and embroiled the rest of the world in war. When the Nazi generals were brought to trial for war crimes, they responded by saying their actions were completely legal within their state. They said, *"We have done nothing wrong. We acted according to our own culture, according to our own mores, according to our own laws. We were told that they could be killed. Who are you to come from another culture, another society, and impose your morals on us?"*[5]

The only way the Allied lawyers could gain a conviction was based upon the universal truths recognized in "Natural Law" (as explained in chapter one), which upholds many of the precepts of Moral Law, for it was implanted by God upon the nature of man. Without moral absolutes, a society has no limitations to the horrors that it can engage in, and upon what basis can it be challenged if each society can create its own truth? Any stable and just society is founded upon moral absolutes and does not seek to create its own truth.

A strong moral foundation in a nation establishes those areas that are nonnegotiable, so that freedoms can be given in other areas without creating a moral decline and corruption. It is moral absolutes that provide for the foundation of religious freedom and a separation of church and state, while still maintaining a national righteousness that God can and will bless, for "blessed is the nation whose God is the Lord" (Psalm 33:12).

God has also said that, "Righteousness exalteth a nation: but sin is a reproach to any people" (Proverbs 14:34).

For a nation to be moral, it must have a constitution and laws that are based on moral absolutes. If a nation recognizes moral absolutes, then it must believe in both the moral law and a Moral Lawgiver.

The Ten Commandments are unique in this world's history as the earliest record of a complete system of morality recorded in alphabetic language that has been in continual usage since its inception. There have been other moral codes that are similar to the Decalogue, but they either are not recorded in alphabetic language (but in the less precise form of hieroglyphics or cuneiform), are no longer used, or are of more recent origin. God's law is unique and superior to all the other moral codes of men. It is universal in its application and is intended by God as a guide for those who will not live by the gospel, but who see the necessity of a moral code upon which men can construct both their personal lives and a national morality.

## THE TEN COMMANDMENTS AND NATIONAL MORALITY

As already noted, the foundation of all national constitutions are based upon an accepted morality, even if that standard is basically the absence of all morality. The question then is whether God has provided a moral standard or whether He has left man to his own devices. The Scriptures affirm that what seems right unto a man is the way of death. For this reason God has written the truth of the moral law even upon the heathen's conscience, even though he knows neither God nor His written law (Romans 2:14, 15). God has intended that all men know His law and observe it in their regular conduct. Even during the time of the new covenant God has promised to write His laws upon the minds and the hearts of men, so that all men from the least unto the greatest might have a knowledge of Him (Hebrews 8:8-12, II Cor. 3:3). But some men have thought themselves wiser than God and have excluded Him from their minds, and thus, while professing themselves to be wise, have become fools, for which cause God has given them over to reprobate minds, and they have become destitute of truth (Romans 1:21-32). For this reason God has provided a written and unalterable law whereby man's laws can be judged.

Were God's law to have ceased, so would have the imputation of sin, for sin is not imputed where there is no law (Romans 5:13). God has said that righteousness exalts a nation, while sin is its reproach; but if there is no law of God for the nations, they can neither be righteous or sinful. How could God justly cast a wicked nation into hell unless He first provided them a standard by which they could have been righteous? But God has affirmed His law as the standard by which men are held accountable. While the civil and ceremonial laws were unique to Israel as a nation, the moral law is universal in its scope.

Through the Ten Commandments the Jews were able to show the light of the truth to the heathen nations (Romans 2:17-24), especially if they themselves observed what they preached.

This law of God, as represented in the Ten Commandments, is God's law for all men and nations of this world. We shall briefly examine some of the national benefits of God's moral code and how it may positively influence civil government.

1. *"Thou shalt have no other gods before me."*

In this precept is the foundation of morality, in that it speaks of a Supreme Being who is the Moral Lawgiver. Unless man acknowledges God, who transcends all earthly authority, they shall invest in themselves supreme authority. The absence of a belief in a supreme God is the guarantee of either anarchy or tyranny, for man and government are not held accountable for their actions.

While not all of America's founders understood the Godhead, they all, whether Trinitarian, Deist, or Unitarian acknowledged a Supreme Being who ruled over the affairs of men. None were atheists. This has been one of the root causes in God blessing America as He has, for its rulers have acknowledged the God of the Bible as being supreme over all human government and laws.

For a government to be the "minister of God" in rewarding good and punishing evil, as God would will it to be, it must acknowledge its right to rule as being God-given.

In this command also is the premise of monotheism (belief in one God). Wherever polytheism (belief in many gods) has been taught to the exclusion of one Supreme Being, the people have been bound by superstition and legend. The clearer a nation has understood the concept of "One God", the more God has blessed that nation. "Hear O Israel, the Lord our God is one Lord," and it is He that should receive an undivided focus and obedience, rather than offering the allowance for a plethora of moralities that derive from the belief in many gods. The concept of multiple deities and their conflicts with one another makes moral absolutes a virtual impossibility. Polytheism in a society has always been the result of a combination of human imagination and demonic influence. The Scripture makes it clear that the demons are behind the worship of false gods ( I Cor. 10:19-21, Deut. 32:17). The Greek stoics and some of their philosophers deplored the Greek polytheism. The stoics were strong advocates of one Supreme Being. This concept was essential for their development of moral absolutes based upon natural law. Acknowledgment of a Supreme Moral Being as the one true God of the Bible is essential to national blessings from God.

2. *"Thou shalt not make unto thee any graven image."*

This precept strongly precludes any type of idolatry, which often is a part of polytheism. It also prohibits any type of prayers to images of the true God or any of His saints. Idolatry has always been a part of commercial religion. Many citizens in some countries are kept poor because of their belief in the necessity to bow before images and icons, casting money before them in order to have their prayers answered and their sins forgiven. Images and icons are an indispensable part of false religion, and so large amounts of money are paid to the religious merchants so that they can be placed in their homes in order to receive protection and blessing. Religious idolaters prey upon the fears and ignorance of men in order to garner amounts of money into their religion's coffers. The truth of God's Word has always opposed all forms of idolatry, lest even a house of prayer become a den of thieves.

3. *"Thou shalt not take the name of the Lord thy God in vain."*

Men have a tendency to invoke God in curses and swearing. God's name is always to be held in reverence. Any attempt to use it lightly diminishes the force of the first precept. Those that use God's name in vain are also given to profanity. When God and His name are held in respect, the speech of men becomes much more respectable. Most nations and societies acknowledge that even freedom of speech must be limited to that which is honorable and respectful. A nation cannot maintain a reverence for God, while at the same time giving no limitations on how men speak of Him.

4. *"Remember the sabbath day, to keep it holy."*

We have already illustrated that the sabbath is for physical rest and spiritual focus. It is based upon an order of natural creation and the need for man to reflect upon the providence of God. The sabbath was made for man, and Christ is yet Lord of it. While Christ clearly set aside its ceremonial observance and those civil penalties attached to it, nowhere are its two basic premises repealed in Scripture. Sabbath keeping in the literal seventh day sense has been replaced with the observance of the Lord's Day, thus illustrating that the principles of the sabbath are not destroyed, but fulfilled.

The Lord's Day, on the first of the week, provides a proper time whereby all the other precepts may be taught and strengthened. It is the time that God has instituted to keep man from forgetting his moral obligations both to God and his fellow man. Even if a nation does not make use of the Lord's Day for spiritual reflection, they will still benefit from observing a law of Creation for physical rest; but a nation that forgets to set aside time to honor God will soon forget Him and then be abandoned by God to reap their own doom.

5. *"Honor thy father and thy mother."*

The basic unit of all stable societies is that of the family. This precept implies that there is a father and a mother for the child to honor. It also implies parental authority and respect for it. A child that is not taught to honor parents will not honor any other authority figure either.

The state should also recognize the institution of the family and not dishonor it by taking away from the parents the authority God has invested in them.

Strong families produce strong nations. Children that are raised to honor their parents will also honor their country. God has promised long life and well-being on earth to those who honor their parents. The breakdown of respect for the family authority will eventually destroy also the higher powers through lawlessness in the land.

6. *"Thou shalt not kill."*

It may be debated as to whether this command prohibits murder or whether it precludes the taking of any human life, but either way, it establishes the fact that human life is sacred and must be respected. It is hard to conceive that this command was ever intended by God to prohibit the taking of any human life, when God at the same time instituted capital punishment for murder (Exodus 21:12).

But yet it is not accurate to say that the government alone has the prerogative to decide when life may be justly taken. Surely no government has the right to legalize the killing of innocent life, such as in the case of abortion. The law is only to punish by death those that are grievous offenders both of God's moral law and man's civil law. Surely also this command prohibits any person from seeking any personal vengeance for wrongs committed against them, by inflicting death.

This precept acknowledges the value of human life, which was created in the image of God, and binds even a nation to observe it. God has brought nations of the world into judgment for shedding innocent blood (II Kings 21:16, 24:3,4). Those nations that do not acknowledge and enforce the sacredness of human life will eventually become despotic and fall under grievous judgment.

7. *"Thou shalt not commit adultery."*

This command helps to preserve the institution of marriage as a covenant that is inviolable. Promiscuity left unchecked will always destroy a nation and a society. The family unit has been so implanted upon the image of man by God that almost all societies, cultures, nations, religions, and even indigenous peoples have recognized the necessity of giving respect unto it. All nations that have developed a system of law have those that address marriage. Not only is marriage blessed by God for all men, but God has commanded that it must be kept sacred and preserved from outside and foreign relationships.

When a nation indulges in immoral lifestyles, a host of problems arise from the break-up of the home. Lawyers wait, like vultures, for the death of a marriage relationship in order to prey upon the financial resources that the parents have laid up for the care of their children.

The price that immorality can cost a nation in terms of moral decline, unwanted children, loss of productive work, mental health, juvenile delinquents, court cases, and violent crimes is staggering and unquantifiable.

The nation who forgets God, He gives up to uncleanness and vile affections and finally will bring them into terrible judgment. The nations of Canaan had become so immoral that God said even the land would vomit them out if they were not annihilated (Lev. 18:24-30). Paul affirms again in Romans 1:32 that they who commit such things are worthy of death.

This does not mean that Moses' civil penalties are to be employed against adultery, for Jesus negated that, but rather that if a nation does not restrain immorality God will bring them into judgment from heathen nations.

Spiritual adultery and physical adultery usually go hand in hand in the moral decline of a nation.

The pagan festivals in honor of false gods were usually a license for sexual orgies (Numbers 25:1-4, Revelation 2:14). God will bless a nation that honors His earliest and most sacred institution given to man.

8. *"Thou shalt not steal."*

This command implies that God gives stewardship of possessions into the care of individuals, and between them and the Lord lies the ownership of it. God recognizes ownership of material goods as lawful gain from the fruit of labor. A society that prohibits theft is promoting a proper work ethic and acknowledging that there are means of acquiring wealth that are improper.

The nations of the ancient world often relied upon the plunder of inferior nations to supplement their wealth. A nation that builds its economy on the spoils of war will eventually be brought to ruin and desolation. All warlike empires of the past have ceased, having been overthrown and judged by their enemies or subjects.

A society that allows theft within it, whether among its citizens or the government, will eventually self-destruct. Unrestrained selfishness or laziness instigates theft. Those who live off the labors of others will eventually become a burden too heavy to be borne and will be cast off.

When a nation's economy is rife with illegally acquired money, not only is it usually squandered until poverty comes, but there is also a sharp increase in violent crimes.

Possession of material goods, proper stewardship of them, and respect for another's ownership are all necessary elements of a sound national economy.

This law also prohibits government from taking unjustly from its own subjects, and employers from abusing their workers. James 5:1-5 warns those that have obtained wealth by fraud and injustice that a judgment is coming that will strip them of their possessions, because of the unjust treatment of their laborers.

9. *"Thou shalt not bear false witness against thy neighbor."*

Communication is essential wherever people live together. Yet communication is only profitable if it be based upon truth. Science and technology are based upon the accuracy of certain data obtained from reliable methods. Progress in any area of mental or physical disciplines is directly related to an understanding of the pertinent truth.

A judicial system can only be effective if it is able to discover the truth of certain events. Men are bound by oaths to truth so that justice can be served. Justice cannot exist in any society unless the citizens are committed to truth. Justice and truth have an inseparable relationship and are indispensable to equitable government.

10. *"Thou shalt not covet."*

This commandment speaks directly to the inward affections of a man, specifically to his selfish nature. Selfishness can be very difficult to curb with law, as man's passions continually drive him to find means to circumvent those restraints. But yet it must be restrained externally.

Covetousness is an insatiable desire to either have more of what is currently possessed or to have what has not yet been obtained. It is the exact opposite of contentment. Men that are covetous have no scruples against using whatever means necessary to accomplish their ends. It can manifest itself in lust for fame, wealth, or an immoral relationship. It is generally conceded by honest men that man's very nature is greedy. His love of money can lead to every conceivable evil.

Nations have seen the necessity of enacting laws to prevent businesses from monopolizing and garnering extravagant profits. Laws must be legislated and enforced that define what profits are fair and equitable in certain areas of enterprise, or even a nation's government can be fleeced by its own citizens or politicians.

Only if principles are held in higher repute than profits can a nation exist that meets the needs of all its citizens. Covetousness must be strongly curbed if a nation is to be universally blessed.

At this juncture a person may wonder how the first four commandments of the ten can be implemented as part of a national morality without the government of a nation becoming a religious institution. Many "Christian" nations in the past have established state churches upon the basis of serving the one and only true God as understood by their own religious persuasion. All other religions were held to be a violation of precepts on the first table of stone. But if it be remembered that all of God's civil and ceremonial laws have been fulfilled in the gospel and are not to be reenacted, then the answer to this question is more readily apparent. A nation who wishes to be under God's blessing may allow certain freedoms of religion that are within this moral code, to all men, while still refusing to govern the nation upon the basis of that which they allow. For example, a Hindu may be permitted to believe and practice his faith in a country, but that country may still refuse to enact laws that are grounded upon Hindu morality. The nation may not deem the cow sacred so that it may walk unobstructed through the streets. The vermin may still be annihilated with no regard to reincarnation, because of a nation's refusal to believe that it could credibly be a person from another lifetime. In this sense the Hindu's religion is restricted by the national morality, but on the other hand he will have a perfect liberty to entertain his own private religious beliefs. If the cow is sacred to him, then so be it, providing it does not forage on another person's property. This then is the balance between religious liberty and the establishment of national morality.

A nation founded upon God's law should not compromise moral absolutes based upon the values of other religions, but yet it should allow those individuals of other religions to privately practice their faith. When a nation accepts all moralities, it loses its ability to define truth and moral absolutes and can no longer hold certain truths to be "self-evident" or guarantee "inalienable rights."

When dealing with the commands of the first table a nation must limit itself to those areas that are visible, externally identifiable, and moral, while leaving all spiritual understanding and instruction to the realm of the Church and the individual conscience. In this same manner the state uses the second table to address physical adultery, murder, theft, and covetousness, and lets fantasy, hatred, tithing/giving (robbing God), and lust to the realm of the Church and individual conscience. The spiritual interpretation of the law is assigned to those who are born of the Spirit, while the state uses the law to enforce external morality. The Decalogue is God's perfect law that was designed to be a "law of nations".

## Moral Government and the Gospel
*Separation of the Two*

Moral government becomes the responsibility of a nation, while the preaching and discipline of the gospel is the work of the Church. A nation has an obligation to compel men to an external standard of righteousness that conforms to God's law. God's Word commands men to be subject to all that are in authority. As long as authority operates within the bounds of moral law, all its precepts are to be obeyed. When a nation violates God's law it removes itself from under God's authority and is not to be obeyed in those specific areas where God's law has been flaunted. A nation also must never usurp any authority that God has given to the offices of the Church, such as defining or disciplining heresy. A nation is under the covenant of works, and rules according to the flesh, while the Church is under the covenant of grace and rules according to the Spirit (Gal. 4:21-31, 5:18).

When the Church operates as the state and tries to coerce men to obedience, it becomes a work of the flesh, and is spiritual adultery (Romans 7:1-6). The law and the gospel cannot be joined together in the body of Christ, for one must die to the law in order to marry Christ. Neither can the nation act as a spiritual leader for the Church while exercising the rule of law. For both the law and the gospel to perform their God-ordained role they must remain separate from one another.

### Effects of the Gospel on Government

While the gospel must remain unfettered and unestablished by the state, yet the state can be greatly and positively influenced through the conscience of men that are sensitive to the requirements of God's law. Wherever the gospel is proclaimed with power under the influence of the Spirit, the fear of God can fall upon society, and the Spirit will reprove the world of sin and judgment to come (Acts 2:43, 5:11, 19:17). The preaching of the gospel has a sanctifying effect upon the general conscience of a nation against evil practices in society. When the light of truth is shed abroad, the darkness retreats. Superstitions are dispelled and deception is exposed. God has never intended that the light of the gospel be hid under a bushel, but rather placed upon a candlestick.

Wherever the pure gospel has come in this world, crime, oppression, and slavery have been overthrown. Men have learned to develop skills for the common good of all mankind. Men learn to live unselfishly for the benefit of society at large. People from all nationalities, cultures, and skill levels are given respect for their contributions. Men learn to be thankful and appreciative of others' help.

A selfish society is always unthankful of its blessings, because it feels it should have more. An unthankful people are full of all sorts of personal grievances and bitterness.

That society which is under God's truth is under a blessing of the Lord, which makes it truly rich.

So, while the Church is separate from the state, yet it performs a valuable service to it. It creates a society that strengthens the state.

One of the greatest of all benefits of the Church upon the state is that it can pray for it and bring God's blessing upon it.

*Government's Provision for the Gospel.*

While the government should not in any way try to use the law to nationally establish the gospel, yet it can and should make some provision for it. The greatest provision any nation can make to advance the cause of the gospel is to give it complete freedom. God has asked the Church to earnestly pray that the state would grant such freedom to the Church so that the good news of salvation may be extended to all men (I Timothy 2:1-8). We are called to lift up holy hands in faith for the welfare of our lands, that God may use our lives to save men through the free exercise of our faith.

Christ has commissioned His Church to carry the gospel into every nation and will bring all those nations into judgment who will refuse it or oppose it. When the state rises up to persecute the Church, they are declaring war against Him that will ride upon the white horse unto victory. Every nation that persecutes the saints is eventually brought into strong judgment. When the saints cry out under the oppression of the state, God will avenge His elect (Luke 18:7, 8).

The Jewish nation began its persecution of the Church and closed its ears to truth, so God brought upon them wrath to the uttermost (I Thess. 2:14-16). The horrors of the siege of Jerusalem, as recorded by Josephus, upon the Jews, were the direct result of the blood of Christ and His saints being upon their hands. The miseries that befell them are unspeakable. Men became mad with hunger and the craze of brutal warfare. Blood ran through the streets. The stench of the carnage was unbearable. Even the battle-hardened Roman soldiers were appalled at the atrocities of the Jews upon their own factions within their ranks. In battle, the Jews fought like crazed men and cast themselves many times to reckless abandon in their attempts to repel the Romans, only to bring upon themselves tremendous slaughter. All this because the blood of Christ and His saints was upon their hands.

Herod, who executed James and attempted to kill Peter, died a horrible and excruciating death by being eaten of worms. Josephus records that Herod knew God's judgment had fallen upon him for his sins, as his body was wracked by pain from an unknown disease that grievously afflicted him after his great oration.

Paul instructed the church at Thessalonica (II Thess. 1:4-9) that those who troubled and persecuted the church, God would recompense with tribulation, and then finally with great vengeance at the return of Christ with His angels. God has kept His word, for all those Emperors of Rome who initiated persecution against the Church died violently.

Nero, that first and great enemy of the saints, was judged by the senate to be an enemy of mankind, and being condemned to be whipped to death, he cut his own throat to avoid the pain of the lashes.

Domitian, the Emperor who raised a second persecution upon the Christians, was stabbed to death with daggers by his own servants, then buried with great dishonor, having his memory cursed, and his ensigns defaced.

Trajan, author of the third persecution against the church, fell into a palsy, lost his senses, and died in great anguish.

Later in history in the land of Bohemia, the judgments of God became so famous and frequent that a proverb was used among the Church's adversaries that if they would initiate a persecution against the saints, within a year God would take their life.

King Charles IX of France gloried in the massacre of saints; but when his day of reckoning came, he died of a painful and debilitating disease, with the blood of his own body issuing out of all its passages.

Hitler, also of modern times, after having shed the blood of many innocent people came to an ignoble end.

God's hand lies heavy upon those who touch the apple of His eye. Christ's relationship to His Church is so close that if a hand is raised against a saint, it is one and the same as if it was committed against Christ (Matthew 25:45, Acts 9:5).

The Psalmist speaks also of those who afflict the saints.

"They gather themselves together against the soul of the righteous, and condemn the innocent blood. ... And he shall bring upon them their own iniquity, and shall cut them off in their own wickedness; yea, the Lord our God shall cut them off" (Psalm 94:21, 23).

God will bless those nations who nourish the gospel by giving it the freedom to be preached and lived, but will curse and cast a blight upon the country that opposes His saints.

## Our Founders, Neither Secular nor Ecclesiastical

Currently there is a battle raging in our country over whether our Founding Fathers were "Christian" or "Secular" in their private beliefs and whether they were seeking to establish a "Christian" or "Secular" nation.

There is much evidence to consider on both sides of this debate. Those who take the position that our founders were orthodox Christians in their understanding of the Godhead, sin, salvation, and the inerrancy of the Scriptures are distorting or ignoring a large body of evidence. However, those secularists who maintain that they were simply Deists and Agnostics are also manipulating history. Some variation occurs among the founders themselves as to what they believed about Jesus Christ, Christianity, and the role religion should play in national affairs.

It is fruitless to try to make any type of judgment upon their personal salvation, as that now lies in the hands of the Lord alone. By their quotations though, we may draw conclusions as to whether they embraced the historic Christian faith or not.

The realm of this subject could be a whole work in itself, but some quotations will be given to substantiate the conclusion that is being drawn from an abundant amount of evidence that has been considered, though not included in this book.

First of all, it is our intent to show that our most prominent and influential leaders, who are generally considered the most liberal of them all, were not atheistic or heathen, though they may not have believed historic Christianity. In fact, most of them embraced a "Christian philosophy" of morality and religion and accepted the Bible as the authoritative source for moral absolutes. Nowhere can it be proved that their morality or form of government was derivative of any other religion or faith than Christianity. They studied the governments of other cultures, but they do not rationalize their own opinions from Zeus, Buddha, Mohammed, or Zoroaster; instead, they are buttressed from a Biblical foundation.

The following quotations substantiate this:

*"We hold these truths to be self-evident, that all men are* created *equal, that they are endowed by their* Creator *with certain unalienable Rights..."* -Declaration of Independence

*"Here is my Creed. I believe in one God, Creator of the universe: That he governs the World by his Providence. That he ought to be worshipped. That the most acceptable Service we can render to him, is doing good to his other children. That the Soul of Man is immortal, and will be treated with Justice in another life, respecting its Conduct in this. These I take to be the fundamental Principles of all sound Religion, and I regard them as you do, in whatever Sect I meet with them."*[6] -Benjamin Franklin

*"... the praise is due to the Grand Architect of the Universe; who did not see fit to suffer his Superstructures and justice to be subjected to the ambition of the princes of the World, or to the rod of oppression, in the hands of any power upon Earth."*[7] -George Washington

*"...the ways of Providence are inscrutable, and cannot be scanned by short sighted man; whose duty is submission, without repining at its decrees."*[8] -George Washington

*"The Christian Religion as I understand it is the best"*[9] -John Adams

*"I say that if I had not steadfastly believed in a Government of the Universe, wise beyond my comprehension, and benevolent beyond my conception, I should have been constantly not only in dejection but in despair, for at least 55 years of my life."*[10] -John Adams

*"Statesmen, my dear Sir, may plan and speculate for liberty, but it is religion and morality alone which can establish the principles upon which*

*freedom can securely stand.*"[11]  -John Adams

"*With respect to the "Genuine precepts of Jesus himself," "I am a real Christian ... sincerely attached to his doctrines, in preference to all others.*"[12]  -Thomas Jefferson

"*Whilst we assert for ourselves a freedom to embrace, to profess and to observe the Religion which we believe to be of divine origin, we cannot deny an equal freedom to those whose minds have not yet yielded to the evidence which has convinced us.*"[13]  -James Madison

"*It is the duty of all nations to acknowledge the Providence of Almighty God, to obey His will, to be grateful for His benefits, and humbly to implore His protection and favor.*"  -George Washington's Thanksgiving Proclamation, 1789

From these quotations there can be no doubt that our most eminent founders, while not speaking clearly for the historic Christian faith, are assured of the necessity of believing in God and obeying the moral requirements of God's law. Thomas Jefferson edited the Bible, taking out of it the supernatural events, and leaving what he believed was its true morality. This became known as the "Jefferson Bible".

They believed in a Moral Lawgiver, the moral duties of man to his Maker, and the immortality of the soul, which would stand in judgment one day for deeds done in the body. Their writings are replete with these concepts. And yet these same men refused to officially establish the Christian faith as a national religion, lest it be corrupted by civil power. The following quotations express these sentiments:

When hearing that the Congregational Church was finally disestablished in Connecticut, Thomas Jefferson rejoiced, "*that this den of priesthood is at length broken up, and that a protestant popedom is no longer to disgrace American history and character.*"

"*Who does not see that the same authority which can establish Christianity, in exclusion of all other Religions, may establish with the same ease any particular sect of Christians, in exclusion of all other Sects?*"[14]

-James Madison

"*What influence in fact have ecclesiastical establishments had on Civil*

*Society? In some instances they have been seen to erect a spiritual tyranny on the ruins of the Civil authority; in many instances they have been seen upholding the thrones of political tyranny: in no instance have they been seen the guardians of the liberties of the peoples.*"[15]  -James Madison

In 1789 some Presbyterian elders asked that Washington consider the fact that the constitution gives no explicit reference to the only true God and Jesus Christ, whom He hath sent; to which Washington replied, *"the path to true piety is so plain as to require but little political direction."*

Not much more needs to be said in regards to early opinions on the establishment of Christianity in our nation, for our constitution clearly forbids it, thus indicating the founders' views on established religion. What may be concluded then, concerning our founders, is that they strongly supported the Christian religion and morality, while at the same time refused to establish it as a national religion.  Some of them were Unitarians and Freemasons (all the Presidents were Freemasons) and would not accept the deity of Christ, and so could not be considered truly Christian, yet because they upheld God's moral law, (by even posting it in the Supreme Courtroom), God has blessed this nation like no other in recent history.

God has ordained a proper relationship between the Church and the state, that when followed, becomes a cause of national blessing. Many of our founders cannot be considered Christian, though they believed in God and morality, and respected the Bible as God's Word. There is a lack of evidence in their writings of acknowledgment of the deity of Christ and reference to a personal new birth experience. Yet in spite of this, at times, they called themselves Christians, not for evangelical reasons but rather for philosophical ones. They regarded the Bible as God's revelation to man, as opposed to any other religious oracle of human composition.

By honoring God as the Moral Lawgiver, recognizing the duty of man to obey His moral precepts, and believing in the immortality of the soul along with a final judgment, our founders instituted a nation upon Biblical righteousness. As explained before, the Bible, especially in the Old Testament, recognizes an external righteousness that results from the observance of moral duties, but in no way equates that righteousness with that which is imputed by Christ to the believer when he is born again. So while our nation may be considered "Christian" in a philosophical or moral sense, it cannot be considered "Christian" in an evangelical sense.

The founders, like the Stoics before them, recognized that a democratic republic operating by the "Rule of Law," must believe in a Supreme Being and moral absolutes (which the Stoics called "Natural Law") in order to avoid both tyranny and anarchy. They went beyond the Stoics, because the light of the gospel in those early days had permeated every level of society, which also helped illumine their understanding with a clearer picture of God's law than what the Greek and Roman statesman had ever comprehended in their pagan societies.

When the state usurps the Church's authority, or the Church the state's; when the state becomes a spiritual minister instead of a moral one; or when the Church uses force to coerce men to faith, God will cast a blight upon that nation for mixing two distinct spheres of power and influence. Our country has divided those spheres according to the Scripture and for that reason God has chosen to bless America.

When the state honors God and His moral laws and gives the Church the freedom to preach the gospel, they will come under the blessing of the Lord. But if the state seeks either to usurp the authority of the Church or restrict its activities, it shall bring corruption into the Church and God's judgment upon the nation. God will not have His Church in union with the law, lest she becomes an adulterer with that which she formerly was dead unto when she was joined unto Christ (Romans 7:4-6).

The Church is joined only to Christ, while the state, in a righteous nation, is joined unto God's moral law; but the two may not become one without committing adultery. Both spheres are ordained by God, but for completely separate functions.

These nations that reject God's law will be judged. Those that will fornicate with the Church will corrupt. Those that honor God's law and grant freedom to the Church will be blessed.

## THE CHRISTIAN AND THE STATE

If the distinctions between the Church and the state are understood, in their respective institutions, does this imply that the individual Christian must also refrain from any association with civil powers? Some may assume that this is a foregone conclusion, but yet that is not so, for Jesus said to render unto Caesar what is Caesar's, and unto God what is God's. This implies that though there must be distinctions made between Caesar and God, there are obligations unto both. There are clear instructions in Scripture of the Christian's duty to the government in the realm of prayer and taxes. This is so clear that it needs very little attention. The great controversies among Christians lie in understanding to what extent beyond that point a Christian may involve himself in civil affairs. Sometimes churches divide over whether a Christian should vote, serve in politics, serve in the military, or practice civil law. We could not possibly look at every area in a detailed manner, and if we did so, we still would not agree in every matter. Many individual consciences within the same body of believers can draw lines at different places as to what is, or is not, acceptable. The intent here is not to answer specifically every question that may be asked, but rather to lay down some overarching principles.

The first proposition is that a Christian is never to compromise "kingdom" principles in order to serve in the civil affairs of this life. Some of these kingdom principles have already been expressed in our examination of gospel doctrines. In order to better illustrate this proposition a specific dilemma could be examined. Possibly one of the most difficult areas for many Christians to delineate is reconciling the need for civil justice, even to the extent of taking human life, while still upholding the sanctity of human life. We will not revisit the whole issue of war, as that has already been examined, but rather look at the issue of taking human life within the realm of domestic civil justice. This includes areas such as capital punishment and law enforcement. While many may argue over the right of the state to execute a convicted felon, few would argue over the right of law enforcement officers to use deadly force if necessary to subdue a violent criminal. The issue is further complicated if we consider whether a Christian who opposes the use of deadly force would not accept protection from those officers of the law who employ it.

If the position is taken that all those offenders of the law may be treated with whatever punishment the state has granted, then the Christian is submitting the decision on whether to take human life to a nonspiritual power. He assumes that since he is employed by the state he may use any power the state has invested in him. If the state is ordained by God, then fulfilling the will of the state is fulfilling God's will. Some may argue that they are not accountable for their actions if the state has granted them authority to take such actions.

A Biblical example of this would be in Romans 12:19 where God says, "Dearly beloved, avenge not yourselves, but rather give place unto wrath." This verse strongly speaks against taking personal vengeance against someone who has committed an offense against you. But yet many would say that though this verse prohibits personal vengeance, it does not prohibit lawful vengeance, for the minister of God is a "revenger" to execute wrath upon him that doeth evil; therefore lawful vengeance is allowable to the Christian. But the passage in Romans 12:19-21 does not give allowance for the believer to take "lawful" vengeance, but rather says that the Lord will avenge our adversaries. The Scripture asks further that we forgive and return good for evil that was committed against us. How does one seek lawful vengeance and retribution and at the same time heap coals of fire upon an enemy's head? It is not denied that the law has the right to punish an offender, or that a Christian may cooperate with the law by bearing testimony to the truth in order to convict and punish an offender. What is prohibited is a believer prosecuting an enemy to the fullest extent of the law in order to take vengeance upon him.

But what if the believer is employed by the state to use deadly force, if necessary, upon a criminal? If he is an agent of the state, may he then take another life and be held guiltless? Under Old Testament dispensation the answer was an unequivocal yes. Under the guidelines of God's moral law the answer still is yes, for the moral law did not preclude deadly force in Israel to whom God gave it. Romans 13 grants the minister of God the authority to take vengeance upon an offender in order to maintain and promote the good of the land. But yet this does not make an assumption that the believer is the minister of God, but rather speaks of the minister of God and the believer as two separate entities (he -"government" and thee- "believer", Romans 13:4). Nor does the passage assume that the minister of God is Christian, but rather speaks of the "Powers that be" as merely existing government. If the believer and the minister of God are treated as two separate entities, then it cannot be said that the believer has the right to participate in all that which God has ordained for the state to do.

Since God has raised up even heathen powers such as Pharaoh and Cyrus to perform His will, it cannot be said that if God ordained the power we may be a part of it. Would it have been right for a Hebrew to have been an agent in Pharaoh's persecution against Israel, since God had raised Pharaoh up? Joseph had served a different Pharaoh for the good of his people. But yet God had raised up a wicked Pharaoh to power as a minister of the state who rebelled against the one who ordained him to power. So though government is ordained of God, a believer should not assume that this gives him the option of being an agent of the state, and whatever the state requires of him, he may fulfill and be exonerated of personal responsibility.

The question then is, if God has prohibited vengeance, and even lawful vengeance to the believer, may he, as an agent of the state execute wrath? It is understood that an agent of the state is empowered to lawfully do what a mere citizen may not, but the question is; may a Christian conduct himself differently, as an agent of the state, from the commands of the gospel, or does the gospel bind him to one rule of conduct?

It has already been proven that the law is for the unrighteous man and is given as a moral guide for human government, but that the Christian may not be joined unto both the law and the gospel. There are two distinct codes of conduct between those under the law and those under grace, for the one is from Sinai and the other from the Jerusalem which is above (Gal. 4:25, 26). The one is after the flesh and the other after the Spirit (Gal. 4:29).

While it can be proven from Scripture that the believer can participate in different levels of authority, it cannot be proven that the believer may live under different codes of conduct; or may live according to both the law and the gospel. What God has forbidden to believers, He has forbidden to them all. We must all stand before the judgment seat and give a personal account of our deeds. There will be no government there to take responsibility for our actions or exonerate us from our deeds when we stand before the Judge of all the earth.

It has often been assumed by Christians that since government is God-ordained, Christians may participate in all her functions and will not be held accountable for misconduct if they are obeying orders from God's minister. This same rationale has led Christians to take action upon other fellow believers when the government proclaimed them the enemy. A man cannot take an oath to the law and still have the freedom to live according to the gospel. Either he breaks his oath or violates the gospel when it does not agree with the law of government.

God has ordained a righteousness of the law (Romans 2:26) for those that walk according to the flesh, and a righteousness of faith (Hebrews 11:7) for those who walk according to the Spirit. The one law is that of sin and death while the other is of life in Christ Jesus (Romans 8:2). The one law pertains to the governments of this world and sinners in general while the other is the order of conduct for the believer. The one law is of works and the other law is of grace through faith (Romans 9:30, 31). For the believer Christ becomes the end of the (moral) law for righteousness (Romans 10:4). A believer who has become dead to the law and alive unto Christ cannot walk according to the conduct of that to which he has died.

The believer is not only delivered from the curse of the law but also may not live any longer by merely its letter, but rather must walk in its spirit (Romans 7:6). Whereas the law forbids murder, the gospel commands love in the same manner that Christ has loved us, which also is in agreement with the spirit of the law which asks us to love our neighbor as ourselves, that is, with all our human capability.

A believer cannot assume then that if he walks in agreement with civil law he is exempt from obeying the gospel's precepts. At that point, the government and not the Word, has become his supreme authority.

But if the government operates according to God's law (which is more rare in recent times) may we not as believers uphold what God has written and the institution that He has ordained? The answer is yes in as much as it does not cause us to violate the gospel in our conduct. What God has ordained for a law of nations is not the rule of the Church. What God has ordained to discover sin and restrain it is not the same as the reign of grace that the believer is under.

Some have advocated a complete separation from any involvement in civil affairs, and yet that position is not a requirement or an endorsement of Scripture. The Scripture calls for every area of our life to come under the Lordship of Christ. When there is a discrepancy between Christ and the state we must follow Christ. The Apostle Paul did not revoke his earthly Roman citizenship, but rather used it to further the gospel (Acts 16:37-39, 22:25-29) and to declare his citizenship rights. It was not that Paul refused to suffer for Christ, but rather that he also recognized that government was ordained of God to protect the innocent.

A Christian may only involve himself in the civil affairs of this life to the extent that it does not entangle him to the point of compromise with his spiritual calling (II Timothy 2:4). God has asked that we support and obey the civil authorities in all their ordinances (I Peter 2:13, 14) that do not violate our commission from the Lord (Acts 5:29).

Many Christians have argued over where that line is to be drawn, many holding either to complete separation from civil affairs, to the other extreme of seeking to christianize the government. The Scripture asks that we support what God has ordained, to the extent that we may do so without compromising any principle of our faith. Our understanding of where that line is to be drawn is largely due to our understanding of the role of the Church and the state.

Some have taken the view that the government exists only for unbelievers. But this is refuted by God's Word, where He speaks of government as being the minister of God to thee (believer) for good (Romans 13:4). The government exists also for the good of the believer as well as the unbeliever. If the government is not to provide public utilities, roads, and bridges for believers, are we then to expect them from the Church? Surely this would involve the Church in affairs that she is to be separated from. Rather, God has ordained that government provide such services for all its citizens. Every believer should render to the government all that is due it in the support of what God has called them to do.

It is also clear from Scripture that God has ordained rulers and nations to perform that which a believer may not participate in. God raised up nations to punish Israel for her sins and then in turn judged the nation that meted out God's justice. Edom was completely cut off for joining forces with Babylon against Israel (Obadiah vs. 10-14). Although God ordained Israel's captivity by other nations, yet He judged those nations for their violence against Israel. God has promised to make a full end of all the nations into which God has scattered Israel (Jer. 30:11). This seems to be a paradox of justice, that God should ordain a nation to fulfill a particular role and then judge them for that act they committed. The foundation of this paradox exists between the sovereignty of God over all things and human responsibility for one's own actions. While God did raise up Pharaoh to perform a certain task that existed in the foreknowledge of God long before it occurred (Gen. 15:13,14); He did not act upon that foreknowledge until He sent Moses to plead with Pharaoh to "Let my people go". When Pharaoh responded with "Who is the Lord that I should obey Him?" and hardened his own heart, God implemented the plan that existed in His foreknowledge and began to harden Pharaoh's heart that he might be a vessel of wrath fitted to destruction. Both the sovereignty of God in His decrees and human responsibility for one's own actions were kept distinct and inviolable, and so it must be in the same relationship between what God has ordained for the state and what man is individually responsible for in his own actions.

In this same manner, Christ's own death was ordained by God and yet God did bring wrath upon both Jesus' betrayer (Judas) and the nation (Israel) that executed Christ (Matthew 26:24, I Thess. 2:15, 16). Jesus' death was ordained before the foundation of the world by betrayal, and yet that one who performed that deed of his own free will, will be judged as having committed a great offense, and will not be honored as implementing God's plan of salvation. Though God ordained Christ's death, it was to be by the hands of sinners and not the Lord's people, but rather by unbelieving Israel and heathen Rome. Jesus told Pilate that he could have no power at all over Him except it were given him from above (God's plan), but yet those of the Lord's people (Israel was under a covenant with God to look for a Messiah from Abraham's covenant, i.e. circumcision) who delivered Him (Jesus) unto him (Pilate) would have sinned. Their sin was even greater than the sin of Pilate, for they were participating in that which God had ordained for wicked hands (John 19:11).

Jesus refers to this principle also in the issue of offenses when He says, "For it must needs be that offenses come; but woe to that man by whom the offense cometh" (Matthew 18:7).

Likewise this principle applies to Christians and government; though God has ordained it to perform certain functions, some of those functions which God has ordained are prohibited to the Christian, lest he fall under God's judgment for disobeying the gospel.

Though this is a paradox, God in His wisdom has ordained that both the believer and the unbeliever fulfill certain roles in this world. Because the unbeliever chooses to live outside of Christ, God uses his personal selfish and wicked motivations and ambitions to accomplish His will in the affairs of this life and yet holds him accountable for them; for it is the result of his rejection of the gospel. The believer, who is born into the kingdom of Christ, is not to involve himself in those roles that God has reserved for unconverted men to fulfill.

If this principle is clearly understood, then it can be understood how government can be a God-ordained revenger upon the wicked, while at the same time the believer is called upon to avenge not against those that wrong him. The believer should not obstruct justice in any way lest he be keeping government from fulfilling their God-ordained role. He should cooperate with the government when they seek to bring an offender to justice, but he is not to seek a prosecution against an offender as retribution for evil done against him, for this is contrary to the Spirit of Christ and His gospel.

It is not possible to always draw distinct lines for everyone in every situation, but if a believer walks by the principles of the Word and the direction of the Spirit, it is always possible to leave a clear testimony for Christ in all our relationships with the civil authorities.

## Conclusion

The first seduction of the Church on a grand scale took place when Constantine married her to the state. She spoiled her wedding garments when she cohabited with the civil authorities. Many Christians were deceived by this seeming triumph of their faith over the religions of the world. While it was a victory in the sense of having spoiled the pagan myths of religion, yet it was also the demise of her spiritual power when it came under civil authority.

No longer was it the elders of the churches who presided over councils, but Emperors and Popes. Whereas in the early years of Christianity the spheres between the state and the Church were distinct and inviolate, now the lines had become blurred, which resulted in the world being plunged into the Dark Ages, and both the state and the Church became corrupt.

All during those years God had remnant churches who did not defile their garments with Rome, who were branded with many different names by their adversaries such as, Paulician, Novation, Donatist, Waldensians, Cathari, Albigenses, Anabaptist, etc. Their history in many cases is still somewhat obscure, for it is written largely by their enemies who maligned them and sought to obliterate all traces of them from the earth. But they have still left a distinct trail; one that is written in blood, for they gave their lives for the faith they professed. It is not denied that the Reformation brought to light many truths of Scripture nor that there are many earnest believers in the Reformed churches, but rather our protest is that the Reformation did not purge the Church of one of the greatest of her pollutions.

Even the Reformers who brought to light many glorious truths of the gospel still sought to annihilate all those believers who would not join the established state churches. They sought only to reform the Church to what it was in the days of Constantine but never attempted to restore it to the original luster of its primitive stages. The Reformed concepts of church and state relationships have still continued to influence Christendom at large, though it may have been rejected to some degree in democratic republics that have instituted religious freedom. Many Christians are still enamored with the possibility of a "Christian nation", thinking that it is achievable through the political process. Tremendous amounts of resources have been spent on christianizing government that could have been spent in the work of the Church, which is saving the lost and discipling believers.

Not only has the ancient error been with us from the past unto the present but once again will it plague the Church at the end of the age through the reviving influence of the Babylonian Harlot.

She represents a revival of ancient mystery religions that were present in Babylon and on down to Rome, and adulterated the Christian faith. According to the Apocalypse, her seat of power was in Rome (Revelation 17:18), where the beast had its power also (Revelation 17:9-12). This accords with Daniel's prophecy of the Little Horn arising out of the fourth world empire. We know that she will reappear when the beast that was (past), and is not (present), and is to come (future), rises up again as a power on this earth (Revelation 17:8-10).

She, as a religious system, rides upon a beast of political power and fornicates with all the kings and nations of the earth (Revelation 18:3).

Not only is she a harlot but she is a "Mother of Harlots," in that she has offspring who are harlots. She may have been the first religion to pollute the Church with her abominations, but she also has other similar religions who have derived from her that also have partaken of her abominations.

Her power over the kings of the earth is directly related to her riding upon the beast of political power. She loses her power only when the political powers turn upon her and bring God's judgment upon her (Revelation 17:16, 17). All her harlot children likewise have sought union with political powers in order to establish their religion. Those churches who seek to unite with civil authorities are nothing more than her harlot offspring who also fornicate with the kings of the earth.

Those churches who unite with political powers are harlot churches on four scriptural charges.

1. *They as a church are married to the law.*

The national churches have always sought to marry Christ's gospel with Moses' law and are therefore proven to be adulterers (Romans 7:1-4). The only way to avoid spiritual adultery against Christ is by becoming dead to the law. They that are joined to Christ before their old spouse (the law) dies shall be called adulterers.

2. *They as a church are united with the world.*

If a nationally established church is to comprehend all of society, then she has included the world into the church. If all men are in the church, the world cannot be anywhere but in the Church; for there is no world at all outside the Church, if the Church comprehends all of the world.

As James says "Ye *adulterers* and *adulteresses*, know ye not that friendship with the world is enmity against God?"

Those churches then that include the world within their ranks have extended to the world their friendship and have exposed themselves to spiritual adultery are harlot churches. One of the greatest evidences of a Church in union with the world is the man-made institution of infant sprinkling, whereby they bring into the Church those that are not yet born again, who often grow up to assume themselves Christians, without ever having been born of the Spirit, and thus bring into the Church the carnality of the world.

3. *All national churches are harlot churches because they are in union with political powers who have all fornicated with the Babylonian harlot.*

In Revelation 18:3 it says that *all* nations have drunk of the wine of the wrath of her fornication; therefore since all nations have been polluted by her, those churches that unite with nations of this earth have entered into relationship with the Great Harlot and are therefore also harlot churches. Though nations may seek to follow God's laws, they are still under the influence of the god of this world, so that even the best of them have supped of some that Babylonian potion. Therefore the Church has been called out from among them to be separated unto God. Until Babylon is destroyed and Christ is ruling the nations the Church must remain separate from all political powers.

4. *Babylonian and harlot churches are all persecutors of the saints.*

The Great Whore is pictured as one who was drunken with the blood of the saints. For "in her was found the blood of prophets, and of saints, and of *all* that were slain upon the earth" (Revelation 18:24).

It is the spirit of Babylon that has caused the martyrdom of every follower of Christ. She has been the inspiration of every national church to persecute those that dissent from them. There has not been a nationally established religion that has not persecuted those saints who wished the Church to remain completely separate from any union with the state; therefore all these churches have shown themselves to be polluted with the Mother of Harlots.

The beast and the Harlot both gain control over the whole earth in the latter days before Christ's return (Revelation 13:7, 18:3). Further, we know that the beast and his armies shall gather all nations of the earth together against Jerusalem (Zech. 14:2) right before the return of Christ. When Christ Himself appears it will be to make war against all the armies of the earth who are commanded by the beast (Revelation 19:17-21).

If saints at this time are still deceived by their desire to be part of the military campaigns of this world, they shall be found in those armies that are gathered together against Jerusalem, who are also against Christ.

This is not merely an assumption of what might happen, but rather a prediction based upon God's Word, that some of God's people will be deceived by the whore and her power.

God issues one final call to His people before unleashing His judgment upon the Harlot; "COME OUT OF HER, MY PEOPLE, that ye be not partakers of her sins, and that ye receive not of her plagues."

There can be no doubt from this statement by God that some of His people are under the influence and deception of harlot churches. So it is not the intent here to pass judgment on those saints who are in those churches who would seek political power but rather to warn them of God's call to come out of them and be part of the bride that walks only with Christ. Perhaps there are some whom God is using in different churches, that God has called to remain faithful where they are and strive for the truth. The accounts of the seven churches in Asia speak of different churches with varying strengths and weaknesses, and yet for each one there is a promise to the overcomers who have washed their robes and made them white in the blood of the Lamb.

The instruction to all is to hear what the Spirit is saying to the churches.

It has never been the intent of this work to discount the glorious truths of the gospel that the Reformation brought to light, nor to discredit the character of godly men of the Reformed faith, but rather to show how that ancient and pernicious evil (Religious Establishments) was never cleansed from the doctrine and practices of the Church by the Reformers, as well as the array of doctrines that are necessary for its support. The Christian world is deeply indebted to the Reformers for bringing God's Word into the language of the people, which did more to overthrow the power of the Pope and false doctrine than any other single act. They also brought to the forefront that salvation is by Christ alone, and not through the Church, Priests, or the sacraments. The doctrine of *Sola Scriptura* (only the scripture) is the great foundation of our faith, which they so ably defended, and which eventually brought the Church to truth and purity beyond that which initially the Reformers sought to establish, such as was realized here in early America. We ask that the reader would carefully consider the truths we have tried to establish in this work and thoroughly examine the Scriptures to see whether these things be so. We may have made some errors in our expositions of Scripture and may have misinterpreted some history, (though in all things we sought to be fair and honest); yet we firmly believe in the truth of the overall views that were propounded, and believe them to be the primitive Christian faith that was established by Christ and His Apostles.

We shall close with the words of the Puritan, Lyman Beecher, who, when the Congregational Church of New England became disestablished as a state church in 1818, cried out: "*I worked as hard as mortal man could, and at the time preached for revivals with all my might........till at last, what with domestic afflictions and all, my health and spirits began to fail. It was as dark a day as ever I saw. The odium thrown upon the ministry was inconceivable. The injury done to the cause of Christ, as we then supposed, was irreparable. For several days I suffered what no tongue can tell for the BEST THING THAT EVER HAPPENED TO THE STATE OF CONNECTICUT. IT THREW THEM WHOLLY ON THEIR OWN RESOURCES AND ON GOD.*[16]

1  *Edwin S. Gaustad, Neither King Nor Prelate p. 66 (1993 WM. B. Eerdmans Publishing Company)*

2  *Ibid p. 92*

3  *Ibid p. 96*

4  *Ibid p. 89*

5  *James Kennedy, Why I Believe p. 95, 96 (1999 Word Publishing)*

6  *Edwin S. Gaustad, Neither King Nor Prelate p. 65 (1993 WM. B. Eerdmans Publishing Company)*

7  *Ibid p. 76*

8  *Ibid p. 77*

9  *Ibid p. 89*

10  *Ibid p. 91*

11  *Ibid p. 92*

12  *Ibid p. 100*

13  *Ibid p. 144*

14  *Ibid p. 143*

15  *Ibid p. 145*

16  *Ibid p. 120*